Leaving Microsoft to Change the World

D1332390

Leaving Microsoft to Change the World

An entrepreneur's quest to educate the world's children

John Wood

Collins

This book is dedicated to my parents, for teaching me to love education, to take risks, to believe in myself, and to serve others.

It is also dedicated to the amazing people of Room to Read – the employees, Board, donors, and worldwide base of volunteers. To be collaborating with such a passionate and fun group of people has been the greatest experience of my life.

ISBN 978-0-00-723703-6

A catalogue record for this book is available from the British Library.
1

Printed and bound in Great Britain by Clays Ltd, St Ives plc

First published in 2006 by Collins US, 10 East 53rd Street, New York, NY 10022

Designed by Nicole Ferguson

Jacket/Cover Design © HarperCollins Publishers Ltd 2008

Front cover quote from Giving by Bill Clinton, published by Hutchinson. Reprinted by permission of The Random House Group Ltd.

CONTENTS

PART 1

DISCOVERING NEPAL;

LEAVING MICROSOFT

CHAPTER 1

"PERHAPS, SIR, YOU WILL SOMEDAY COME BACK WITH BOOKS"

AN ICY WIND BLEW OFF THE MOUNTAIN AS I ZIPPED MY FLEECE jacket against the encroaching night. Looking up from my journal, I watched the sun sink behind the soaring snowcapped Himalayas. Clouds appeared massed behind the ridgeline, ready to march into the valley like night sentries. A young Nepali boy interrupted to offer a drink. This eight-year-old appeared to be running the small trekker's lodge on his own; I had seen no one else during my two hours at the table.

I asked if they had beer.

"Yes!" was his enthusiastic reply.

As I wondered about child labor laws, and whether this might be the youngest bartender I'd ever been served by, he ran off.

On a normal day I would be ordering another coffee at sundown, preparing for the three or four hours left in my workday as a marketing director at Microsoft. Today was blissfully different—the first of 21 days of trekking in the Himalayas. I wanted the beer to toast the start of my longest holiday in nine years, and a break from the treadmill of life in the software industry during the breakneck 1990s. Ahead lay three weeks without e-mail, phone calls, meetings, or a commute. Three weeks where the biggest challenge was walking 200 miles over "donkey trails" with all my gear on my back. On day ten, the trek would reach a Himalayan pass at 18,000 feet. This would be the highest I had ever climbed to in life. The challenging mountain pass and the long break would be a fitting reward for years of nonstop work.

My bartender returned with a dusty bottle of Tuborg, which he wiped on his black shirt. *"No chiso, tato,"* he said, apologizing for the beer being at room temperature. Then his face lit up. *"Tin minut,"* he said as his spindly legs carried his body recklessly down to the river. As I waited the requested three minutes, he plunged the bottle into the icy glacier melt, smiled, and waved.

A middle-aged Nepali man at the next table laughed aloud at the boy's clever, low-tech solution. "Who needs a refrigerator?" I asked as a way to start conversation. "Are all the children in Nepal this clever?" He replied that the people here needed to learn to make do, because they had so little. For example, dinner was cooked over a wood fire because people lacked luxuries like stoves and ovens.

The boy returned with a very cold beer—and a look of triumph.

Pasupathi appeared to be in his mid-50s, with thick glasses, weather-beaten dark pants, a Windbreaker, and a traditional Nepalese *topi* cloth cap. The sun and wind had carved fine lines of wisdom into his face over the years. The Nepalis, I quickly learned, are a friendly and welcoming people, and I struck up conversations with almost everyone.

Pasupathi was eager to tell me about Nepal, so I asked him what he did for a living. "District resource person for Lamjung Province," he explained. He was responsible for finding resources for the 17 schools in this rural province. I noticed his worn-out tennis shoes. In Nepal, that meant that most of the schools were off the main road and far out on the dirt paths I had spent the last seven hours trekking.

I told Pasupathi that I had always loved school as a child and asked whether Nepalese children were eager learners.

"Here in the rural areas we have many smart children," he replied with a rapid-fire assessment. "They are very eager to learn. But we do not have enough schools. We do not have sufficient

school supplies. Everyone is poor so we cannot make much investment in education. In this village, we have a primary school, but no
secondary school. So after grade five, no more schooling takes place
unless the children can walk two hours to the nearest school that
teaches grades six and above. But because the people are poor, and
they need their children to help with farming, so many of the students stop education too early."

As Pasupathi poured himself tea, he told me more.

"Some days I am very sad for my country. I want the children to
get a good education, but I am failing them."

Eager to learn more, I peppered him with questions. I found it
hard to imagine a world in which something as random as where
you were born could result in lifelong illiteracy. Had I taken my
own education for granted?

Pasupathi told me that Nepal's illiteracy rate, at 70 percent, was
among the world's highest. This was not the result of apathy on the
part of the people, he insisted. They believed in education. The
communities and the government were simply too poor to afford
enough schools, teachers, and books for their rapidly growing population. His job could be frustrating. Every day he heard about villages that lacked schools, or schools where three children were
sharing a textbook. "I am the education resource person, yet I have
hardly any resources."

He had many dreams. For example, he wanted to help one village move up from a one-room building in which grades one to five
were taught in shifts because the school was crammed into a small
space. His enthusiastic voice dropped as he next described the reality of having no budget. All he could do was listen to the requests
and hope that one day he could say yes.

Our conversation drew me into his world and incited my curi-
osity. Here was a potential opportunity to learn about the real Nepal, rather than the trekker's version of the country. I asked where
he was headed next. I lucked out. He was leaving in the morning to
visit a school in the village of Bahundanda, which was along the
trekking route. It was a three-hour walk up steep hills. I asked if I
might join him. He agreed. "I would be proud to show you our
school. Please meet me here again at seven for tea."

. . .

I DIDN'T EXPECT TO BE IN THE MIDDLE OF THE HIMALAYAS AT THIS POINT of my life. My notions of a serious adulthood didn't include backpacks and hiking boots. But I was doing more than recapturing my lost adolescence when I went to Nepal.

One factor was exhaustion. I had been working at Microsoft for only seven years, but it felt as if decades had passed. I joined the company shortly after graduate school. The period from 1991 through 1998 was one of tumultuous and exciting growth for the technology industry, and for Microsoft. But the only way to keep up was to work crazy hours. My job had an additional complication. I was a specialist in international markets, and as a result I was always trying to be in seven places at once. It was like a game of Twister played on a global scale. *Be in Johannesburg on Friday and Taiwan on Monday, ready to do presentations, take meetings, and do press interviews.*

The job was financially rewarding but full of high pressure and stress.

It seemed as if my mantra was "You can sleep when you are dead and buried."

Seven years in, though, that nagging question continually popped up: Is this all there is—longer hours and bigger payoffs? I had adopted the commando lifestyle of a corporate warrior. Vacation was for people who were soft. Real players worked weekends, racked up hundreds of thousands of air miles, and built miniempires within the expanding global colossus called Microsoft. Complainers simply did not care about the company's future.

I was, however, increasingly aware of the price I was paying. Relationships—starved of my time and attention—fell flat as a result. Family members grumbled when I canceled yet another Christmas reunion. I was a regular last-minute dropout for friends' weddings. Whenever friends proposed an adventure trip, I would usually have an immovable meeting standing in my way. The company could rely on me, but friends and family could not.

I remember a late-night return to my Sydney flat after a ten-day business trip to Thailand and Singapore. "The answering machine must be broken," I thought. "The light is not blinking." I push the button anyway. "Beep. You . . . have . . . no . . . new . . . messages," the mechanical voice announced. It might as well have added the word "loser" at the end.

With the software industry doubling every year, and Microsoft fighting to capture market share in every major category, the stakes seemed high enough to justify self-sacrifice. The corporate culture reinforced this mania. It wasn't until I finished a set of meetings with Steve Ballmer, Microsoft's hard-charging, demanding, and voluble second-in-command, that I convinced myself that I had earned a break. Ballmer was in Sydney reviewing our work in Asia. When we finished his business-review meetings, a two-day-long event where Ballmer tended to shout and harangue, a colleague— Ben—suggested we unwind by going to a slide show about trekking in Nepal given by a local adventure travel company.

Seeing those unbelievable mountain ranges squared it away. I was long overdue for a holiday. When the presenter mentioned that the Annapurna Circuit was a "classic trek that takes three weeks, covers two hundred miles, and gets you as far out in the Himalayas as you could imagine," I mentally began booking the time off. Next stop, Nepal. Over a Mongolian hot-pot dinner with Ben, I joked that *maybe* if you went high enough into the Himalayas, you could not hear Steve Ballmer screaming at you.

BACK IN NEPAL, CROWING ROOSTERS WOKE ME JUST BEFORE SUNRISE. The Timex Ironman read six o'clock. I debated snoozing a bit longer before meeting with Pasupathi for tea. The Himalayan dawn was cold; the four-season North Face bag felt like a pizza oven. But excitement over finally being in Nepal won out. I put on a warm thermal layer before leaving the bag.

Fog blanketed the river valley. The lodge's stone patio was deserted. The eight-year-old host delivered a steaming cup of *dudh chia* (milk tea). I clutched it beneath my face. From the battered cardboard menu I asked for a cheese omelet with toast. The boy ran back to the kitchen where his mother was stoking a wood fire.

As I waited for Pasupathi, I studied the day's route on the Annapurna Circuit map. The trail to Bahundanda followed the Marsyendi River. We'd be walking upstream, between the deep canyons the strong, icy river had carved over centuries of its headlong rush toward the Indian plain and the Bay of Bengal. The first two hours of the day's trek looked to be relatively flat, after which we'd ascend thirteen hundred vertical feet in just under a mile. At the top of that climb lay Bahundanda, the village where we would visit Pasupathi's school.

Along with a sizzling omelet, my young host presented the bill for my stay. I felt guilty over its size. I had been given a bed, a beer, dinner, breakfast, and unlimited cups of milk tea. Five dollars. Tipping was considered an insult, and I wondered what else I could do to thank this boy and his family. My musings were interrupted by Pasupathi, who appeared out of nowhere, wearing the same clothes he had been in the night before. He said that he was ready to start moving, so I quickly scarfed down the eggs and grabbed my pack.

No day that starts with a trek in the morning sunlight can be a bad day. We walked along the boulder-strewn river. A surprisingly large volume of water rushed downstream. Green, terraced rice fields were carved impossibly high into the steep hillside. As the sun burned off the morning chill, the only sound was that of the river and two pairs of feet making good time along the dirt trail. All seemed right with the world.

After two hours of flat terrain, we confronted a steep series of switchbacks—the approach to Bahundanda. It was the first of the dozens of difficult ascents I'd experience with burning pain in the legs over the next few weeks. The village clung to a lofty perch on the side of the hill, looking down into the river valley.

Pasupathi, twenty years my senior and on his third cigarette of the morning, was still in front of me. He crested the hill and without waiting marched toward the school. Children clad in uniforms of dark blue pants and powder blue shirts ran by us as a clanking bell signaled the start of the school day. They smiled at and greeted the foreign backpacker. "Namaste." "Hello, sir."

Pasupathi introduced the headmaster, who offered a tour. The first-grade classroom spilled over with students. There were 70 in a room that looked as though its capacity was half that. The floor was packed earth, and the sheet-metal roof intensified the late-morning springtime sun, baking the room. The children sat on rows of long benches, crammed close together. Lacking desks, they balanced notebooks on bony, little knees.

We visited each of the eight classrooms; all were equally packed. As we entered, every student stood, without prompting, and yelled, "Good morning, sir," in perfect English. The headmaster next took us to the school's library. A sign outside the door proudly announced SCHOOL LIBRARY, but inside, the room was empty and the only thing covering the walls was one old, dog-eared world map. It showed, ten years after the fall of the Iron Curtain, the Soviet Union, East Germany, Yugoslavia, and other countries that had ceased to exist. The books were noticeable only in their absence.

I phrased my question in the most polite way possible:

"This is a beautiful library room. Thank you for showing it to me. I have only one question. Where, exactly, are your books?"

The headmaster stepped out of the room and began yelling. A teacher appeared with the one key to the rusty padlock on the cabinet where the books were locked up.

The headmaster explained. Books were considered precious. The school had so few that the teachers did not want to risk the children damaging them. I wondered how a book could impart knowledge if it was locked up, but kept that thought to myself.

My heart sank as the school's treasure trove was revealed. A Danielle Steel romance with a couple locked in passionate and semi-clothed embrace on the front cover. A thick Umberto Eco novel, written in Italian. The *Lonely Planet Guide to Mongolia*. And what children's library would be complete without *Finnegans Wake*? The books appeared to be backpacker castoffs that would be inaccessible (both physically and intellectually) to the young students.

I asked about the school's enrollment and learned there were 450 students. Four hundred and fifty kids without books. How could this be happening in a world with such an abundance of material goods?

Without prompting, the headmaster then said:

"Yes, I can see that you also realize that this is a very big problem. We wish to inculcate in our students the habit of reading. But that is impossible when this is all we have."

I thought that any educator who used the word *inculcate* in a sentence deserved to have better teaching materials. I wanted to help, but would it be considered condescending if I offered? The headmaster saved me the trouble of thinking this through. His next sentence would forever change the course of my life:

"Perhaps, sir, you will someday come back with books."

THE TEACHERS INVITED PASUPATHI AND ME TO "TAKE TEA." I BEGGED off, insisting that they needed to be back in their classrooms. They insisted harder.

We talked about the library. Two teachers repeated the request for books. "I'd love to help. But in Sydney, where I live, or America, where I am from, I would only be able to collect English books. Would they be useful?"

The grade-eight teacher assured me that these books would be eagerly accepted. The school—as per the government curriculum—taught English from grade one, in addition to Nepali.

Once I nodded and smiled, the floodgates opened. The teachers were not shy in outlining their wish list: storybooks, books about animals, ABCs and 1-2-3s, geography, basic science, colors. I asked if 200 to 300 books would be enough, and the teachers, in chorus, assured me that this would make a huge difference for the school.

One teacher looked skeptical. He asked for confirmation that I would honor my pledge. "Many trekkers come through this area, and many have said that they will help us. But they do not come back and we do not hear from them again." I assured the teachers of Bahundanda that I would be true to my word. As I left, the school's English teacher shook my hand. "Please, sir, when you come back with books, you will be very welcome. The children, their heads will hit the ceiling because they will be jumping up and down with excitement."

I imagined what that day would be like. I pictured loading several hundred books onto the back of a rented yak and returning to a warm welcome. This morning's hike had been beautiful. How much more fun would it be if I was anticipating our arrival at the school? I remembered my own childhood excitement every time my parents bought a new Clifford the Big Red Dog or Curious George book and wondered how these students might react to similar brightly colored books.

This image of my return, accompanied by a yak with hundreds of books on its back, burned in my mind.

"I promise you, we will meet again."

CHAPTER 2

AN IDEA BURNS BY CANDLELIGHT

I SAID GOOD-BYE TO PASUPATHI. HE WOULD BE TREKKING FOR THREE hours along a side trail to another school. I thanked him for introducing me to the education system in Nepal. "I will not say good-bye," he said with a smile. "Instead, I will say *pheri bhetaunlaa.* This means 'until we see each other again.' If you come back with books, please remember that we have seventeen schools here in my province. This school is one of our better ones; the others are in worse shape. Please come back. *Pheri bhetaunlaa.*" With that he lit a cigarette, pressed his palms together and bowed, and walked off. I strode in the opposite direction, higher into the hills.

During the four-hour afternoon hike, my brain spun with the possibilities. *Could I get my local library to donate books? Hold a book drive at work? Hit one of those "Buck a Book" surplus stores and buy several hundred? How soon could I get back to Nepal?*

That night I stopped at a small lodge run by a charming Nepali woman in her late 50s. I was exhausted by eight hours of hiking with a heavy pack, but mentally energized by the challenge given by the teachers. The menu offered some intriguing dinner options:

Trivous Roast Briten
Fielt of Blat Steaks
Winner Esnetur
Hungering Gulsh

Had someone translated the menu from Nepali to English to German to Hungarian? I used my limited treasure trove of Nepali to ask the owner if she could make egg fried rice. *Mito cha,* she said, telling me that I had chosen a delicious dish. I wondered if she would have said that had I ordered the Hungering Gulsh.

I sipped tea and began talking to a Canadian woman at the next table. She asked why I had such a big grin on my face, so I eagerly told her about the school and my plan.

She asked me how I planned to get books to the village. I admitted that I had no idea, but that it did not seem beyond me to figure it out. She then pointed out several potential problems—the cost of shipping books from overseas, the potential difficulties with Customs, import taxes, and other things that could go wrong. I never enjoy listening to people talk about why things cannot happen, so I changed the subject.

After dinner, I went back to my $2-per-night room. The drafty walls made me thankful for my faithful sleeping bag. The lodge had no electricity, so I rummaged through the backpack for a headlamp and a book. My current read was the Dalai Lama's *The Art of Happiness.* It seemed tailor-made for me after the visit to Bahundanda. The Dalai Lama had written extensively about our duty to others and made a persuasive case that one of our primary duties on this earth is to look out for people who have less. "The basic fact is that all sentient beings, particularly human beings, want happiness and do not want pain and suffering." He suggested that if we were lucky enough to be living a good life, we should recognize this gift and thank God for it by looking out for others who need our help in breaking out of the cycle of poverty.

I was inspired to briefly meditate on these words, and to record my thoughts. In my journal, I wrote, "It does not matter if we have material wealth. What really matters is—what do we do with it? I have attained financial success at a young age, but that was mostly luck. I just happened to join the right company at the right time. The fact that I have money does not make me a better person. What really matters is what I do with it."

The other trekkers were sleeping. The sound of pen on paper broke the silence. My headlamp was the only illumination. I returned to the book.

The Dalai Lama wrote that when we gave something away, we actually got something back in return: happiness. If we were to use our money simply to buy ourselves things, there would be no end. Acquisition would not produce true happiness, as we'd never have the biggest boat, the nicest car, and would be stuck in a perpetual materialist cycle. But if we gave something away to those who are less fortunate, we'd get nothing in return except for a warm feeling in our heart and the knowledge in our brains that we had made the world a better place.

The Bahundanda visit had put me in a frame of mind to be receptive toward this teaching. I visualized 450 students without a proper library. Would I stick with my goal? Or would I forget this school as soon as I returned to the frantic pace of my career? I had always vowed in the past to "do more for charity." I had usually failed; work had won out. I vowed that this time, it would not.

I turned to a different section of my journal. Accompanied only by the sound of barking dogs and snoring trekkers, I began drafting a list of everyone in my life who might be willing to help me collect books for Bahundanda.

MY EXCITEMENT FOR SETTING UP A LIBRARY CAN BE TRACED DIRECTLY to my childhood. My earliest and most vivid memories involve reading. On Sundays, my mother would spin a story from the comics section of the newspaper for my enjoyment. My eyes followed the colorful drawings and I committed the stories to memory. At bedtime I would insist upon countless rereadings of classics like *Go, Dog. Go!*; *Green Eggs and Ham*; *There's a Wocket in my Pocket!* During long family car trips, my nose would be stuck in a book while my brother and sister were otherwise engaged punching each other.

I read so voraciously that my parents' limited budget could not keep up. Being a pragmatic engineer, my father designed a cost-effective solution. My parents bought me a bike as the "big present" for my tenth Christmas. I thought the bright green, banana-seated vehicle was the coolest set of wheels in town. Our small public library in Athens, Pennsylvania, was only three miles from our house, and so once we experienced spring thaw, I proudly began my weekly trips.

There was only one small problem. The library allowed only eight books to be checked out at a time. I have never been shy about making suggestions for how things could be done better, so I asked the kindly and matriarchal librarian if the limit could be raised. My zeal for reading won her over. We agreed that it would be our little secret that for selected customers the new limit was twelve.

On occasion I'd earn the ire of my teachers when they discovered the storybook hidden beneath the class textbook. I'd sneak furtive glances at childhood classics such as *Touchdown for Tommy* while also listening in on the class discussion. This seems to have ignited a lifelong penchant for multitasking and an obsession with productivity.

Thankfully, my grades did not suffer as a result. When I brought home a report card full of good marks, my parents would offer me a reward of my choosing. All those library books required extra hours to read them, so my choice was always a week of extended bedtime. I can remember nights when my older siblings and parents were asleep. The house was silent as an empty country church, the quiet broken only by the sound of turning pages.

This love of reading, learning, and exploring new worlds so predominates my memory of youth that I simply could not imagine a childhood without books.

DURING THE NEXT SIXTEEN DAYS OF TREKKING, MY MIND KEPT THINK-ing about the proposed school library project. One day I talked to a Nepalese guide named Dawa Sherpa and mentioned the project. Dawa was a short man with a muscular frame influenced by years of portering on Everest expeditions. He was fond of baseball caps, thumbs-up signs, and English-language colloquialisms. "See you later, alligator" was his favorite. He laughed constantly, and this influenced those around him to share in his joy. Dawa reminded me of Dostoyevsky's quote—"if you wish to glimpse inside a human soul and get to know a man . . . just watch him laugh. If he laughs well, he is a good man."

I asked for Dawa's feedback on whether a book drive would be a good idea. "Yes, I think so. You see, in Nepal we think that education is the key to the future of our country. One reason nations like yours are rich is because all children grow up going to school. Here we do not have that advantage."

But what about English books? Were they needed in a rural school?

"Nepali people want to learn English. It is the language that will let us communicate with others. Not many people speak the Nepalese language. But so many people speak English. I am one example of this. If I did not speak English, you and I could not communicate. Trekkers would not hire me to be their guide. Most people in Nepal make a very small amount of money, maybe fifty rupees [75 cents] per day. But as a guide, I make eight or ten dollars a day. Tourism is the biggest industry after farming. So if you can help children learn English, then maybe you help them to have more opportunities and a better life."

A mix of excitement and fear started to run inside me. The adrenaline pumped when I thought about how many books could be gathered and put into children's hands. At the same time, I doubted myself. My friends could flake, and work demands certainly wouldn't make it easy to follow through on my promise of returning. I could picture day one back at the office, immediately being pulled in a million directions at once. I needed to find a way to stay true to my vision.

That night, at 12,000 feet elevation, the cold set in the moment the sun ducked behind the mountains. The only artificial light was from a loud and hissing kerosene lantern. I zipped into my bag and was alone with my journal and my thoughts.

I thought back to life in Sydney, where I enjoyed a comfortable income, a Saab convertible; a two-bedroom, two-bath apartment on the harbor all to myself; and so much "stuff" that I was renting a storage locker. Maybe, I thought, my life is screwed up if I can't fit everything I own into a 2,000-square-foot apartment.

I debated whether doing just one school library was enough. Pasupathi's closing reminder that his province had 17 schools had stuck with me. Why not think bigger and start 10? Or 20?

I reached into my backpack to grab one of the seven books I'd brought along to read during the trek. Almost as if to answer my questions, a line from Søren Kierkegaard appeared on the first page to which I flipped:

"There is nothing with which every man is so afraid as getting to know how enormously much he is capable of doing and becoming."

I felt as though a challenge were being made, albeit from a dead Danish philosopher. I turned the headlamp off as visions of Kierkegaard danced in my head. Lying in the dark and staring out the small window at a half-moon, I thought about this project as a litmus test: Would I be willing to use my good fortune to help others? It would be a shame not to respond to these needs in a big way.

AFTER THREE GLORIOUS WEEKS OF TREKKING, I RETURNED TO KATHmandu. I had loved the freedom of being in remote mountainous areas, and of being cut off from phones, e-mail, newspapers, and the accoutrements of modern Western society. There was, however, an urgent e-mail that needed to be written. I immediately went in search of the nearest cybercafe.

Pulling up Hotmail, I counted over 100 people stored in my online address book. Clicking on the "Mail All" button, I prepared to make the best sales pitch of my life.

From: John Wood
Subject: Books for Nepal—Please Help
Dear Friends,

   Congratulations. You have been selected to participate in one of John Wood's random ideas. Unlike most of my rambling stories from the road, this one will not take long to tell and will do a lot of good for a large number of children whose lives are less fortunate than ours.

While trekking through the Nepal Himalaya, I was invited to visit a local school. Over dinner at a small trekking lodge, I had met Pasupathi, a man who administers 17 local schools in the remote province of Lamjung. In the West the term "school administrator" might bring visions of a deskbound bureaucrat, but Pasupathi walks ten miles of donkey trails every day to visit the rural, dirt-floor schools set up to educate children in small mountain towns. His goal is to help children to gain an education, and his job is made difficult by lack of resources.

Nepal is one of the world's most beautiful countries. It is also one of the poorest. It's hard to support a population when the majority of the terrain is mountainous and barely inhabitable. It's hard to grow crops at 12,000 feet and impossible to do so at 17,000 feet. A measure of the poverty—GNP per head is $400. A starker reminder—pay a local family $2 and you have a bed for the night.

The lack of resources in the schools is sad. I showed the teachers a battered postcard of Sydney and they asked if they could keep it to augment their world map, which was the only decoration on the wall of the classroom. The "library" we visited, despite being in the largest school in the district, had no more than twenty books, and those were backpacker castoffs that are not at the appropriate reading level for the 450 children in grades 1–8. Think how much books meant to you as a kid, or to your own children. Then imagine taking that away. It would have a profound impact on your life path.

Therein lays the crux of this mail. I need your help! I asked Pasupathi and the headmaster what they needed most and was told desks to keep up with the population growth, and books. I contributed cash to buy some desks and have vowed to return with enough books to set up a good library that will keep their students busy gaining a lifelong love of reading.

If you'd like to help, there are three things you can do:

—Send any books you have which would be suitable for a

young student learning English, up to age 12. There are collection points in Australia and the U.S. (thanks, Mom and Dad!) listed at the bottom of this e-mail.

—Forward this mail to friends or family who may have books their own children have outgrown. Everyone knows someone who has an old copy of *Goodnight Moon* or *Hop on Pop* lying around. If sent to Nepal, it will be read dozens of times by eager students.

—Stick $5 or $100 in an envelope and send it along. I'll buy kid's books in bulk (ten for a dollar) from online retailers and bookstores. I will personally match all cash donations, dollar for dollar.

I will pay all costs of postage and handling to get the books to Nepal. Please remember the energy, creativity, and hunger for knowledge of youth, and do something to help these children. Get your friends involved! We all want to make a difference in life. Here is an opportunity to do so in a way that may seem small to you, but will have a big impact on kids who have been denied an education by the poverty and isolation of their homeland.

The worst option is to do nothing.

Thanks in advance.

Warm regards from Kathmandu,

John

ON MY FINAL MORNING IN NEPAL, I FELT GLUM ABOUT HAVING TO LEAVE. The country had captured my heart. I consoled myself with the thought that I would return. I would be coming back with books. I would rent that yak. As I paid the bill, I chatted as usual with the lodge owner and his two friends who seemed to be always hanging out. I commented that I had enjoyed our conversations over the previous three days. "I will be back. See you next year."

Tilak, in his mid-20s, with jet-black hair and a perpetual smile, asked me how I would get to the airport.

"No problem, I will jump in a taxi."

"Oh, no! I will take you on my motorbike. Your backpack, no problem, it's a big bike with lots of room."

We weaved through the chaotic streets of Kathmandu. Tilak dodged diesel-belching buses, cows, and cars that were not moving fast enough.

Fifteen minutes later, the airport. I jumped off the bike and hoisted the heavy pack onto my back. Tilak shook my hand. "Good-bye, Mr. John, please come visit us again next year."

"Wait, wait, let me give you some money for the ride!" I fished frantically through my pockets.

He shook his head and waved his hand, palm down. "You do not have to pay me anything. You are my friend." Before I could utter a word of protest, he smiled, waved good-bye, and sped off into traffic.

This was my final positive impression of Nepal after three weeks that had been full of them—the quiet dignity of a people who are poor, but who value friendship over money. I knew that there was no way I could ever repay all the kindness that had been shown to me.

CHAPTER 3

YOU NEED TO GET HOME SOON!

BACK IN AUSTRALIA, WORK QUICKLY RESUMED ITS FRANTIC PACE. Centripetal forces immediately yanked my attention from Himalayan libraries to the competitive world of technology. Microsoft was preparing for a fierce battle against IBM to win the electronic-commerce business of Coles Myer Ltd, the largest retailer in Australia. One could call CML the Wal-Mart of Australia, except that their market share there was larger than Wal-Mart's share of the American market. During 1998 IBM had spent billions of dollars promoting their e-business initiative. This was yet another case of Microsoft being perceived as "behind the times" during the booming Internet era. Even within the normally overconfident Microsoft Australia, there was a widespread impression that we would lose this contest against IBM.

Not if I could help it. I told Anthony Joseph, the Microsoft sales executive handling the account, that he could count on me to help win the business.

"I don't want to pitch a technology solution to CML," he replied boldly. "I want to give them an entire business plan for e-commerce, of which Microsoft's technology is but one facet. We can do a total end-around on IBM. While they're trying to explain to the client why their server is better than our server, we will instead be giving the client an entire business plan. It's simple. We engage the client at a strategic level. We win the business."

I told Anthony that it was a great strategy, but that writing a business plan to take a multibillion-dollar business onto the Internet was not exactly a simple undertaking. But this was Microsoft, the land of no excuses. We knew there would be no better way to broadcast our e-commerce capabilities than by winning one of the world's biggest retailers. Within a week of my return from Nepal, I was buried in studying the e-commerce market into late in the evening.

One night my e-commerce studies were interrupted by an e-mail from my father. When my parents had agreed to be the U.S. collection point for our book drive, my father asked how many books I thought they'd receive. "I don't know, probably one hundred or two hundred."

Subject: You need to get home soon!
Dear John,

I am writing to invite you to come pay us a visit in Colorado. Your book drive has succeeded beyond any of our imaginations. The UPS guy is here at least twice a day. I have moved one of my cars out of the garage to make room for the books. I think that we have about 3,000 books here, but we have lost count.

You might want to pay a visit home and help me sort through them. I do not know what the schools over there want, and we also need to figure out a way to ship the books over.

Please let us know—your mother says she will make lasagna for you since you will need energy to sort through and pack all these books!

Love,
Dad/Woody

IN 1998, USE OF THE INTERNET AND E-MAIL WAS BECOMING WIDESPREAD, but was not the overwhelming force it is today. The success of our book drive was an early manifestation of the power of this network.

Several dozen people had sent me questions, and as I scrolled down, I realized that some of the initial recipients of my mail from Kathmandu had forwarded it to 50 friends, who had then sent it along to dozens more friends. Two years later, we were still receiving mail from people reading my original plea for books. Somewhere in cyberspace, my request may still be circulating.

SIX WEEKS LATER I MADE THE 25-HOUR JOURNEY TO COLORADO. BITTEN by the literacy bug, I had printed off a thick sheaf of United Nations reports on the state of education in the developing world. They made for compelling, yet depressing, reading. As we sped across the Pacific from Sydney to Los Angeles with all the modern conveniences such as movies, cocktails, and hot meals even at 35,000 feet, I read about the sad reality for many of the world's children.

What struck me first was the UN's estimate that 850 million people in the world lacked basic literacy. I had to read the number three times to convince myself that it was not too large to be true. The world's population was around 6 billion people. That meant one out of every seven human beings lacked the ability to read or write a simple sentence.

Of the 850 million lacking basic literacy, the UN estimated that two-thirds were women. This had a terrible carryover effect, as it's typically the women who are rearing the family's children. If the mother is educated, it is much more likely that education will be passed on to the next generation. I knew this from my own experience, given that my mother and my grandmother had both read to me from an early age. Too many children in the developing world started life disadvantaged from day one because their mother had not gained an education.

The UN report was not yet done depressing me. The next section revealed that over 100 million children of primary-school age were not enrolled in school. One hundred million. Mao once said that a single death is a tragedy, but a million deaths is a statistic. Now I understood his point.

I was frustrated. These children would not get a second chance—next year or a decade from now would be too late. Somebody should do something! Lack of action would simply perpetuate the problem.

The depressing litany of statistics forced me to begin questioning my project. Helping a small number of libraries serving a few thousand Nepali students would represent just a drop in the ocean of illiteracy. The UN report proved also that books would not be enough. It was obvious that the developing world also needed primary schools, and effective ways to increase female enrollment.

Three hours outside of LAX, I pulled the window shade down for a siesta, and a respite from contemplating a problem that appeared to be much larger than I could tackle on my own.

On the connecting flight to Colorado, my mind switched from focusing on the problem to contemplating the solution. A friend had responded to my plea for books by sending me $100, along with a story clipped from the pages of the *International Herald Tribune*. The article focused on the Queens Public Library system. It was the busiest in the United States, due to the large immigrant population. The article profiled a recent immigrant from Taiwan—Pin-Pin Lin—who brought her two sons to the library twice a week. She insisted that they read in English rather than Chinese and would check out up to 20 books per visit. I thought of my own childhood library trips, and my parents being just as excited as Pin-Pin Lin about the possibilities inherent in reading.

The article continued, "The extraordinary love affair between immigrants and libraries is a century-old story in New York. . . . The most crowded libraries have always been in neighborhoods with the largest population of recent immigrants."

This was the power of Andrew Carnegie's legacy. He had used his wealth to set up over 2,000 public libraries across North America. Three generations after his death, they were continuing to pay dividends. These new American citizens were fortunate that Carnegie had thought long-term. For the Taiwanese boys, Carnegie had created the hardware, and their mother the software. This bode well for their assimilation and success in America.

Could we do the same for the people of Nepal? How about other countries in the developing world? My travel experiences had taught me that parents around the world are similar at least in one respect—they want their children to have a better life than they have had. I did not possess Carnegie's wealth. But I had a thirty-year head start on him. I would not wait until I was old and retired. I was still young, and full of energy. In Colorado, spilling out of my parents' home and into their garage, we had at least an initial down payment on this dream.

I ARRIVED IN COLORADO EXHAUSTED FROM THE JOURNEY. MY FATHER had been awaiting my arrival for weeks. So we dove right in. I had been forewarned, but I was still surprised at the huge quantity of books that had piled up. A number of handwritten notes had been sent. With typical engineer's precision, my father had saved these in chronological order in a manila file folder.

> Dear John:
>
> I received your request for books from our mutual friend Gail Darcy. I want to thank you for doing this. In 1995, I had the pleasure of trekking in Nepal for a month. I was saddened by the crushing poverty and wanted to do something to help the people. But I had no idea how to start. Then your note arrived. I recruited all of my colleagues here at Scholastic, and we cleaned our bookshelves and closets. We're really happy that these books will find a good home.
>
> Thank you for giving me a way to finally achieve my goal. Let me know if I can help pay for shipping of these books over to Nepal.
>
> Namaste,
> Ellen

Another friend of a friend wrote to say that she could not imagine a world without books. She had sent us several dozen Dr. Seuss books, along with money to help pay for shipping. A third note was from a mother discussing how much it meant to her when her children insisted on reading bedtime stories. The e-mail from Nepal, she said, had opened her eyes to a problem and made her all the more thankful that her children's lives were full of books.

We spent two days sorting the donations that had come in from all of our new friends. The first step was to separate the wheat from the chaff. Thankfully, over 95 percent of the books were usable. We had an occasional laugh over some of the detritus that had found its way to us. My favorite was titled *How Computers Work*. It was written in 1973.

Our next step was to box them up in a sturdy manner so they could survive the 8,000-mile journey to Nepal. That task reminded both of us of a major strategic gaffe: we didn't have a plan to get the books to Bahundanda. The school was a two-day walk from the nearest road. Simply writing the school's address on the boxes and sticking them in the mail was not going to do the trick. I kicked myself for not having thought about logistics in more detail.

AT DINNER THAT NIGHT, MY FATHER PROPOSED A SOLUTION. HE HAD gone online and found contact details for the Lions Club in Kathmandu. He was a member of his local club and proposed that we ask the Kathmandu club for assistance. I was skeptical that a group of strangers halfway around the world would want to work with us.

My mother chimed in, "Woody, I think you might be barking up the wrong dog."

"*Tree*, Mom."

"What?"

"The expression is 'barking up the wrong *tree*.' "

"Well, your father knows what I mean."

After a few decades of marriage, every couple has its own unique shorthand.

My father was ignoring our discussion. He had already gotten up from the table to unilaterally overrule us. From his downstairs office, he sent an e-mail describing our project.

The next morning, as I ate homemade banana bread and read the *Denver Post*, my father trotted upstairs. He had a reply from Kathmandu:

Dear Lion Woody:

    We received today your inquiry about sending books to Nepal. We appreciate your willingness to help our country. The Lions Club of Downtown Kathmandu has two focuses—preventing blindness, and children's literacy. We would be happy to help your project. When you are ready to send the books, please let me know. I will give you instructions. One of our fellow Lions works in the government, so he can be sure that the books will get through Customs without any delay or need to pay duty.

Because you have so many books, I would respectfully ask that you consider donating them to a number of schools. All of our schools here have shortages, and I believe it would be valuable to help five or ten, rather than just one. This is to be your decision, but I offer it as what I hope is a helpful suggestion.

Thanking you from Nepal,

Lion Dinesh Shrestha

My father was kind enough not to do an "I told you so" dance. Instead, he poured himself a cup of coffee and joined the breakfast table. He said that he had been thinking constantly about this project, and that he wanted to join me in Nepal. He was excited by the idea of helping to deliver the books to Bahundanda and other schools in the Himalayas. I tried to talk him out of this idea by explaining that travel was difficult in Nepal—sanitary conditions were lacking, one slept on uncomfortable beds in drafty teahouses, he would not be able to eat meat, and there would be no television. He commented that he was not aware he had raised such a condescending son, then reminded me that he had survived the Depression and World War II.

There were other concerns I did not share aloud. My father and I have never been overly communicative, and I had a fear of traveling alone with him for two weeks. We had not spent much one-on-one time during my adult years, and I was worried about being together with few distractions. Would we find things to talk about? He had seen the developing world from the deck of a cruise ship, but not in hiking boots and with a pack on his back. I knew he was tough, but still, he was seventy-three. Wasn't trekking in the Himalayas a younger man's game?

I stalled. "I'll think about it, Dad. I am not sure when I will be going over. We should delay a decision for the time being."

. . .

burned as we prepared Microsoft's competitive pitch against IBM.
One evening my preparation of the final slide deck was interrupted
by an e-mail from my father:

> Dear John:
>
> I wanted to let you know that today I posted 37 boxes of
> books to Nepal. The total weight was 967 pounds [he was always
> one for details!]. The total cost was $685, so please send me a
> check when you get a chance.
>
> You should be very proud of this project. It's going to help a
> lot of children get a chance to read.
>
> > Love,
> >
> > Dad
>
> PS—Can you please explain to me again why I can't go with you
> to Nepal?

A long pause, followed by another read of the mail. Tears started
flowing. I felt like such a jerk. Why had I resisted the idea of taking
him on this trip, given all the work he had done on the project? I had
been thinking only of myself. I had an illusion that it would be best
to "travel light" and be free of responsibility for someone who was
not experienced at hardship travel in a place like Nepal.

I immediately hit Reply. I let him know that I was sending a check
for $3,685. He could hold the extra $3,000 in reserve to buy a
business-class ticket to Kathmandu. "We'll need to give the books a
few months to get there. We will follow soon behind. It's winter there,
and I have a full plate of work projects, so let's plan to go in March or
April. I never thought I'd say these words, but—see you in Nepal!"

I shut down my PC and pulled out my journal. Sitting on the
living-room sofa and staring at the lights on the Sydney Harbour
Bridge, I recorded how thankful I was that my father had pushed
back. The book drive had been a father-son project. He deserved to
enjoy the experience of putting the books into the hands of the students. The next step was to enjoy a once-in-a-lifetime experience traveling together to remote mountain villages. Bahundanda beckoned.

CHAPTER 4

WOODY AND JOHN'S

EXCELLENT ADVENTURE

PRAYER FLAGS FLAPPED IN THE BREEZE, THEIR BLUES, GREENS, AND reds in stark contrast to the soaring snowcapped Himalayan peaks. The Buddhists believe that prayers can be answered if they are written on flags that are hung outdoors. As the wind passes over the flags, the prayers are lifted up to heaven.

On this particular morning the winds made prayer traffic quite heavy. I pulled my ski cap tighter and inhaled deeply. The smell of cedars mixed with the smoke from the fire over which milk tea was brewing. The homecoming, nearly a year since my pledge to the teachers of Bahundanda, made me feel that all was right with the world.

The morning serenity was a welcome antidote to my current life amidst the noise and pollution of Beijing. Microsoft had posted me to a new role as director of business development for the Greater China Region. We had won the Coles Myer business against IBM, and part of my new and expanded role would be helping to start our dormant electronic-commerce initiatives in mainland China, Hong Kong, and Taiwan. I was excited by the role, and the promise inherent in the world's fastest-growing technology market. But there were already problems with life in Beijing. The athlete in me was suffering from life in a bitter-cold and polluted city. The lack of public space for running or cycling was in sharp contrast to my prior life in Sydney and Seattle. My weight had shot up by ten pounds after just two months. I had a constant cough as pollution stuck in my throat.

Morning in Nepal felt enlivening, life-affirming, and peaceful.

My father was with me. I poured cups of milk tea as we greeted the day. I had not ever expected to travel with him to a place this remote. Events had conspired to make him every bit as enthusiastic about the Bahundanda library project as I was, even though he had never set foot in Nepal.

We drank tea, ate cheese omelets, and discussed how excited we were that each student in Bahundanda would soon have access to books. I asked if he had ever thought that our book drive would be such a success that we'd have to hire a "donkey train" to carry them all. Eight beasts of burden were tied up in the field next to our small lodge. The "donkey driver" was loading two over-stuffed boxes of books on each animal. They munched on grass in preparation for the day's labor. I told my father about the original vision of renting a yak. "Our book drive was such a success that one animal would not be enough."

We soon set off on the trail, the donkeys and their driver following behind. The donkey bells, hung around each neck to warn susceptible hikers of their stubborn approach, clanged in a chorus. We followed the ice-cold and fast-flowing Marsyendi River upstream, crossing it several times on rickety bridges. Unbeknownst to us, preparations were being made for our arrival a few hours up the trail.

THE SUN BEAT DOWN RELENTLESSLY AS WE CLIMBED UP A SERIES OF steep switchbacks. Sweating profusely, I stopped at a small stream. I was so far ahead of the donkey train that I could not hear their bells. After washing my face, I looked up to see a Nepalese man joining me to take a drink from the icy waters. Wearing a baseball cap and a broad smile, he offered me a warm "Namaste." I answered, *"Kasto cha,*" Nepali for "How are you?" His answer came in a rapid torrent of broken English.

"Today, sir, I am very happy. Today is a very big day for our village. There is a man coming here today with books for our school. We do not know how many, and we do not know where he is from. I think he is from Holland—that is what somebody told me. So our students are waiting, and I am going there now to greet his arrival."

A chill convulsed my body. Did our little book project mean this much to the community? I extended my hand. "My name is John. I am from America. This is Woody. The books are right behind us. Can you show us to the school?" Sushil said he would be happy to be our guide.

Woody and Sushil chatted. I fell several steps behind, focusing on my thoughts. The next hour would be the culmination of a year of planning. I wondered if it would live up to our expectations. Would the children be as excited as we'd imagined? Who were we to be showing up in this remote village with a bunch of used books? We had spent so much time, traveled so far. There were many reasons to be optimistic, including Sushil's enthusiasm. Still, I wondered whether anything could make the reality as wonderful as the scene that had played out in my imagination over the last year.

AS WE GOT CLOSE TO THE SCHOOL, A CACOPHONY OF VOICES COULD BE heard. Our pace quickened. In the dusty schoolyard, children were running around. Teachers were shouting. The headmaster approached and gave me a warm hug.

The students had formed a human corridor through which we were to walk. Sushil urged me to go first. I pressed my hands together, bowed, and said, "Namaste," to the first child, a five-year-old girl. She had jet-black hair and an ivory-white smile. She hung a marigold garland around my neck. Laughter ensued as several other girls competed to be the next to hang their garlands. We moved slowly through the line. Every moment of contact with each student was to be relished. The youngest ones had picked flower petals in the forest. These small offerings piled up in our hands. By the end, we could have opened a small flower shop.

We were led to a makeshift podium. The teachers were waiting to greet us. I recognized faces from the prior year. We shook hands and exchanged "Namastes." The children were hushed, and the headmaster made a brief speech:

"This is a very big day for our school and our village. We now have a library full of books. Inside books you will find hidden the mysteries of the world. With books, you can learn, and you can make a better future for your families and for our country. We wish to thank Mr. John and his father, Mr. Woody, for giving us such a precious gift, and we promise to always take good care of the books." I made a mental note to ask him not to lock these books up and wondered whether I should assure him that we'd return each year with new books to replace those that had been damaged.

And with that, we relieved the donkeys of their burden. As we unloaded the books, children rushed toward us, eagerly grabbing for the new treasure. As boys do, one of them bonked his friend on the head to secure a better spot in line. Except that there was no line. Only chaos. The students' excitement indicated that this was their first encounter with brightly colored children's books. They were wide-eyed as they gazed at photos of giraffes and hippos. They motioned eagerly to friends to point out the rings of Saturn. A girl's face was frozen in fear at her first encounter with the teeth of a great white shark. A small group giggled at a picture book of Labrador puppies.

As we watched, a teacher joined us. He took my hand in his. His brown eyes were moist and his face wore a wide smile. "You have given our children so much. We have so little to offer in return."

I had a lump in my throat. Words were hard to find. I struggled to explain that the school had filled my heart with a feeling it had never before experienced—that I had made a difference in the world, or at least one very small part of it. For these children, there was a bit more opportunity today than there had been yesterday. All of this had come about because of a simple request a year ago—"Perhaps, sir, you will someday come back with books." Woody and I made our best attempt to respond. But the real heroes were our friends around the world, old and new, who had helped us not to show up at this party empty-handed.

WE WALKED BACK DOWNHILL, THE UNBURDENED DONKEYS MAKING double time. At the guesthouse, I paid our donkey driver with a fistful of Nepalese rupees and a generous bonus. He bounced happily down the trail. I offered to buy my father a celebratory beer. We sat outside, on the lodge's rough and weather-beaten wooden picnic table. As the sun warmed us, a breeze from the river provided some relief.

For today at least, my fears about lack of father-son communication were not relevant. The day had provided many topics of conversation. As I poured our Carlsbergs into dusty glasses, I began to inundate him with my thoughts. I explained that I had so enjoyed the experience of delivering the books, but that my mind was also racing with questions about what else might be possible. This was too fun to stop now.

He asked what I thought was possible.

"Well, I was doing some research before we flew here, and I read that Nepal has twenty-three thousand villages. I was amazed that a country that looks so small on a map of the world could have so many. I wonder how many of these communities face a problem similar to that in Bahundanda. The illiteracy rate here is around seventy percent, so obviously this is not an isolated problem. And I know from my travels in places like Vietnam, Cambodia, Zambia, and Guatemala that they face similar issues. So I just wonder how to take this small project and move it beyond just a few villages in Nepal."

The fiery sun was dipping below the nearest peak for its 12-hour siesta, so I went inside to retrieve our jackets. I did not want the conversation to end, and upon returning to the table I kept asking questions. I started by inquiring whether Woody could remember how important the library was to me during my childhood.

"Yes, very much. We could not afford all the books you wanted.

You were a voracious reader, but money was always tight. At the library, you were always trying to check out more books than the allowed maximum."

He smiled at the memory. I knew he was proud of me. I was surprised that he had this vivid of a memory of my childhood. He had always worked so hard and was so quiet. But just because he did not talk did not mean he was not paying attention. I silently toasted this new era in father-son communications by draining my beer.

"Dad, think about all the villages in the world where children don't have that option. How many millions of kids will not have the opportunities I have in life, simply because they were denied an education at a young age? It's almost like there is this 'lottery of life.' At a young age children are arbitrarily deemed to be winners or losers, based upon where they were born. You're born in Scarsdale, you win the right to gain an education. You're born in Bogotá, you're denied that opportunity. It's arbitrary. It's not fair. I think it's in our power to do something about it."

"True. But it would take a lot of time and effort to do so. And what about your new job at Microsoft? Don't you have Bill Gates visiting next month?"

"Oh, yeah, right, I forgot. That real-life thing." Out in the Himalayas, one can forget about reality.

This did not, however, dampen my enthusiasm. This was important work. It was life-affirming. There could be no excuses. I'd work nights on this project. Weekends. Holidays. Whatever it took.

I went to bed that night with fantasies of subsequent trips delivering books to the schools of Nepal. I vowed that next time we would need even more donkeys, or perhaps we'd upgrade to a team of yaks.

CHAPTER 5

DEBATING A RADICAL CHANGE

TWO DAYS LATER, MY FATHER AND I WERE BACK IN KATHMANDU. I AM not a morning person, but on our first day back I woke just after dawn. I walked the quiet streets in search of some clarity on ways I could continue to set up libraries while still holding down my day job.

Instead of clarity, I found a group of monks, clad in saffron-colored robes, filing into the monastery for morning prayer. I wanted to follow them, to listen to the chanting, and maybe even find some time to meditate about life. But I did not know if one had to be a meditative monk to gain entry to the inner sanctuary.

As if to answer my question, an old monk approached. He shuffled slowly and extended two large and weather-beaten hands. They engulfed mine. His eyes, deep and warm, stared into mine with a look that was profound and peaceful, putting me at ease. He motioned me to follow him inside.

He offered a small yak-hair carpet to protect from the cold stone floor. He then motioned to a young monk of about eight years. The boy's face was frozen in concentration at his task—pouring tea from a huge pot at least half his size. The young monk handed me a brass bowl, then filled it with steaming yak-butter tea. My hands, stiff from the cold, clutched it in eager celebration. I nodded my thanks. They left me alone to join the other monks for prayers.

The tea took the edge off the cold. I doubt that Starbucks will ever sell *grande yak butter lattes,* but the salty and bitter liquid tasted great to me. As steam drifted over my face, I felt warmed by the monks' gesture of inclusion.

A bell rang, followed by a few seconds of silence. Then came the low, guttural chants of 30 monks. Hundreds of candles flickered in the darkness. I wanted to join the monks in meditation, to empty my mind of all thoughts. The only problem was that my Western, non-Buddhist mind had other ideas. Not only could I not empty my mind, I couldn't stop the flood of images and ideas streaming through my head since I'd arrived in Nepal seven days ago.

Instead of inner peace, I had inner turmoil. In my mind were two forces that were both powerful, but in diametric opposition. Microsoft had posted me in a new role, and in two days I was scheduled to journey back to that life. In the opposing corner stirred my quickly changing priorities. Did it really matter how many copies of Windows we sold in Taiwan this month when millions of children were without access to books? How could I get fired up about our electronic-commerce initiative in Hong Kong, or antipiracy efforts in China, when seven of ten kids in Nepal faced lifelong illiteracy?

Did my job really matter? A successful year would only help a rich company get richer. I would add some padding to a bank account that already exceeded anything I had dreamed possible by age 35.

Granted, life at Microsoft was nothing to complain about. I had a well-compensated position with a fast-growing company, a full-time car and driver, stock options, and carte blanche to travel around the world on an expense account. For years, I had taken intense pride in working for the *bellwether* technology company. Now my entire belief system was being challenged.

My inner voice nagged, "Look, you should admit to yourself that Microsoft will miss you for a month or two. Someone will quickly fill the void. It will be like you never worked there. Ask yourself, Are there thousands lining up to help poor villages build schools and libraries? *That* job is not being done. You should rise to this challenge."

Around me, the room had grown silent—the monks had finished. I took a sip of tea and realized too late that it was now cold. Checking my watch, I realized that half an hour had vanished during my internal debate.

The old monk returned. He took my hand in his, and we walked out into the sun. Distant white peaks and blue skies filled my sight line. The prayer flags being whipped by the wind invigorated my spirit.

My mind felt as if it had clarity. I was inching closer to a decision. I felt as though I was willing to give up the security of a corporate life. I might have life after Microsoft. It might take place here in Nepal.

I laughed to myself as I thought, "Oh, no, this is going to sound like a terrible cliché: Western guy walks into monastery and changes the course of his life. Do the Buddhists call it an epiphany, or is that a Catholic term?"

Despite my fears, this felt like the right thing to do. I knew my life would be happier, even if I did not yet know how to survive financially as a global do-gooder.

However, I would still have to announce my decision to the world and prepare for those who would try to talk me out of it. The world is full of risk-averse people. I knew that a lot of them would not be shy about offering their opinion that I should stick with the known, safe path. I wondered whether I'd be as brave, and as certain, once I'd been transplanted from the serenity of the monastery back into the real world.

TWO DAYS AFTER THE MONASTERY VISIT, I WAS IN A SLIGHTLY LESS happy frame of mind. At the Kathmandu Airport I glared at the Thai Airways jet that would carry me to Bangkok, then on to Beijing. I dreaded what lay ahead.

For most of our lives, we are taught to act in accordance with society's expectations. I would soon defy them. My entire life had been on a predictable trajectory dominated by a couple of university degrees and thirteen years of white-collar employment. My identity was defined by my career. I now planned a radical shift, a big leap into the unknown: from corporate executive to unemployed guy setting up libraries in the Himalayas. I prayed that I would be decisive and follow through on my gut instinct.

CHAPTER 6

LONELY IN A CITY OF

12 MILLION STRANGERS

TWO MAIN FEAR FACTORS LAY IN MY IMMEDIATE FUTURE—SOPHIE and Michael, my live-in girlfriend and my boss. I spent most of the four-hour flight to Beijing thinking about them. It would take a great deal of courage to tell them both that my life was about to veer off on a surprise trajectory. I felt more like the Cowardly Lion.

Sophie and I had been together for the last year. We had originally appeared to be on the fast track to marriage—so much so that I had agreed to be the "trailing partner" and move with her to Beijing when her advertising agency had asked her to run their China office.

I hated the thought of leaving Sydney. I loved the city. But I loved Sophie more.

In early January 1999, after three-and-a-half years of sun-drenched bliss, I said good-bye to my adopted hometown. On that last day I played tennis with my friend Mike as the sun rose over perfect grass courts, then bodysurfed at Manly Beach. Two flights and 74 degrees of latitude later, I arrived just in time for the second week of Beijing's brutal winter.

This was the first time I had optimized a major decision for someone besides myself. At first it felt great. Our initial months in

China were a bold adventure. We wandered the markets practicing our rudimentary Mandarin Chinese skills on amused vendors, searched for the city's spiciest Sichuan restaurant, and dove into our new positions leading large parts of our respective companies' growth push into the world's hottest new market.

But lately we had run into problems. Our differing attitude toward career was the main one. I wanted to devote more time and energy to my passions outside of work. These included travel in remote parts of the developing world and a significant focus on sponsoring education projects. Sophie was averse to taking the time away from her job. A bigger issue was that she had no interest in joining me on my travels. Her preferred holiday was more Four Seasons than Third World.

A six-foot, blue-eyed blonde from rural Kansas, Sophie reveled in our glamorous expatriate lifestyle. In her words, she had escaped the rural Midwest and embraced the world. After too long being in junior roles, she had busted through the glass ceiling and now ran the China operations for an international advertising agency.

I was proud of her. But her focus on career was defining most of our existence. When we'd fallen in love, much of our time was spent hiking, discussing great books, exploring Australia, reading, and making bold and exotic travel plans. Over the last six months, things had changed. As she focused on her role in China, many of our shared passions had been thrown overboard.

The previous Christmas had been but one example. We planned to spend two chilled weeks on the islands of Indonesia. We'd start on the salubrious beaches of Bali and Lombok, with a week to decompress, sleep in, and enjoy each other's company again after a few months of only sporadic meet-ups as Sophie commuted between Sydney and Beijing. Next, we'd hike volcanoes on the island of Flores. We'd close off our Indonesian triathlon traversing the Gili islands in a rented sleep-aboard sailboat. Diving, reading, and fresh seafood would be the focus of our days.

I had spent hours planning the trip in detail. Flights and hotels were booked. Sailboat deposits were made. Dive spots were researched. The backpack was loaded with books.

I was also bringing along a surprise. As a profession of faith in our shared future, I had filled a hardbound vellum journal with a long list of the life adventures I envisioned us enjoying during our lives together. It was my profession of faith that we'd always be a couple.

On the eve of our departure, she canceled. Her client (Coca-Cola) needed her at a high-level planning meeting, she explained. I proposed that instead of 14 days, we go for 10, but there was another work-related excuse. She counteroffered with what I considered a pale substitute—an unadventurous three-day weekend at a resort in southern Australia. Annoyed and defeated, I set to work canceling our Indonesian reservations. A sad thought crossed my mind: How many of the "Journal of our Shared Future" 's prophecies had any chance of coming true?

Now, three months later, my decision to leave Microsoft and to focus my life on education projects would place my future in the world's poorest communities. This would have serious repercussions on our relationship; in fact, it might even end it. Upon my return to Beijing, I'd be announcing to Sophie that I wanted to spend the majority of my time in places where she had no interest in joining me. I doubted that our union could sustain this much time apart.

As if this was not enough, one other person was on my mind: my boss, Michael. He headed the Greater China Region for Microsoft and had hired me as his right-hand man within days of hearing that Sophie and I were planning a move to Beijing. He was already dependent on me to help him keep up with a massive workload. I liked and respected Michael. As coworkers, as drinking buddies, and as tennis opponents, we had a great time together. I was learning a lot from him. He was one of the smartest and most effective execs I had met at a company of superstars. I was also honored that he had placed so much trust in me.

I felt awful as I contemplated letting him down. He had trusted me. I would not be upholding my end of the bargain.

For the time being, I would have to keep my life-changing news to myself. Bill Gates was scheduled to visit China. It was my responsibility to assure that the visit was productive and well executed. This was not the time to make disruptive announcements. For a few weeks my plans would be bottled up inside. As soon as Bill was gone, I could let this genie out of the bottle.

. . .

THE BAGGAGE CLAIM AREA OF BEIJING'S TIRED AND DILAPIDATED AIR-
port was crowded and chaotic. Acrid cigarette smoke hung in the
air. All rules about personal space had been repealed. Perhaps they
had never existed. An elderly Chinese lady shoved me out of her
way in the excitement of seeing her bag. Welcome home.

My attention was diverted by a slap on the back and a loud
"Ni hao." My driver, Liu Wei, had managed to find me in the baggage scrum. He was clad in a solid blue shirt with red-and-white-
striped sleeves and blue stars on the collar. I hugged this living
Chinese version of a large American flag and handed him a bottle of
duty-free whiskey. "For later, after you drop me off and after you
get home, okay?"

It was an unusually warm spring evening. I opened the window
as I told Liu Wei about the trip in a combination of English and
broken Mandarin. Within seconds the pollution outside grated on
my throat and burned the eyes. The window went back up. A depressing mood descended. Where had the fresh air and the possibilities of the Himalayas gone?

Within twenty minutes we were at Sophie's and my shared
home. I asked Liu Wei to pick me up early the next day. There was a
full slate planned for Monday morning.

Inside our spacious and subsidized expat compound, Sophie
greeted me with a huge hug and several kisses. Her blue eyes spar-
kled with a welcome that said, "You're home." With a "Ta-dah!"
motion she produced a bottle of Cricket Pitch, my favorite Australian Shiraz. The smell of Enchiladas Casa Sophie, a dish she had
learned to make while living in Mexico City, wafted through the air.
It was touching that she had made my favorite food; the dinner conversation that lay in front of us would be gut-wrenching.

From the moment we had met at a cocktail party at my Sydney
flat a year earlier, in the spring of 1998, we had communicated
openly and candidly. There was almost nothing we would not share.
Whereas some former girlfriends had described me as being de-
tached, things were different with Sophie. I felt extremely comfortable with her and told her everything. As I poured us two glasses of

the ruby red Shiraz, I started to regale her with every detail of the trip.

I started slowly, describing what it was like to travel with my father. I told her about our visits to the schools, and the feeling of joy I had upon seeing the students' reaction to the books. Next came a description of how great my father had been about trekking through challenging conditions, and how happy he seemed while out in the mountain.

She interrupted to ask about the conditions—did you have showers? Hot water?

"Well, yes, there were showers, but the water was not hot. No electricity. Nothing quite like a cold shower after a hot day of trekking," I nervously chuckled in my best Boy Scout–leader voice. She attempted a sympathetic smile.

I reminded myself that despite her international postings, her strong preference was for the glamour of the expatriate life in a big city like London, Prague, or Paris. Large paychecks, housecleaners, and a full-time driver on call could make any city feel even better than home. My desire to strap on backpacks and "go walk about" in the developing world held no appeal to her. We were both "international," but in very different ways.

This did not make either of us a better or a worse person than the other. It wasn't as if this was "new news" to me; she had been up-front about this from the beginning. I could also not blame her for enjoying a comfortable life, especially since she had studied and worked extremely hard to get to this position. How many Americans had mastered French, Spanish, Czech, and Mandarin Chinese by age 33?

Sophie brought me back into our world by repeating for the third time how happy she was to have me home. As she served the steaming enchiladas, my angst increased as I cautiously broached the subject:

"Look, I think I should tell you that I may not be home as much as you expect. I am thinking about returning to Nepal on a fairly frequent basis."

"But what about Microsoft? You've already used up so much vacation time on this last trip to Nepal. And I want us to go to a beach resort in Thailand this year."

I suggested that since our last trip had been to a luxury resort, perhaps we could next have a Himalayan holiday. I told her that it would mean a lot to me if she could see our work and deliver more books.

Silence. Then words that sucked the oxygen out of me: "John, you can go to Nepal as often as you want, and I will always be waiting for you when you get back. But you know me—I don't want to trek, and I don't think of nights in a sleeping bag as a great vacation, or particularly romantic. So just make sure that if you do go, you still have enough vacation time for the Thai beach."

I decided to just throw it out there. But first—a large gulp of wine. "I am not sure how to say this, but I think that Microsoft's vacation policy might not be that relevant. I am thinking about quitting."

She looked shocked. She reminded me that we had just arrived in Beijing, that I was kicking butt in my role, and that I might one day be able to run the entire China region.

I explained that my title and my career no longer seemed important to me. I might need to leave them behind. Something had changed inside me, and I wanted to be true to that desire.

Again, a cold, hard dose of reality. "But how are we going to live? Microsoft pays for this house, and the rent is ridiculously expensive."

"Maybe we downsize? Or I do some consulting work on the side? I really have no idea. I have not fully thought this through. Right now what I need is to think about what would be possible, not all the reasons I can't make a change."

We sat down to a rather quiet dinner. In just ten minutes we had gone from a happy and conversant reunion to a tense silence. I wondered if the next few months would witness many more of these awkward stalemates.

CHAPTER 7

GATES IN CHINA

FORTUNATELY, THE FRENETIC PREPARATIONS FOR BILL'S VISIT PRO-
vided immediate and much needed distractions.

The morning after my return from Nepal, after a night of fitful
sleep, I arrived at the office early. The focus on Bill's upcoming visit
meant a day of dawn-to-dusk meetings.

I started the day with a check of e-mail. I was happy to see a full
in-box. Our subsidiary was definitely in all-hands-on-deck mode.
Michael and I were exerting pressure on the sales teams to line up a
few big deals that we could close either before or during Bill's visit.
Johnson, our head of sales, had copied me on a mail he'd sent out to
his team:

"Sensitive of urgency, salesman shall be a wolf. A wolf never
waits the result."

I rang Johnson on his cell to cheer him on. "You should not be
shy about keeping the heat on your guys." The subsidiary had
missed its sales goals during the prior half year. Now that I was on
board, I had no intention of showing Bill anything but rapidly improving results. I reminded Johnson that all we needed were two or
three large deals. "Big companies are already using our software.
They are just not paying for it. You should tell them that sooner or

later, they are going be pushed by the government to legalize. This is our golden opportunity—nothing focuses people like a deadline. This is the only time Bill will be in China during the next year. Use that to our advantage. If it helps, we will carve some time out of Bill's schedule so that any executive who signs with us can have a short chat and have his picture taken with Bill. Tell them we will have press at the event. Maybe their photo will be in the newspapers. That might help to close a few deals."

It may seem a strange inducement: a photo op as part of a six-figure deal. Yet it was actually an attractive offer to many company executives. In China circa 1999, senior managers did not earn their positions by being great capitalists. Most of the big companies were government-owned, and Communist Party leaders would often be rotated through senior positions based more on their political connections than on business acumen. Few things could matter to a political figure as much as getting his photo with a famous person, whether it be Chinese president Jiang Zemin or Bill Gates, seen by millions in the newspaper. It was an odd quid pro quo to offer, but one that I felt confident would yield results.

A chiming noise interrupted. The Microsoft Outlook calendar warned that I was running late for a meeting with our public relations agency. Tomorrow was our press conference to announce Bill's visit. We'd brief fifty journalists on the expected highlights and itinerary for his two days in China.

My main concern was to put Bill's visit in a "Chinese context." Michael and I were both very aware that Microsoft's local subsidiary was not perceived as a good Chinese citizen. Issues of nationalism, patriotism, and pride all intersect in Chinese corporate culture, and we knew that our treatment by the government would be more positive if we were viewed as being "the Chinese part of a global company."

Because of my experience in Australia and the Asia region, the team turned to me for my opinion. During my tenure as marketing director, Microsoft Australia had been voted by readers of *BRW*, the nation's most influential business magazine, as the second "most respected Australian company." Qantas had won, and the Foster's brewing house had placed third. We were proud to have been considered as "true-blue" as these two Aussie legends. I was asked how Microsoft China could pull off the same coup.

I explained that I was really too new to China to have an informed opinion.

"Everything is so different here. I don't yet speak the language. And I don't understand your customs."

"We're not that different," Alex, the marketing director, challenged.

"Yes, you are. There are parts of this memo that are somewhat incomprehensible to me, like the idea of closing the press conference with a song. What's up with that? No offense, but we have enough PR trouble in China already without me torturing the press with my voice."

"Do you not sing songs at press conferences in America? Or in Australia?"

To buy time until I could come up with the right answer, I stared at the memo. "To close the press conference, the Microsoft management ensemble sings a song—with accompaniment by the band [Band? Had I approved the budget for a band?]. The song should show the vigor and vitality of Microsoft employees."

I tried to imagine Jack Welch and his cadre of senior GE executives crooning a tune to the assembled press—"We're just wild about shareholder value, and our shareholders are wild about us." Or Donald Trump singing, "Give my regards to Broadway, as I am planning to buy it soon."

I suppressed my smile and changed the subject.

"We have to make sure that Bill is well briefed and is constantly citing examples of the great work Microsoft is doing in China. We are spending millions of dollars on programs like technology scholarships for promising students. We're building a massive research office here. We're developing new products that will launch in China and then propagate to the rest of the world. But nobody talks about these investments and initiatives. In every meeting with the government here, they tell us about how we need to do more to help China develop a technology industry. We're not getting any credit for our efforts. Chinese companies are having a field day by saying it's more patriotic to buy software from them rather than from a 'foreign enemy.' If there's only one thing we do right, it has to be making sure that Bill is on message that Microsoft is a good corporate citizen."

I volunteered to lead an ad hoc group that would write up Bill's briefing notes and left the rest of the team to work on the closing song.

TWO WEEKS LATER, I FLEW TO THE SOUTHERN CITY OF SHENZHEN, racked with fear. Bill was scheduled to arrive the next day, and there was so much that could go wrong. Microsoft had taken a beating in the Chinese press for suing a local company for software piracy. Unfortunately for us, it was a company with good political connections. The Chinese have a word for this, *guanxi* — "connections that can be very useful." This company had unleashed the forces of *guanxi* in a vicious counterattack. The pliant local media had been convinced to portray Microsoft as an "evil foreign company that is only here to exploit the Chinese." We had some image adjustment to do.

In addition to being fearful, I was also fascinated by how it would all play out. The juxtaposition we were about to witness could not have been greater. Bill Gates, the world's most successful living capitalist, was about to visit the most populous Communist stronghold.

On the plane, drinking a lukewarm cup of Chinese tea and munching on steamed pork buns, I did a back-of-the-envelope calculation to determine the wealth disparity between Bill and the average Chinese. Using the Microsoft stock price as a proxy, Bill's net worth on that day was about $60 billion, give or take a mere billion. In contrast, the average annual GNP per Chinese citizen was $725. Bill's wealth was thus the equivalent to the annual earnings of 83 million Chinese citizens.

By March of 1999, nobody really believed the old orthodoxy that the country was purely Communist. A saying popularized by past leader Deng Xiaoping was "To get rich is glorious." As if to prove it, we had a backlog of requests for meetings with Bill so long that a month of his time could not have met the demand. The level of enthusiasm the Chinese had for the world's greatest capitalist spoke volumes. In one generation, the Chinese had gone from viewing a person like Bill as a "running dog of capitalism" to elbowing each other out of the way to get their photo taken with him. Although I was nervous, there was also a happy realization that regardless of how things went, I would eyewitness an interesting bit of history.

Eager to get my mind off the visit for at least an hour, I dove into a book that had nothing to do with technology, Microsoft, or China. *The Unfinished Presidency* promised to tell the story of Jimmy Carter's "journey beyond the White House." I was immediately drawn into the story of Carter the humanitarian. His work building homes with Habitat for Humanity and monitoring elections around the world provided inspiration—and showed that people could turn the page and start a new chapter of their lives. This was even true for a man like Carter, who had previously held the most powerful office in the world.

The current chapter focused on efforts led by Carter in the early 1990s to eradicate the guinea worm. This microscopic parasite made life miserable for millions across wide swaths of Africa and Asia. It would enter the human body through contaminated drinking water. Once inside it grew up to three feet. Unlike a tick that burrows into the skin, the guinea worm would actually burrow *outside*. A farmer would be going about his or her day when suddenly a hole would open in his or her ankle or foot and out would pop a fattened worm. Even after the shock, the swelling, and the pain of slowly removing the worm by wrapping it around a stick, the affected patient would be left with a burning blister made worse by toxins secreted by the worm. With few treatment options available, it would quickly be covered in flies. Diseases like tetanus could result.

A small amount of money could prevent this problem. For pennies, people could be saved from misery. Inexpensive microfilters to provide safe drinking water were available. At a health conference, Carter asked a simple question: "If the guinea worm is so easy to eradicate, why is it not being done?" Told that it was mostly a matter of political will, he decided that he'd lend his own connections to the fight against this parasite.

In early discussions with others interested in the disease, officials began by talking to Carter about whether to focus on Ghana or Nigeria or Pakistan. Carter, thinking big, suggested that instead of eliminating the worm in just one country, they should aim for a *worldwide* eradication of this parasite. Together with William Foege, the former head of the Centers for Disease Control, Carter "convinced the World Health Organization to select guinea worm disease as the second disease to be eradicated from the earth—after smallpox." *

I loved that Carter thought big. He also got results: the world's poor benefited from a 97 percent decline in the reported cases of guinea worm disease, from 900,000 in 1989 to fewer than 30,000 by 1995.

I was so captivated by this success story that I had not noticed our approach to the airport. Our bumpy landing brought me back from remote Africa to southern China. It was time to leap back into work.

THOUSANDS OF DETAILS HAD TO BE IRONED OUT IN ADVANCE OF BILL'S arrival. We had planned every minute of his day, down to two three-minute bathroom breaks. This schedule had to be approved by his team in Redmond, Washington, two weeks in advance of his visit. Our team in China had walked every inch of the booked hotel, arguing whether the walk from the Grand Ballroom to the restaurant where lunch would be served would take two minutes or three. I broke the tie. "He's high energy, impatient, and manically focused. Go with two."

One part of Bill's trip planning had to be the ultimate travel luxury. A staff person in Redmond sent a garment bag full of clothes that arrived in each city a few days before Bill. When Bill entered a hotel room, his clean and pressed clothes were already hanging in the closet, with a tie that perfectly matched the suit. Lucky duck.

Prior to this being standard practice, his sartorial splendor left much to be desired. He would sometimes start the day by donning the rumpled clothes from yesterday off the floor. The official Microsoft PR spin on this practice: he is so focused on solving bigger issues that he doesn't pay attention to little things like how he dresses. I will leave the unofficial spin to the reader's imagination.

Bill was in Hong Kong, speaking at a CEO conference. The plan

* *The Unfinished Presidency*, 1998.

was for him to spend the night there and make the drive to Shenzhen early in the morning. It's about a ninety-minute drive from Hong Kong to Shenzhen if you are a mere mortal. However, if you're the richest man in the world, then certain arrangements can be made to cut that time in half. In Bill's case, this meant no need to dawdle at the Hertz counter as the clerk tried to sell him overpriced insurance. Instead, he walked out the front door of Hong Kong's glorious waterfront Grand Hyatt to find a convoy of vehicles waiting for him. We're talking major-league motorcade. Black limos, SUVs with smoked-glass windows, motorcycles, and police cars. Sirens blaring, lights flashing. *CHiPS* meets *West Wing*.

The motorcade was courtesy of the Chinese government, which had also reserved the border crossing between Hong Kong and the mainland for Bill's exclusive benefit. A lane on the highway was also blocked for his private use. It was enough to make me wish I'd flown down to Hong Kong to join in the fun.

As Bill set the new *Guinness Book* record for cross-border commuting, we were nervously waiting at the cavernous government-owned hotel that would host the day's events. The lobby was a sea of reporters, government functionaries, hotel management, assorted groupies, and Microsoft employees. An excited buzz went up among the 100-plus members of his welcoming committee as Bill's limo sped up the heavily manicured driveway, right on time.

The limo door opens. A hush descends. Bill steps tentatively into the lobby. The crowd applauds. Bill looks perplexed. His face says, "All I have done is walk ten steps from the limo to the lobby. These people are clapping as though I just nailed a half gainer off the high-dive board."

I had not seen Bill in person in over three years. The first thing I noticed was that the legend was right. His hair really was a mess. His haircut was definitely not befitting a billionaire. Go into Supercuts, ask for their newest employee, tell her that you're in a terrible hurry, that you will tip based on speed rather than on quality, and you get something like this as a result.

The second thing I noticed was that Bill did not look at all happy to be here. Panic set in—I was partially in charge of the next event, and I did not want an unenthused CEO onstage.

But there was no time for thinking about any of this, as we had to immediately usher him into the first event—the official launch of Microsoft Venus. We were using a rather loose interpretation of the term *launch;* this product was so mired in the "still-on-the-drawing-board" phase of its life cycle that it did not even have a real name. Venus was the code name, and in truth we were at least six months away from product availability.

Microsoft Venus was a device custom-designed for the mainland Chinese market. We were trying to exploit one of the world's largest market gaps. In China, hundreds of millions of families had risen high enough up the economic ladder to own a television. Internet penetration into the home, meanwhile, was about a hundredth of that level. So rather than trying to sell Chinese families an alien device, a PC, for their home, we would instead convince them to attach the "Venus" box to their television. Venus would allow them to access the Internet. But, wait, there's more—it would also play DVDs.

In other words, it was the kind of product that made total sense in theory and on paper. The reality of bringing the product to market was proving to be more difficult. What we'd be showing today was what I euphemistically described to a member of the press as a "working prototype." It was the only working prototype in existence. In my mind, the official list of components boiled down to metal casing, two chips, duct tape, and a prayer.

Nevertheless, the hall was packed like a rock concert. This, after all, was the crazy Internet-bubble era, when pretty much any product announcement that could string together buzz words invoking the Internet, connectivity, and China would meet an enthused reaction and hoards of cash. We had over 1,500 people in a room that any fire marshal worth his salt would have capped at half that number. The noise was deafening. Chinese tech geeks were standing on chairs to get a better view. Flashes flashed and photographers climbed over each other and threw elbows to get close to Bill. Reporters yelled questions in competing bursts of Mandarin and Cantonese. China had clearly caught Venus fever.

After watching Bill bump into a few photographers as he struggled to make his way to the stage, I joined the "human wall" that stood between him and the thrusting, impatient paparazzi. He finally got to the podium, but could not quiet the crowd. I pictured him thrusting his fists in the air and yelling, "Hello, Cleveland, are you ready to rock?"

He burst my fantasy bubble by instead clearing his throat and telling the crowd that he was happy to be back in China. The crowd quieted and he talked about our team's vision of delivering customized information to millions of Chinese via the Venus device. He explained why the product made economic sense for the manufacturers whom we were trying to convince to produce it, and for consumers whom we'd ultimately ask to buy it.

We moved on to the product prototype demonstration. To lend authenticity to the demo, I'd convinced the team to set up a "typical Chinese living room" on the stage. My goal was to have people see the Venus device in the context in which it would be used. Our set designers had, however, come up with a living room that was more W Hotel than "rural Chinese peasant," and one had to wonder how much we were paying to get Scandinavian-designed sofas airlifted in. Nevertheless, it was amusing to watch Bill amble across the stage to join our two Chinese presenters in their "living room," as though a khaki-clad Bill just happened to be strolling in their agrarian, rural neighborhood and had dropped by for a quick product demo.

The session went well, at least by the standards of the "low bar" I had set (e.g., the prototype does not blow up onstage and immolate the presenters). Within ten minutes, it was all over, and Bill was being ushered off to sign a few contracts that Johnson's team had secured. I joined the Venus team onstage and we exchanged numerous high fives and hugs. The day had started off strong.

Alas, the sum total of Venus devices eventually sold was zero. The project was canceled, for undefined "technical reasons," less than a year later. On its official launch day one would never have guessed how quickly a product could move from "the device of the future" to the scrap heap of history.

THE PART OF BILL'S VISIT THAT REQUIRED THE MAJORITY OF MY FOCUS was his scheduled television interview with Shui Junyi. Junyi (the Chinese put the last name first, first name last, so one addressed him as Junyi) was one of China's most famous television journalists, and he would be recording the interview that day for airing the following week on China's leading television network, China Central Television (CCTV). CCTV is *the* network in China, holding the market power of ABC, NBC, and CBS combined. If anyone in China has a television, there's about a 99 percent chance he or she has access to CCTV. As Microsoft had lately experienced severely negative press in China, we made it a high priority to give Bill a chance to talk directly to the Chinese people. The stakes were high, as was my blood pressure as I contemplated introducing the world's most successful capitalist to the world's biggest Communist country via a one-on-one chat with a journalist none of us had met.

I felt in over my head. After a short time in the Middle Kingdom, what did I know about the Chinese media?

My immediate reaction was to call my friend Dave and propose that we blow off steam over a drink. At the bar, I flagged down our waitress, who looked no more than 16 years old, and ordered a Scotch on the rocks.

I told Dave, "This is such a huge opportunity for Microsoft. You know the old adage 'You never get a second chance to make a first impression'? Well, we will be making a first impression on *at least one hundred million viewers*. Think about it—it's like having forty percent of Americans watching an interview. All these people in China are going to have an indelible impression of Bill, and therefore Microsoft, burned into their brain, all based upon this twenty-minute interview. And having been in China for all of two months, I am in charge. I cannot screw this up."

The next morning I decided that the logical first step was to meet with the journalist covering the story. Shui Junyi was famous and popular in China. The prior year he had filmed one-on-one interviews with Bill Clinton and Tony Blair. My team described him to me as "the Peter Jennings of China." This only increased my fear.

Over the phone, I suggested to Junyi that we meet for a coffee and get to know each other, then discuss how we would work together. We set a meeting for the following Saturday morning at Beijing's Intercontinental Hotel.

My team and I arrived early and staked out a large table in the middle of the lobby. It was an unusually bright day for winter in Beijing, and the atrium's massive garden and abundant sunlight made me feel as though we were in Bali rather than Beijing. Junyi and his team arrived right on time. He strode to our table confidently. Dressed in jeans, boots, and black leather jacket, he looked even younger than his 35 years. His face showed a complete absence of stress.

He smiled broadly as he introduced himself in perfect English. Our respective entourages were introduced. It seemed to be a common rule in Chinese business that one should bring three times as many people to each meeting as were necessary. Fully two-thirds of participants in most meetings never spoke nor seemed to take notes, and I often left having no idea why they had been included.

The 12 other meeting participants leaned inward to Junyi and me, indicating that we were to talk while they listened. In order to learn as much as possible, I immediately began asking questions of Junyi. "Junyi, it's great to meet such a famous journalist who is known by hundreds of millions of Chinese viewers. We're thrilled that you're going to interview Bill. Can you tell me more about CCTV's goals for the interview, and also your own?"

"I am a big fan of technology," he responded. "And I think that Microsoft, with other companies of course, has brought technology to millions of people who can now use it to be more productive. I also want to help the Chinese people understand more about what makes someone like Bill a great businessman. We do not have many examples of homegrown entrepreneurs. Yet there are millions of young kids here in our country who say that they want to be the next Bill Gates. China will only advance if we become a technically literate nation, and one that encourages the formation of new businesses. I think that Bill can be an inspiration to my viewers."

Hmm, maybe this wouldn't be too difficult, I thought. I was used to the Chinese press vilifying Microsoft, and now here was a journalist who seemed to respect our leader. So I went with this feeling, breathed deeply, and took a risk:

"Mr. Shui, I share your perspective. I think that Microsoft does some great work and I am proud to have spent most of my career working there. But I see a lot of criticism of us in the Chinese media—we are often portrayed as being an imperialistic American company that has 'invaded' China. But in actuality ninety-nine per-cent of Microsoft China's employees are Chinese natives, with ob-vious exceptions like me, of course. (This drew a laugh from Junyi.) Bill has publicly stated that one day China will be one of Microsoft's three biggest markets, along with the U.S. and India. The company is investing tens of millions of dollars in a research lab here in Bei-jing. There are only three places on earth where we do pure re-search—Seattle, Oxford, and Beijing. I view this as the ultimate sign of respect for the intellectual prowess of China's young computer scientists. I'd like for us to be able to tell that story—the 'Chinese version of Microsoft'—to your viewers."

Junyi agreed that this would be the right approach, and we be-gan brainstorming on questions that would touch on these sub-jects. It was a productive hour, one characterized by candor and cooperation. We got along so well that we agreed to meet again in two weeks. Shui asked that we meet "one-on-one, no entourages, no note takers."

Two weeks later we had dinner at the Louisiana restaurant at the Beijing Hilton. Over a bottle of cabernet, we continued to discuss "the Chinese version of Microsoft," and Junyi was kind enough to tell me about the questions he planned to ask so that I could make sure Bill was prepared. We had a celebratory cognac, toasted the success of the interview, and parted into the chilly streets of Beijing with an excited promise to meet up again in Shenzhen.

RARELY HAD I FELT SO GOOD ABOUT MY PREPARATION FOR AN ASSIGN-ment. At 3 p.m., as I walked into Bill's suite to prepare him for the interview, I thought of the adage that James Baker III, the for-mer U.S. secretary of state, said had been drilled into him from a young age by his father: "Prior preparation prevents poor perfor-mance."

My mood quickly turned from quiet confidence to outright panic. It became obvious during the first thirty seconds of talking to Bill that he had not done his prior preparation. He was asking basic questions, including the name of the reporter and the network. Knowing how busy Bill is, I gave him the benefit of the doubt and began to explain some of the key facts about Microsoft in China that I hoped we could get across during the interview. As I talked, he stared at the floor and rocked back and forth in his chair. Suddenly I felt insanely insecure—was he impatient? Bored? Few things can yank the carpet out from under one's confidence as much as one's boss not paying attention. I continued on, discussing some of the investments being made in China by Microsoft that I hoped he would discuss during the interview. Again, I got no reaction, and the worn gray carpet seemed to evoke more interest than my ideas for a successful interview. I cut myself off from the briefing and asked, "Are you ready for this—do you feel that you know the China-specific answers to Junyi's questions?"

"Yes, let's go" was his curt reply.

So we went.

I had gotten Junyi's permission to remain in the room and positioned myself behind the cameraman to be out of Bill's and Junyi's sight lines. Which is a good thing, because my face would probably have given away my disappointment. Bill's answers were not even close to those that we had suggested, and they had little to do with China. Junyi's first question focused on our R&D spending: "Microsoft invests over two billion dollars per year in research and development. How much of that money is spent in China?"

Bill's suggested answer (per the briefing notes): "Our investment in China is significant. As a matter of fact, this is one of only three markets in the world where we've opened a research laboratory. The other two are at Oxford in Great Britain, and in Seattle. We're doing a lot of work to make it easier to enter Mandarin characters, both on a keyboard and via pen-based computing. Personally, as a guy who grew up writing code, I have a great deal of respect for the brilliant scientists educated at Chinese universities, and they are doing work that will affect how Chinese people use computers for the next several decades."

Bill's answer (paraphrased): "Well, I can't give you an exact number, but it's large. We invest heavily because we believe that research is really important to the future of computing."

I was incredulous, and disappointed, and it only got worse as the interview went on. As each China-specific question was asked, Bill gave a generic answer.

Later in the interview, Junyi discussed how Chinese youth looked up to Bill: "In fact, on the way in here I met a five-year-old girl outside the hotel who was crying because she wanted to meet you. She said that you are her hero, but she could not get past security." Bill missed a golden opportunity to show his human side to 100 million Chinese citizens. Rather than saying "That's a shame, I'd love to say hello to her after the interview," he instead acted as though the subject had not been raised. He said nothing, there was an awkward pause, and then Junyi went to the next question.

I was tempted to stop the interview, except that this would also have stopped my career. Instead I sat in my chair, quietly pondering why CEOs sometimes decide that they are too smart to listen to the rest of their team. After hours of preparation, and getting as close to a journalist as is ethically allowed, my advice had been ignored. I thought of Paul Theroux's line written while on a cruise ship: "After a man has made a lot of money, he usually becomes a bad listener."

As the interview wrapped up, I tuned out. In my thoughts, I gave Bill the benefit of the doubt—after all, he is traveling constantly, we do business in more than fifty countries, we're growing by leaps and bounds, and he has a lot to keep up with. The interview had been important for me. For Bill, it might have been just another in a series of meetings and interviews that were all strung together as he frantically crisscrossed the globe.

Yet my mind remained fixed on the idea that for Microsoft, the company to which I still felt loyalty, it was a missed opportunity to win over a skeptical Chinese public.

I had thought it would be exciting to spend time with Bill. But my focus was on results, not on proximity to power. The experience confirmed that pulling the plug on my career was the best idea. As the company got bigger, there was less correlation between efforts and outcome.

I had put long hours into this interview, and that time could not be gained back. But I knew it was important not to focus on Bill's performance. There was no way I could ever run a company this large, so I was in no position to be judgmental. What seemed more important was the signal this sent to me. If I could not make a big difference at Microsoft, then perhaps this gave me even more of a green light to bail out. I could launch my own start-up and focus my hyperkinetic energy on the growing slate of Nepal projects. Rather than being in Shenzhen, I could be in Kathmandu. The children of Nepal obviously needed me more than my employer did. It was time to jump out of the plane and run my own show.

BILL'S BATBOY

Despite the demotivation inherent in Bill's China visit, I can't help but respect him. Not only did he start a great company at a young age, but the work he and Melinda are doing through the Gates Foundation will positively influence the lives of millions.

I am well aware that even though it was risky to leave Microsoft to start my own charity, I had a nice "safety net" in place because of the company's stock-options program. Many people use the word *generous* when talking about this compensation scheme, but I think of it as visionary. The way Bill and his management team set things up was quite clever, because they attached a quid pro quo to the options. To work for the company, one had to accept a rate of pay that was significantly below what one could make at other companies. For example, when I joined Microsoft in 1991, my base pay was $17,000 lower than it had been in banking. In return, I was given 3,250 share options in the company.* The message this sent to employees was that if the company did well in the long term, they would also. But there were no guarantees, and only hard work and smart strategic thinking would increase the odds of this calculated risk paying off. Like much of history, it seems obvious in retrospect that this was a fantastic trade-off, but at the time none of us knew.

* I still have the original letter, signed by Melinda Gates, and will one day auction it off as a charity fund-raiser.

continued

By 1999, those of us who had been at the company for a long time had done quite well. I give most of the credit to Bill and Steve Ballmer for their visionary leadership and their tenacious attention to detail. The two of them reminded me of a theory of Warren Buffett's that I had read—whom you work for makes a big difference. Buffett recalled that a long time ago, baseball players like Babe Ruth and Lou Gehrig voted a full share of their World Series proceeds to their batboy.

"The key to life," said Buffett, "is to figure out who to be the batboy for."

Few people get to be batboy for the Yankees of the Ruth-Gehrig era, or the Microsoft of the Gates-Ballmer era. I am grateful for the serendipity.

Of greater importance to my long-term success were the management and leadership lessons I learned during nearly nine years at the company. These will be discussed in a later section of the book.

CHAPTER 8

WALKING AWAY

KNOWING THAT I WAS GOING TO LEAVE DID NOT MAKE IT ANY EAS-ier to contemplate the fateful moment when I'd need to hit the switch. I would be severing my ties with everything that was important in my immediate world—Sophie, Michael, Microsoft, and China. As I had only been in Beijing for four months, there was no support structure of friends to turn to for advice, comfort, and solace. I knew that the coming months would be one of the roughest periods of my life.

Making things even harder was an inherent trait: I hate to disappoint people. From a young age, I had always been a "good kid" who was loved and respected by my parents, their immediate circle of friends, and my teachers. Something I think of as the "make-other-people-happy-with-you gene" was part of my DNA from a young age. Now, rather than pleasing Sophie and Michael, the two people closest to me in China, I would instead be breaking away from them.

I knew that I would be at a loss to explain why my life plan had changed so radically and why they did not fit in with it. We were united in our glamorous lives as expats and our chosen careers; to opt out would be to abandon one's tribe.

As much as I knew how painful the separations would be for all of us, I also knew it had to be done. The feeling of excitement for my life outside Microsoft had increased to such an extent that my mind was blazing with thoughts and ideas about a post-Microsoft life. I knew that I'd go back to Nepal to see the schools we were building and the libraries we were setting up and to plan future growth. I was becoming interested in projects that helped refugees to resettle successfully. Friends were suggesting that I do consulting projects for their start-ups and use the lucrative fees to fund more schools and libraries.

I knew that I had to free myself from any constraints that would prevent the pursuit of these dreams.

A STRONG SIGNAL THAT I NEEDED TO MAKE A BREAK CAME A WEEK LATER during a meeting in Hong Kong of Microsoft's top PR people in Taiwan, Hong Kong, and mainland China. One of the subjects on the agenda was a regionwide charity initiative that we'd kick off later in the year. I was excited at the prospect of instilling a greater sense of philanthropy into the region, and hopefully one that would remain even after I had left. I arrived at the meeting five minutes early and began filling the first three pages of a yellow legal pad with my ideas for helping some of the 200 million people in the Greater China Region living in poverty.

My teammates' ideas were, unfortunately, quite different from my own. Within ten minutes, the mainland-China team had laid out their plan to help a few dozen students from a middle-class neighborhood in Beijing transfer from public school to an elite private school. I challenged Alice, the team leader.

"With all due respect, and you know the China market better than I do, I am not sure that this plan has much of an effect on those who are truly needy. You are helping kids who are middle-class, and who are already in a public school system that by Asian standards is pretty solid. Kids who live in the capital city get a much better education than those in the rural areas, where the local governments lack resources. This plan you are proposing simply allows those students to go to an even better private school. The school is more elite, yes, but is this really the best way to use Microsoft's resources to help those most in need in China? Isn't there a way we can help those who are really poor? Like maybe kids in rural areas who don't even have schools to go to?"

"Helping the poor does not really help us," Alice shot back.

I invited her to explain further.

"If we help the poor rural kids, that really does not matter to the company. If we help the middle class to go to good schools, then they will learn technology and become consumers of computers and software. We need them to join the upper class, or they will not really help our business. That should be the aim of this charity program."

My heart sank. I'd had such high hopes for this meeting. Hoping that the Hong Kong team would have more inspiring ideas, I asked them to go next.

Their team proposed an initiative under which Microsoft employees would spend time training senior citizens on how to use computers. The Hong Kong staff would strongly be encouraged to spend one night, or a Saturday, in a senior citizens' home. One benefit, I was told, was that we could spend much less money than budgeted, since "we are already paying our employees anyway." The hope was that the funds earmarked for the charity program could instead flow to the subsidiary's bottom line.

I did not know where to start with my critique, so I dove right in. "But, don't you think that this will look very self-serving? It would be like Exxon buying a gas-guzzling vehicle for a poor family, in hopes that they'd fill the tank every week. Our critics are having a field day by saying that we're not a good Chinese corporate citizen. If we want to prove otherwise, we should think about doing something for seniors that does not involve computers. Can we improve their home? Serve them a hot and nutritious meal? Take them out on field trips?"

My ideas were met with silence. To the meeting's participants, corporate social responsibility was only relevant if it helped the business in the long term. I stopped arguing and reminded myself that philanthropy that extended beyond one's family was still a relatively new concept in China. These young employees had been trained to act like capitalists. So it would be hypocritical of me to criticize them. Nevertheless, I continued to daydream about what it would be like the day I ran my own show and could relentlessly focus on helping those most in need. A day when charity did not involve quid pro quos.

I WAS CHEERED UP BY AN E-MAIL FROM DINESH, OUR FRIEND FROM THE Lions Club in Kathmandu. Two villages in Pasupathi's district had made proposals for school construction projects. Dinesh had visited both and wanted to proceed.

"I told them we will only help them if they will help themselves," he wrote. "This means that you (or any donor you find) will buy the bricks and the cement. The community will donate land and volunteer labor. I will also work for free and oversee the projects. I promise you I will make the eight-hour trip to visit both villages on a monthly basis to make sure progress is being made."

The amount of money needed to fund the construction materials was relatively small when compared to the benefit to the children: $10,000 would build both schools. I replied immediately, telling Dinesh he could count on me for funds. My plan was to surprise my parents by dedicating both schools to them, as a thanks for my own education and their continued efforts to collect books and financial contributions for our projects.

BACK IN BEIJING, I PANICKED. I HAD JUST PLEDGED $10,000 BEFORE I had even determined whether finances would allow me to radically change my life. It was time to run the numbers to answer the important question: Could I afford to abandon my job, my paycheck, and my stock options?

Reviewing what I had in the bank, and my monthly spending, things looked good. I could most definitely survive for at least five years without fully depleting my savings. Then I realized one problem. In my haste to prove to myself that this was a good idea, I had forgotten to factor in that Microsoft had been paying our rent. I adjusted my monthly cash outflow higher, then went online to do a sanity check on rents in San Francisco (my hope was to base my new organization in a wealthy American city with strong ties to Asia). Damn, what an insanely expensive city. Another adjustment, but the spreadsheet showed that I could invest four years of my life into my charity without taking a paycheck. I would just have to cut back on my spending or take on a few small consulting projects to help with cash flow.

The numbers forced me to confront one reality. All my life I had been in saving mode, and now my nest egg would be severely scarred. I then rationalized to myself, what good are savings if you can't use them to fund your dreams?

TWO DAYS AFTER MY INITIAL FINANCIAL ANALYSIS, PANIC SET IN. SLEEP was lost over the idea of spending years watching my savings dwindle toward zero. I forced myself to write down a Plan B. That felt good, so I wrote down Plan C.

Plan B: Take consulting gigs in the booming dot-com economy. As an ex-Microsoft exec, I could probably command a high hourly rate. Cut living expenses. Spent one-third of time consulting and two-thirds of time on my education projects in Nepal and possibly another country like Vietnam or Cambodia. This way, clients who paid me for consulting would end up subsidizing my charity work.

Plan C: Work on education projects during the day and bartend at night. I am a personable guy, a hard worker, and a fanatic about customer service. Therefore, my tips would be good, and rather than spending money on good wine (one of my hobbies) I would negotiate a little employee discount!

I really liked Plan C, but it led to another panic—that of lost status. Was I actually willing to go from being an exec to tending bar?

At any social gathering in America, the first question asked by a stranger is usually "So, what do you do?" How would it feel to say "I tend bar down at McGee's Pub"? I pictured myself on the job wearing a Northwestern hat, or a Microsoft polo shirt, accompanied by the sound track from Springsteen's "Glory Days." How would it feel to have my answer to that question, for the first time in thirteen years, be about something other than the business fast track?

I tried to remind myself how pathetic it was to rely on labels and easy clichés to define my identity. I recalled advice my father had given me in junior high school. One night as we raked leaves, he asked if he needed to sign the permission form for junior varsity football. No doubt to his surprise, my response was to start crying. I explained to him that I had no interest, that all the kids who had signed up were bigger than me, and that my visions of the Darwinian playground had convinced me that I would be best off sticking with my paper route as my after-school activity.

As usual, his advice was simple and straightforward: If you don't want to play, then don't play. I countered that this was easy for him to say, but that I would have to face all the kids who would call me a wimp. "John," he parried, "you are old enough to know that the only person you have to satisfy in life is yourself. Even your mother and I no longer matter. Don't do anything to please us. Do what you think is the right thing to do and get used to answering only to yourself."

I REHEARSED, IN MY MIND, AN ANSWER TO "WHAT DO YOU DO?"

"I have this little project setting up libraries."

Kind of tepid. I tried again.

"I deliver books on the back of a yak to rural villages in the Himalayas."

No, wouldn't work. Too flippant, and it made it sound as if I were one of those rich "trustafarian" kids with dreadlocks who have spent too much time traveling in the Third World.

Third try.

"I build schools and libraries in poor communities in Nepal."

Not bad. I liked it. I walked over to the bathroom mirror, imagined myself at a dinner party, and tried saying it aloud.

"I founded and run an organization that builds schools and libraries in poor communities in Nepal."

I was projecting my voice and standing straight. It was clear that I would be proud to say this. If anyone judged me harshly, I would ignore it. Their problem, not mine. Besides, one does not meet a lot of status seekers in the far reaches of the Himalayas.

LONELY AND WITHOUT MANY PEOPLE IN BEIJING TO WHOM I FELT CLOSE enough to ask for advice, I worked the phones.

I discussed with my father the dilemma of leaving the company. "What do you think it means that I am more excited by e-mail about a donation of a few hundred used Dr. Seuss books than I am about a million-dollar deal to license Windows to a major Chinese telecommunications company?"

With paternal wisdom, he replied, "It just means your priorities have changed. You've always been very independent, and it's probably time to do your own thing rather than working for someone else."

My friend Mike in Sydney offered the best piece of advice I received: "Look, there are two ways to remove a Band-Aid: slowly and painfully, or quickly and painfully. Your choice."

Mike was right. It was time to stop the navel-gazing and leap into action. I was tired of dinking around, debating, writing in my journal, running the numbers, and whining to my friends. These were smoke screens and stall tactics. I knew what I wanted. It was time.

ON A BEAUTIFUL MAY MORNING IN BEIJING, I WAS ACTUALLY HAPPY TO be stuck in traffic. Anything that would delay my appointment with Michael was welcome. As Liu Wei navigated the crowded streets, I sipped from a large commuter mug full of Chinese tea and looked out the window of the backseat. Of particular interest was a worker standing between two lanes of traffic with a shovel, filling potholes. He had chosen to dress in camouflage fatigues. I wondered if he preferred to *not* be seen by oncoming traffic. I felt bad for chuckling at this thought, yet also thankful to have momentary relief from the images playing in my mind of my own impending head-on collision.

Arriving at Microsoft, I refilled my mug of tea and headed

straight for Michael's spacious office. With a deep breath I knocked on the door, walked in without waiting for an invitation, and sat down in one of his guest chairs.

I got straight to the point:

"Look, you are not going to like what I am about to tell you, and I am not going to enjoy it either because I hate to disappoint you and let you down. But the reality is that I can't work here anymore. I don't like this city, I don't like my life, and my priorities have shifted pretty radically." He tried to interrupt but I bulldozed over him. I had practiced this speech for days and did not want to lose my place. "Nobody has been able to understand me over the last few months as I've tried to explain why this life no longer works for me. I don't want to be an expat anymore, nor do I want to be a tech executive. I know this will be disruptive to the subsidiary, and I apologize for that. But there is no use trying to talk me out of leaving. We can negotiate my end date, and I will do whatever I can to do the right thing for you, and for the company. But there is no talking me out of this decision. I've been debating it for a few months now, and the concrete has dried. I'm sorry."

He looked shocked. He had realized that something was on my mind over the last few weeks, but he did not expect this radical or sudden of a shift on my part. I felt awful; I knew I was letting him down. I was abandoning him when he needed me to be his right-hand man. I listened in a miasmic fog as I heard him use words like "shocked," "confused," "disappointed," and "pissed." He reminded me, not that I needed it, that he had taken a risk by bringing me to China in such a senior role, and that I had now made him regret having had faith in me. "You're the guy who covers for me on so many meetings and issues. You're the guy I send to every meeting that needs someone smart to make the key decisions. You're one of the few guys who know what it's like to work in an Asian subsidiary, but who also knows how Redmond HQ works. I can't invent another one of you."

I blurted out that I could not talk about it right now, that it was too emotional of a decision, and that we'd have to discuss details later in the week. I again said that I was sorry. With that, I busted through his door and rushed back to my office. I packed up my laptop, called Liu Wei to meet me with the car, and slunk out of the building via a side exit, feeling like a traitor to the cause.

I was scheduled to fly to a meeting in Hong Kong that afternoon. Eager to escape my normal life, I decided not to go home and instead to drive directly to the airport with a plan of whiling away a few hours in the Air China lounge prior to departure. During the drive, I thought that it was pretty pathetic to live in a city with so few comfortable and welcoming public places that one had to go to the airport to find peace and serenity.

Landing in Hong Kong felt like deliverance. The sky was bluer, the air was cleaner, the architecture was more inspiring, and the city had a bustle to it that was all too lacking in slow-moving Beijing. And here, just a few hours' flying time south of home, was a city that was not full of my personal problems.

I arrived at the waterfront Grand Hyatt, with its panoramic floor-to-ceiling vistas of the busy harbor and the grand sweep of the city's skyline, and asked the clerk to extend my reservation from one night to two. I craved a break from life in Beijing and was dreading the inevitable conversation with Sophie upon my return. I'd book a few meetings to justify the extra day in Hong Kong, but in reality my mind would not fully be engaged in those conference rooms.

By day, I talked with our teams about long-term initiatives that I would not be around to implement and felt guilty for faking it. At night, I walked the bustling streets of the city, stopping on occasion in a pub to have a beer and write out thoughts in my journal. Over a background din of Ricky Martin hits and raucous Australian expats cheering on their beloved Wallabies in a rugby match against New Zealand, I wrote for pages on end about the pain of ending one's current life. I did not feel as though I was living *la vida loca* right now. Yet there was promise in what lay ahead. I counseled myself to remain fixed on the true north I had decided upon, and to remember that Sophie, as well as me, would be better off if we simply admitted that we were on different life paths. She did not want my new life of Third World travel and philanthropy any more than I wanted our old life of glamorous and lucrative expatriate careers. Neither of us was wrong. It simply was what it was. We had different priorities. I still respected her greatly and loved watching her excel at her chosen career. I just no longer wanted to optimize my life for the same set of variables.

TWO DAYS LATER, BACK IN BEIJING, I TOLD SOPHIE THAT I WOULD BE leaving our relationship, our home, our shared city, and our joint career path. It felt like such a cruel fate to attain total freedom by doing irreparable harm to someone I loved deeply. I knew this was the right thing, and that we both needed to find a mate who wanted to share our path in life. But this knowledge did not make it any easier. My tolerance for pain is extremely low, especially when I am causing it for others.

To escape, and to live the life I desired, I was abandoning her. A positive for me was a severe negative for her.

Sophie had once surprised me with a painting on which she had labored for weeks. It was a warmly colored watercolor of a wooden park bench, resting in the comfortable shade of a large oak tree. She told me that it represented the solitudinous place where we would peacefully sit at the end of our long lives together. The painting and its glass frame now lay shattered at the base of our bedroom wall, against which it had been flung.

That, and my move into the guest bedroom, augmented a short-term future of pain and loneliness. I resolved to finish up my work as soon as possible in order to begin the next chapter of my life.

SIX WEEKS LATER: THE CESSATION OF PAIN. THE MOVERS ARRIVED ON A Wednesday; I packed up my office on a Thursday; and I was on a flight to San Francisco on Friday morning.

Ten minutes before takeoff, the United 747 is fully loaded and ready. My mountain bike and two backpacks are in the cargo hold. Out the window are Air China and China Eastern jets. I muse that this might be the last time I will see the adopted city that I never quite managed to adopt.

A stewardess asks if I'd like a glass of champagne. It's 11 a.m., so I decline. I pull out my journal to record my thoughts at this major inflection point of my life. As I begin writing, I think about that offer. I ring the call button. When the stewardess returns, I ask sheepishly if it would be possible to get a glass of the bubbly after all.

The effervescent drink tickles my nose as the 747 lumbers down the bumpy runway. We lift off tentatively, then burst higher on a steep and powerful trajectory. I silently toast our liftoff from Chinese soil and the cessation of my existential angst. My decision has finally crystallized, been announced, and been implemented. There is no turning back.

For the next five minutes, I watch the city of Beijing, enveloped in its usual cloud of coal dust and smog. It gets smaller and smaller, and farther and farther behind. Everything negative and stress-inducing fades as the plane gains altitude and flies east. For the first time in months, I feel relaxed, happy, and forward-looking. We were escaping gravity. My mind-set was positive and buoyant. Onward and upward!

PART 2

STARTING OVER

CHAPTER 9

THE START-UP YEARS: AN OBJECT
IN MOTION REMAINS IN MOTION

IN DECEMBER OF 1999, I RECEIVED NOTICE THAT THE IRS HAD AP-
proved charity status for my new organization. Its official name
was Books for Nepal.*

My immediate thought was "Now what?" I was a corporate
refugee who had never worked for a charity in an official capacity. I
had always viewed my education projects as a hobby, not a voca-
tion. Although I was eager to get started, I had no idea how to
start.

I was so green I sometimes embarrassed myself. An old college
friend, Jim, was an experienced philanthropist who sat on the board
of his family's foundation. The prior year I had told him of my plans
to leave Microsoft and spend more time on my education projects
in Nepal. He asked when I would have 501(c)(3) status.

He rolled his eyes as I asked what this meant. He explained that
this was the designation my fledgling organization would need for
donations to be tax-deductible. I explained that I'd rather keep
things simple, avoid bureaucracy, and leave the IRS out of this. An-

---

* The name would eventually be changed to Room to Read; see page 125 for
background on the name change.

other roll of the eyes, and another lecture. He explained that no-body would donate in a significant way if I could not prove that we were a real organization.

Next, he offered incentive. Once we had this mysterious 501(c)(3) status, he and his wife, Jen, would write a $10,000 check.

That worked. I called an attorney, who had been recommended by a friend. Christopher Beck answered on the first ring. "I'm a lawyer, but also a frustrated international relations major who never got to use his degree. You can count on my help. I heard you were in Seattle this week, so how about if we meet at the Starbucks in Belltown? They have comfy chairs, which is good as I'll need several hours of your time."

I hoped we could fast-track the IRS process, and figured that massive amounts of caffeine might be a good place to start. My fledgling organization desperately needed the money.

Dinesh had suggested that we hire a few young Nepalese guys to work full-time on our projects. Our first schools were under construction. More books were coming in from individual donors, and a large publisher had pledged a donation of 25,000 books. Over 100 schools had requested to participate in our library program. Dinesh was willing to hire and manage the new employees, while himself remaining an unpaid consultant.

He said that we could hire local college graduates for about $200 per month. Jim and Jen's money would be more than enough to al-low us to build a team in Nepal. It was a tentative start to what would eventually become a perpetual whirlwind of hiring. But even these small steps meant we were becoming a real organization.

NOT EVERY POTENTIAL DONOR WAS AS FRIENDLY, ENCOURAGING, AND generous as Jim and Jen. I was frequently turned down during the first few years of Books for Nepal's life. This bothered me only slightly. Anyone in a sales career knows that if you're not getting rejected, you're not casting your net widely enough. What did get to me was the condescending manner of some of the people I met during the early years. Had I been less confident, some of these in-dividuals would have dealt crushing blows to my enthusiasm.

One of the first meetings I sought was with the San Francisco–based American Himalayan Foundation (AHF). The American version of Sir Edmund Hillary's Himalayan Trust, the organization had sponsored numerous projects in Nepal over the previous 25 years, ranging from bridges to hospitals to schools. I had visited some of their schools during my third trip to Nepal and was impressed with their work. I was therefore thrilled when one of their senior directors agreed to a meeting at their well-appointed San Francisco office.

My excitement, alas, was premature. The executive, in her mid-40s and elegantly dressed, was friendly enough upon greeting me. But warning signs soon began flaring. Twice on the way to her office she stopped for conversations with colleagues that lasted for several minutes. She did not bother to introduce me. I assumed she was having a busy day. The skies darkened further when we got to her office. Within two minutes of explaining my goals, I was cut off.

"I am not sure why we should be talking to you. There are hundreds of little groups doing what you do."

"I agree. There are many organizations working in Nepal, and that's a good thing, because the country needs a lot of help. One thing that makes Books for Nepal different is that we have plans to take this project to a pretty massive scale. If I learned one thing at Microsoft, it's to think big. Most charities build one or two schools. I want to build hundreds. There are a lot of charities that have set up a few libraries, but nobody has emulated Andrew Carnegie by setting up several thousand of them in the developing world."

"And what makes you think you have what it takes to do so?"

"Good question. To start, I'm ambitious and have a ton of energy. I'm not afraid of hard work. There is a huge network of people I know from my technology days who can all be pitched to donate to the cause. Finally, I am not the least bit shy about asking people for money or favors. For example, I just received word from Carol Sakoian, vice president of international business development of Scholastic, that they are donating twenty-five thousand children's books to our program. She said that this is just the beginning of their support, and that she will introduce me to other publishers."

The executive looked at me with the same indifference with which a cow on the side of the interstate views a passing car. She checked her watch, even though we were only ten minutes into our meeting. Undaunted, I forged on.

"I would think that the news on Scholastic would be of interest. I know that AHF has built forty schools in the Everest region. I have visited a few of them and was impressed. But one thing I noticed was that they have the same problem that most every school in Nepal has—an empty library. So I got to thinking—what if we put some of these new books to good use? My organization could help your schools by setting up forty new school libraries. That, to answer your earlier question, is one of the main reasons I wanted to meet with you."

She made another not-so-surreptitious time check. "I don't know. You'd have to talk to my people about that. Those are all details that I don't follow."

"Great," I naively replied. "With whom should I talk? Are they here in the office today?"

"I'll have to put somebody in touch with you. But for now I really need to get to lunch."

Now it was my turn to check my watch. I forced myself to refrain from making a sly comment that it must be nice to be part of an organization that took lunch at 11:15.

IN THE NEARBY NEIGHBORHOOD OF NORTH BEACH, I LICKED MY WOUNDS at a coffee shop. I hoped that a steaming latte would compensate for the frosty reception in the meeting. The café had wireless Internet access, so I pulled out my laptop to write a thank-you e-mail. I felt that I had been treated rudely. But I was a novice. I needed every favor I could get.

I reminded the AHF executive that she'd promised to put me in touch with the officer in charge of the school program in Nepal. I sharply rapped the keyboard as I hit Send. It was obvious that she would not respond.* It was extremely frustrating. I hoped this

---

* She never did.

was not how my new world worked. I was so used to the world of business, where we were constantly in motion and trying to "GSD"—Steve Ballmer's acronym and constant reminder to "get shit done." People leaped onto good ideas because, if they did not, their competitors might. The charity world, more immune from market pressures, apparently did not play by these rules.

I wondered whether this was emblematic of my new status in life. At Microsoft, I had grown used to having calls returned, a staff that would execute my plans, and all the resources I needed. I was now a fish out of water. I felt small and feckless. With no experience in the complex world of international nonprofits, I had a grand vision but few results and even fewer contacts. I felt demoralized and wondered if my transition had been a mistake.

As I gazed out the window at the sidewalk cafés beginning to fill up with their lunch crowds, a New Mail chime sounded on my laptop. Dinesh was working hard as usual. It was 2 a.m. his time. The Subject line was irresistible: "Good News from Nepal."

"Dear John, attached are photos of two of our new schools under construction. As you can see, the parents are helping by clearing the land, digging the foundation, and helping to carry the bricks to the building site. The headmasters of the two schools have requested that you be here this fall for the official opening ceremonies. Can you come?"

My heart immediately went from nearly empty to overflowing with optimism. In Dinesh's mail lay a reminder that I could not let the naysayers get me down. The only way to move forward was to focus on the positive. I immediately forwarded photos of the projects to a few dozen friends, in the hope that they might know someone willing to invest in our dream. Next, I dropped a mail to my travel agent to inquire about flights.

SEVERAL WEEKS LATER I LEARNED ABOUT A POTENTIAL "DREAM investor"—the Draper Richards Foundation. DRF was born out of a venture capital firm founded and run by legendary venture capitalists Bill Draper and Robin Richards Donohoe. Having hit several home runs with their fund, they had decided to plow some of their winnings into the "social entrepreneur" sector through endowed fellowships. The foundation had just been formed, and little was known about its goals. Two facts, however, stood out clearly—they were looking for organizations in their infancy, and to those they liked they made a three-year pledge of $100,000 per year. Best of all, the money was completely unrestricted—i.e., the chosen "fellow" could do whatever they wanted with it. Most foundation grants came with multiple strings attached, so unrestricted funding, especially a multiyear commitment, looked to me like manna from heaven.

A fellow Kellogg School of Management alumnus made the introduction to DRF's executive director. I was a bit gun-shy after my AHF experience, especially upon walking into DRF's 29th-floor offices with sweeping views of the Bay Bridge. It looked like another AHF-type organization with a five-star office and a zero-star personality.

Jenny, the executive director, immediately put me at ease. She was friendly and encouraging. Rather than immediately asking me questions, she started off by explaining their business philosophy:

"Our niche as a venture capital firm was finding great early-stage businesses. Kana. Hotmail. Tumbleweed," she said, reeling off a quick troika of multimillion-dollar investment wins. "Now we want to take some of that money and do something similar for the betterment of the world. We are looking to fund early-stage charities. We want our portfolio to be full of young organizations that are going to scale up and change the world. Ideally it will be early enough in their life cycle that a relatively small amount of seed funding will have a huge effect as the organization grows. The key for us is to find people who are natural entrepreneurs."

Portfolio. Scale. Seed funding. Entrepreneurs. She was speaking the language of business. I wanted to hug her.

That feeling lasted for about a nanosecond. Next, she told me the bad news:

"I like what your organization does, but you are too far advanced for us. We only like to invest in early-stage ventures."

"But, but, but . . . we are early stage. We're still in our infancy, we're just getting started, we've only taken baby steps," I blurted out, searching desperately and pathetically for more euphemisms for *young*.

"I don't know. You already have a decent number of schools and libraries built. You are talking about expanding beyond Nepal. I think you might be too far along in your life cycle for us."

I put up my best defense—some would refer to it as "pleading."

"Two schools and twelve libraries are total tip-of-the-iceberg," I replied. "And, yes, I am talking about going into other countries, but at this point it's just talk. We can't do anything without the funds. Think of this as being like a great business idea, but one where the entrepreneur can't afford to hire employees yet."

She said nothing, so I continued.

"Look, can I be really honest with you? Every other foundation with which I have spoken has told us that we are too young, and that they only fund organizations that are further along. And now you are telling me that we are too old. Do you know how much this kills me? I feel like a cartoon character who has just gone off the cliff and is running in place in midair. I really need this funding. We have dozens of communities asking for new schools and libraries, and I don't have the capital to say yes. The way you should look at us is that we are in year two of what will be a multiyear build-out. So we're still comparatively young."

Jenny gave nothing away. She'd let me know if we made it to their next stage of due diligence.

I walked out of their office with a feeling in my gut that was akin to being in love. I wanted so badly for it to work out and was fearful of how it might feel to be rejected.

TWO WEEKS LATER, ON A PERFECT SUNNY AFTERNOON, I HUNG UP FROM a phone call with Sarah Leary, an old friend from my Microsoft years. She had just agreed to endow a school in Nepal to honor her father. An hour's run along the beach would be my celebration. After that, a return to work for what was certain to be a late night. Just as I was grabbing my gym bag, the phone rang again.

"Hi, John. This is Rhonda from Bill Draper's office. Bill heard

from Jenny about your work. He would like to come into your office and meet you tomorrow."

Excellent! I told her that I was totally flexible on timing.

"He and Jenny can show up around two. We should probably
allocate three hours, as he wants to go through your business plan
in detail."

"Yes, our business plan. Excellent. We'll look forward to reviewing it with him. In detail. Thanks."

When a legendary venture capitalist sets aside three hours to review the business plan, any entrepreneur would be nervous. Especially an entrepreneur who doesn't actually *have* a business plan. I
mean, there were bits and pieces of a business plan in various loca-
tions—in my head, on random sectors of my hard drive, in e-mails
that Dinesh had written on his hopes for massive program growth.
We had some sketchy notes on our planned expansion into other
Asian countries. But we were always in "do" mode and had never
taken the time to actually pull everything together into one coher-
ent document. Did I really just agree to meet, in less than 24 hours,
with one of the world's foremost venture capitalists?

Realizing how much was on the line, and with the clock ticking,
I raced home. I grabbed my sleeping bag, a pillow, and a change of
clothes. Returning to the office, I brewed a large pot of coffee. Now
was the time for heroes.

WITH THE PRECISION OF A FINE SWISS WATCH, BILL AND JENNY WALKED
into our cramped office in San Francisco's Presidio National Park at
2:01 p.m. I handed over two copies of a 35-page business plan still
warm from the printer.

My first all-nighter since graduate school had been successful. I
had slept on the floor from 2 a.m. until 6 a.m. As I listened to the
lugubrious foghorn protecting the Golden Gate Bridge, I thought
about how my faithful sleeping bag had been with me on that initial
trip to Nepal and was now also here during the hard part of putting
ethereal dreams into solid reality.

I resumed work at 6 a.m., fueled by the omnipresent fear of fail-
ure. I typed frantically, making a mental note to spell-check later. At

1:45 I dashed off to the local YMCA to shower, shave, and don fresh clothes. Screeching into the parking lot, I saw Bill and Jenny pull up in his red Mercedes convertible. I ducked into the office ahead of them. On the printer's output tray sat two thick copies of our business plan. I felt like Reggie Miller sinking a clutch three-pointer with a second on the shot clock.

A large bear of a man, William H. Draper III was perpetually tanned from his daily tennis game. He has large bushy eyebrows, silver hair, a friendly twinkle in his eye, and a fierce intellect. He had recently turned 70 but looked a decade younger. In a camel-hair blazer, crisp white shirt and red silk tie, and with patrician posture, he looked as though he had stepped right off page five of the Brooks Brothers catalogue.

I began by walking Jenny and Bill through our business plan in sequential order. Bill had already flipped ahead to page 17. He wanted to know all about my background, that of our employees, and more about our volunteer fund-raisers. "I invest in people. Tell me first about your people, because if you have not gotten that right, then there is no hope for your organization. You mention that you are starting volunteer chapters that raise funds for you. Who are they? Name names."

"This model is built on the knowledge that not every person who wants to change the world is going to quit their job to do so. My goal is to allow anyone, be they an investment banker, a consultant, or a school teacher, to raise funds to help us to get more schools and libraries built. All of them can sneak in an hour during their work day or work at night or weekends to plan fund-raising events or campaigns. For example, a group of volunteers here in San Francisco threw an event last fall that raised $35,000. That does not sound like a lot of money. But in Nepal it's enough to construct four schools. This model motivates the volunteers and also the people we invite to the events because they know exactly where their money goes. I have some old friends in Seattle who have offered to do an event next month. The beauty of the model is that we don't have to pay them a dime, so we can keep our fund-raising costs low."

"That's excellent—good thinking. I like low overhead," Bill thundered. I breathed a sigh of relief. But it was a quick one, as Bill immediately veered back to page one, on which I had codified our mission statement after several hours of trying to distill my vision for changing the world down to just one sentence: "Our team works in partnership with local communities in the developing world under a coinvestment model to catalyze the creation of new educational infrastructure, including schools, libraries, computer labs, and long-term scholarships for girls."

Bill's stentorian voice boomed, "I like this. Coinvestment makes total sense. You know that I also used to run UNDP [the United Nations Development Program], right? I always thought that the only way these aid programs would work is if the local people were required to also donate labor and small amounts of money. Otherwise the project is just a free gift bestowed by outsiders, and nobody will value it because they have nothing at stake."

I seized on the pause, which I knew would be brief. "I agree. Do you know the quote by Michael Porter from Harvard Business School?" Bill and Jenny nodded no. "He points out that in the entire history of the travel industry, nobody has ever washed a rental car. If they don't feel ownership, they won't do any long-term maintenance. That's the way I feel about our projects."

The random walk through our business plan continued for a few more hours. Bill was voluble, enthusiastic, complimentary, and full of his own anecdotes about international development work. Obviously, the best approach was to give up control of the meeting. Bill would drive.

After several more questions and digressions, Bill said that he was impressed and that he'd look forward to working with us. He suggested that I start thinking about how I'd invest the money. At which point Jenny cut him off: "Bill, we still have a lot of due diligence ahead of us. This is not a done deal. We need to check their references, and I have some more questions that I'd like to ask, and Robin has still not met with them. That can take four to six weeks."

"Not for these guys it won't. They obviously have their act together. But, yes, you can check their references." Behind her back, he winked at me.

On the way out the door, he eyed my bright yellow North Face sleeping bag. Feeling the need to explain, I told him, "On some nights, when we have important deliverables, this is my home." Bill laughed with the roar of a lion, slapped me on the back, and said, "That's what I like to hear. We want people who aren't afraid of hard work. Too much of the nonprofit sector has a nine-to-five mentality."

At that point, I knew with absolute certainty that the fellowship was mine. I immediately began to envision how much we could do with the increased capital, and how great it would be for our young organization to have this blue-chip stamp of approval.

ENTREPRENEURIAL FROM A YOUNG AGE

Bill Draper also grilled me on what made me an entrepreneur. I said that from an early age, I had always started and run small businesses. Even at age five, I played the role of CEO and VP of sales.

During my childhood in Connecticut, one of my favorite activities was painting. But I did not practice "art for art's sake"— rather art for the sake of commerce. My parents had always praised my work, and so my five-year-old mind decided that if they had such high regard for my paintings, well, then, naturally other adults in the neighborhood might also enjoy them.

One afternoon my mother noticed me counting a pile of nickels and dimes.

She inquired, a bit suspiciously, where I had found this pile of loot.

"I sold my paintings."

"What do you mean, you sold them? Where? To whom?"

I told her that I had gone door-to-door selling to our neighbors. "I did two kinds of paintings—sailboats and barns. Sailboats are much better, people like them more. I sold hardly any barns. So next time I am going to paint only sailboats. And maybe some horses. No more stupid barns."

She sternly assured me that there was not going to be a next time. She forbade me from going door-to-door again.

continued

She was quite naturally surprised when, a few days later, she saw me counting an even bigger pile of coins with a wild-eyed zealousness that would have impressed Warren Buffett.

Again she asked about my suddenly enlarged financial stockpile.

I happily informed her that the latest batch of sailboats, all twenty of them, had sold.

"I thought I told you that you were not allowed to go door-to-door selling your paintings."

I replied that I had not.

"Well, then how did you sell them? Surely the neighbors did not come here to the house asking to buy more paintings."

"No, I had Jimmy [my best friend from next door] sell them. He gets a penny for every one he sells, and I keep four cents."

Some internal maternal alarm must have gone off, alerting her that this was not going to be an easy child to raise. She would have to read the fine print, define her terms carefully, and closely monitor my compliance.

It was the first of many enterprises that would help prepare me to build what I hoped would be one of the biggest nonprofits in the world.

CHAPTER 10

MAKING THE ASK

I WAS THRILLED TWO WEEKS LATER WHEN BILL AND JENNY ANNOUNCED that I'd been approved as the second Draper Richards fellow. The funding would be a boon for the organization. We could use their unrestricted funding for general operating costs and use our strong "Adopt a Project" model to have donors fund the direct cost of schools, libraries, and scholarships.

DRF's commitment, while large, would not be enough. I had big dreams and did not want to be overly dependent on any one funder. I would have to keep pitching relentlessly to bring new donors on board.

One of the often overlooked but most important skills that any young charity must have is the ability to sell its vision, its business model, and its programs to potential donors. And I do mean "sell." Most people in the nonprofit world hate to ask others for money. They need to get past this barrier, quickly, or their organization will suffer.

People associated with nonprofits, be they board members, employees, or donors, justifiably love talking about their program delivery. They can chat for hours about their results, whether the number of meals served to the homeless or their campaign to convince more women to screen for early signs of breast cancer. The people who start nonprofits usually do so because they are passionate about their cause, and so these leaders tend to focus their conversations on programs.

The part of the business that gets talked about less frequently is equally important—raising the money to pay for the meals, the screenings, and the employees who deliver these services. I have been surprised at the extent to which the charity world treats fundraising as some dirty little task that is best ignored. Like Victorians who refuse to talk about money or sex, many charities act as though funding comes from a black box that is not well understood and certainly best not discussed.

Ignoring reality will not make it go away. If a business loses money on every sale, it will eventually go under. Many charities are cash-flow negative, yet they keep their head buried in the sand, assuming a white knight will emerge to save them. That is a formula for disaster.

I knew from day one that I had to be a salesperson as focused on cash inflow as I was on program delivery. We could not build schools if we did not have people willing to *fund* schools, nor could we sponsor long-term scholarships for girls if we did not have commitments from donors to endow them over the long term.

I knew these facts because they had been burned into me from a young age. In college and graduate school, I was blessed with professors who were fanatical at imbuing in each student the importance of capital. They forced us to learn cash-flow models with the intensity of a rabbinical student studying the Torah. It was logical that this would help me in my business career, given that capitalism is all about capital. But this focus was an even bigger competitive advantage in the charity world.

EVERY YOUNG ORGANIZATION NEEDS TO BRING ON EMPLOYEES WHO have both tenacity and sales skills. Cash in from donors means cash out for programs. No cash in means no programs. Period. The younger the organization, the less likely it can take for granted that it will win enough business to pay bills, grow the organization, and survive. Whether it's a new charity seeking donors or a start-up software company trying to land its first customers, it's critical to have people on your team who are not afraid to "make the ask."

More important, it must be in their DNA to not take no for an answer, to return to the prospect again and again. My reaction to rejection was "No? Can I ask you to instead say 'Not yet'?"

Few organizations epitomized this trait as well as Microsoft during its early days. I will leave it to others to debate whether the company has been too tenacious. All I knew when I interviewed there in 1991 was that unless one could prove tenacity during the interview, one had no chance at a job offer. And the company was even more selective than Harvard, accepting less than 5 percent of applicants.

As if this was not enough to make me nervous when I interviewed at the company in 1991, I also learned upon my arrival on a misty Seattle evening that my final interview would be with Melinda French. At the time, Melinda was the girlfriend of Bill Gates, and the all-too-common rumor that she would marry him turned out to be an accurate prophecy. Bill was not the type to date anyone unless she had a razor-sharp mind, so the pressure on me increased. Because the position for which I was interviewing reported to her, she would make the final decision on whether I was hired.

The morning of the interview, I awoke early to head out on the wooded trails of Microsoft's campus for a run. My intention was to clear my head, but unfortunately it was instead filled with questions that Melinda might ask:

- Why is your background in corporate finance relevant to Microsoft? (The first answer that popped into my head was "It completely isn't. Not in the least.")
- Prove to me that you have even the remotest understanding of the software industry. ("I really don't. But, uh . . . I am willing to learn?")
- Why should we hire you instead of one of the other five finalists for the position? ("I'm not sure, as interview protocol prevents me from having met any of them, and I am sure they are all fine people.")

Clearly I had to do better. I needed to be self-confident enough to sell myself. So what if I came from the world of finance? After all, my job at the bank was to develop relationships with new clients, and I had been quite successful at this. If I could sell something as boring as a bank line of credit, I could certainly knock the ball out of the park with a product as exciting as software.

Too focused on the interview, I almost landed in midstride on a squirrel darting across the path. I forced my mind back to the interview. I knew it would be a battle, as Microsoft was notorious for asking tough questions. I had heard through the rumor mill such zingers as "Explain why manhole covers are round" and "Estimate the number of basketballs that you think are sold in the U.S. every year, and then walk me through your methodology and assumptions in arriving at this estimate."

My head was spinning as the questions clogged my brain. But I love challenges and enjoy grappling with hypotheticals. My pace quickened, my feet hit the pine-needle-covered trail at a rapid turnover, and evergreen trees whizzed by in my peripheral vision as I psyched myself up for battle.

My battle armor was, unfortunately, a banker's suit and a Brooks Brothers tie, which made me feel like a dork as I strolled across Microsoft's leafy campus. Barefoot developers in baggy shorts and polo shirts were sitting by the side of the duck pond named Lake Bill, and many cast amused glances at the poor interviewee. To this day I do not understand why the masochists who run the HR department don't tell interviewees to dress casually. In the pre-Dockers early 1990s, it was still a really big deal for a multibillion-dollar company to have a casual dress code. The HR department always stressed during campus recruitment that there was no need to upgrade one's wardrobe and claimed that employees enjoyed working in a casual environment in which their brain was free to roam. Yet, when I asked whether I should dress up or dress down for the interview, I was told, "It's really your call." Now, as I took my walk of shame across the campus, I regretted my sartorial selection.

Fortunately, when I arrived at the unimaginatively named Building 16, Melinda put me immediately at ease by telling me that I had an impressive résumé and was a strong candidate. She was younger-looking than I had expected, and very attractive. Sparkling brown eyes played against her tanned skin and shoulder-length dark hair. She was dressed casually in a short-sleeved tennis shirt, khaki pants, and open-toed sandals. I apologized for being overdressed. She laughed and said she didn't understand why the HR department didn't tell interviewees to tone it down. I began to agree, but was knocked back against the wall by her first question.

"Commercial banking does not seem like an industry that attracts aggressive or tenacious people. Tell me a story from your career at Continental Bank which illustrates that you're different."

I drew a deep breath, did an internal high five in my brain since I had anticipated a question like this, and shared with Melinda a story about how I'd landed a large and difficult account: Weirton Steel.

DURING MY THIRD MONTH OUT OF GRADUATE SCHOOL, IN 1989, I FIN-ished Continental Bank's internal training program. The last day was the most tense, as the thirty trainees knew that our two-year rotations would be assigned. One's graduation gift could be a gold-plated prize, or a dud.

During my exit interview from the program, I was excited to hear that I had been assigned to a group called Mideast States. As a committed internationalist and world traveler, I was excited about the prospect of doing business in places like Dubai, Saudi Arabia, and Kuwait. My training manager quickly pricked the bubble, and my gold-plated prize turned into a dud as he informed me that the bank's definition of *Mideast* stretched from West Virginia to Pennsylvania, then westward into Ohio and Kentucky. In other words, no passport required.

My new boss, Rick, gave me a list of companies in this region with which he wanted to build a relationship, but had not had any luck. I recognized one of them, Weirton Steel, because they had recently saved their mill from bankruptcy through an employee buy-out. This strategy was similar to that of United Airlines, and popular business journals were touting employee ownership as the next big thing. I grabbed a phone, dialed the PR department at Weirton, and asked for the date of their next annual meeting. Two weeks out. It looked as if I'd be making my first trip ever to Weirton, West Virginia.

FEW EXPERIENCES IN LIFE CAN BE AS MISERABLE AS WAKING UP IN TIME to catch a 6 a.m. flight out of O'Hare, especially when every seat on the plane is full, and every one of those people is fighting for space in the overhead racks. Ah, the glories of business travel. The American Airlines stewardesses were no more happy about it than were the passengers, and because they controlled the supply of orange juice and coffee, our fate was in their hands. Alas, the plane went into its descent before the poor slob in seat 47F was served, so I arrived in Pittsburgh tired, hungry, and wondering when in life I could graduate to the front of the plane.

After a full day of meetings, I made the hour drive west through industrial Pittsburgh to even-more-industrial-and-blighted Weirton. Their main steel mill was at the town's epicenter, and judging by the lack of economic activity and the noticeable number of vacant shops with BUILDING TO RENT signs, it was obvious to me that this town needed its mill and the 2,000 jobs it provided.

I walked into the annual general meeting without knowing anybody, so I asked around and eventually located Rick, the friendly PR guy with whom I had originally talked. He offered to walk me to the snack tables, which featured an array of Ritz crackers and Iron City beer in cans. We both grabbed a fistful of crackers and a beer, and as we chatted, I commented that I was impressed to see the local television news crew filming the annual meeting. He asked what I was referring to, so I pointed to a video cameraman. Rick explained that this was actually an employee filming the annual general meeting for a program called *Weirton News and Views.*

"*News and Views* is a daily show, no more than a few minutes in length, that is broadcast to all of our employees at the start of each day. Because every one of them took a pay cut in order to assume an equity stake, we want them to stay informed of how the company is doing. Because many of them start work early and have families, they can't be at this meeting, but at least they can hear the highlights tomorrow morning."

I expressed admiration for the idea and said that I wished my own employer was so enlightened as to report progress to us each and every morning. I asked if management also watched *News and Views,* and Rick said they did. Then an idea popped into my head.

"Rick, you're the guy in charge of PR, both internal and external, so you're in control of the broadcast, right?" He nodded. "Without overstepping any bounds here, do you think it would be relevant to the employees that a banker from Chicago was so impressed with the ESOP [employee stock ownership plan] that he flew in to learn more about the company?" This time Rick did not nod, but instead made a frantic motion to wave the cameraman over to us.

Three minutes later, it was showtime:

Rick: "So, John, tell us why a banker would fly all the way out from Chicago to visit a steel mill that most of the world had given up for dead."

My reply: "The fact that Weirton employees all took pay cuts in order to participate in an ESOP made news throughout the country. It's not very often that management and employees come together to make a financial bet that expresses their faith in their company's future. Continental Bank looks for innovative companies to which we can provide funding, and Weirton has definitely impressed us with its enlightened approach to having management and labor work together to build a competitive company and a strong community at a time when so many mills are shutting down. We'd be very interested in talking to management about ways we could forge a strong banking relationship."

I was sure I had sounded dorky, but Rick assured me that we had nailed it on the first take. Which was a good thing, given that the business part of the meeting was starting and the crowd was filing into the conference space. Soon thereafter, I made the drive back to Pittsburgh through the dark night.

The next morning, my secretary called to say I had received a fax from Weirton's assistant treasurer, Mr. "Pat" Pasupathi.* He suggested that we set up a lunch meeting on my next trip to the region. She could barely finish the sentence before my boss grabbed the

* No relation to Pasupathi from chapter 1.

phone out of her hand. "How did you manage to crack these guys so quickly?" he asked.

"I had better tell you in person—it's too good of a story to not share face-to-face. But suffice it to say that our bank's name is now well-known to the company's management."

Three months later, we signed a contract to provide the company with a $25 million line of credit.

Melinda must have liked the story; I received a job offer within a week of returning to Chicago and I joined Microsoft full-time in April 1991. Tenacity would be a theme of my career at Microsoft, and later at Room to Read. At Microsoft we worked long hours to grow our market share in the Office Suite (Word, Excel, etc.) category from single digits to over 85 percent in less than two years. But the intense focus would never be more important than during the first few years of Room to Read, when I had big ambitions but scarce financial resources. In those days, I viewed every encounter, whether it was with an old friend or the people on either side of me at a dinner party, as an opportunity to talk about our projects. My hope was that my passion to change the world through education would resonate, and that the individual who was the focus of my pitch would enthusiastically agree to help the cause.

AS MUCH AS I TRUSTED MY SALES SKILLS, I WAS STILL NERVOUS ABOUT asking people for money. Nobody likes asking others for favors. It's one thing if you're requesting to borrow your neighbor's jumper cables, but something else entirely if you're soliciting a large donation for which the donor will get no quid pro quo (unless you count good karma or the feeling of having done the right thing). To help psych myself up for the early days of making the ask, I wrote out five core principles that I would review before key meetings with prospective donors:

- If the donors have money, then chances are good they have been helped in their own life by education. Play up the fact that they now have the opportunity to give that same gift back to hundreds of children in the developing world.

- I can show donors a direct connection between what they give and what gets done as a result. There is a causal link between an $8,000 donation and a new school in Nepal. Some people don't like to give money to charity because they don't know where their money will go. In our case, we can show them *exactly* where their money went. It's so tangible that we can send them photos, or they can visit the school or library in person.
- We keep our overhead low, so donors will know that 90 cents on the dollar goes to the projects, not to administrative and fund-raising expenses.
- Passion sells. There is not enough of it in the world, so when people meet a passionate individual, that person really stands out. When I tell donors that I quit a lucrative career in the technology world to devote myself to this cause full-time, and for zero pay, that will resonate.
- People are looking for more meaning in their lives. Funding education provides a great feeling that you have helped to change the world for the better.

This list was reviewed before key meetings. Donors responded. I heard many more yeses than nos. The more positive the response, the bolder I got.

I was flattered that so many people supported Room to Read, but it also made me realize how hard I would have to work. If someone was putting money down because they thought I'd spend it wisely, then my personal and professional honor were at stake. A positive reputation is a hard thing to gain, and an easy thing to lose. If I proved to be true to my word about deploying donors' funds effectively, the possibilities for Room to Read would be limitless. We'd also be in a virtuous circle—satisfied donors would donate again and would also tell their friends about "my school" and encourage them to also invest. The additional capital would mean even greater results, and bigger results would attract more investment. Ultimately, this dynamic would make it all the easier to make the ask. But in the early days, my pulse still quickened every time I knew that the meeting was approaching the end of its alloted time, and I'd soon need to request support. To help, I'd visualize a village that needed a new school or a library, or a girl who was not in school due to economic discrimination. I pictured them cheering me on. With those images, it was always possible to dig deep, banish the fear, and close every meeting with the words "We have big dreams, and I need to ask for your support to help us reach them."

HOPE AND OPTIMISM, NOT DOOM AND GLOOM

I will do almost anything to raise money to help Room to Read to build more schools and libraries. However, I consciously avoid one technique that other charities use, apparently to good effect—what I refer to as the "Sally Struthers Weep-a-Thon."

Everyone knows that there is poverty in the world, and almost all of us are saddened by it. Some charities find it effective to show photos of a child covered in flies, or a malnourished family lying in the dust. With all due respect to Ms. Struthers, I think it demeans the world's poor to use pity when soliciting donations. These images negate the inherent dignity of each human being. I might be wrong, but I think that guilt should not be used as a marketing tool.

This is also in the financial interest of the charity, because potential donors want hope and optimism in their lives. They want to see solutions. If we accost them with images of a poor person, they are likely to be sad, but they may not take action. If you instead present a photo of a kid from the inner city in his graduation cap and gown, a little girl smiling as the result of a successful cleft palate operation, or farmers in Honduras using their new well, then people are more likely to share in that optimism by donating to the cause.

I realize, of course, that we need to make citizens aware of the terrible conditions in which much of humanity lives. But I leave that to CNN and the BBC and assume my donors are smart enough to know about the state of today's world. I'd much rather lead with a solution and ask potential donors, employees, and volunteers to be a part of it. The tears we shed should be tears of joy the day we open a new school or present 50 girls in rural Vietnam with their long-term scholarships.

CHAPTER 11

EXPANSION BEYOND NEPAL

IN 2001, AS OUR NEPAL PROGRAMS GREW, I SET MY SIGHTS ON OPEN-
ing Room to Read in a second country. With so many nations
facing staggering illiteracy problems, I wanted to think big and set a
precedent of perpetual growth for the organization. I often visualized the places I had traveled that lacked schools, libraries, books,
even simple things like pencils.

Vietnam intrigued me. Ravaged my numerous wars, and for so
long poor and isolated, the nation had every reason to be pessimistic and inward-looking. Yet their citizens had faith and optimism
that education was the ticket out of poverty. The average person
might earn only $1 per day, but people believed that they would
soon make $2, then $3, if only they could educate their children.

But the main reason I wanted to help Vietnam to build its educational infrastructure was due not to economic statistics, but instead
to a young man named Vu.

IN 1997, I HAD WALKED ONTO A SYDNEY HARBOUR FERRY, OVERSTUFFED
backpack slung across my shoulders and a huge grin on my face. I
was bound for a flight that would transport me to the start of a solo

two-week trip through Vietnam. A business trip to Hanoi the previous year had piqued my interest, and during my frantic 48 hours there, I jealously eyed all the backpackers who were seeing the country at a slow pace. While I was running to meetings, they were sitting in cafés drinking strong Vietnamese coffee, slurping *pho* (noodle soup), and leafing through the Lonely Planet guide to plot their next destination. Sure, I was here in Vietnam on an expense account, seeing the country for free, but was I *really* experiencing it?

A year later I went back to see the country for real. With a backpack full of books and a blank journal, my goal was to travel from the south (Saigon) through the long, thin, banana-shaped Communist wonderland. I was relieved to have a break from Microsoft's frantic pace. More important, I was eager to contemplate my future. Indeed, my intention was to fill the blank journal with ruminations on my life and what came next.

The days in Vietnam were quiet and uneventful. I started most mornings writing in my journal over a strong, piping hot cup of Vietnamese coffee with the viscosity of motor oil. In Hue, on day four, my morning ritual was interrupted by a Vietnamese teenager, about 17 years old, who asked if he could sit with me.

I made a universal "Please be seated" hand gesture. He immediately accepted. He had neatly cut jet-black hair and a kind face on which the troubles of the world had not yet drawn lines. He was dressed in blue cotton trousers, a crisp white short-sleeved shirt, and plastic sandals.

"My name is Nguyen Thai Vu. But call me Vu. That's easier."

"Nice to meet you, Vu. Please, please, sit. My name is John. I am from America."

"Good, because I want to practice my English with you. Is that all right?"

"Certainly. But I am not sure how much practice you need, because your English is flawless."

"Oh, no, it is not so good," he said with genuine modesty. "You see, this is a small hotel, so there are not many guests, so I do not have as much practice as I would like."

"You work here?"

"Yes, but perhaps you have not seen me because I work the night shift. But I see in the register that you will be here for three days, so perhaps you will be my friend and every morning we can practice my English."

I was eager to help. But my idea of a vacation was to get away from meetings and commitments, and he was proposing a standing appointment each day of my stay. I quickly changed the subject by pointing to a worn, dog-eared book he had placed on the table entitled *Learning Microsoft Excel* and asked if he was studying computers in addition to English.

"Oh, yes, I study computers as much as I can. Computers are important for Vietnam to continue to develop and be linked to the rest of the world."

"Do you know something, Vu? I actually work for Microsoft, and part of my responsibility is for sales of Microsoft Excel."

His eyes lit up the way that American teenagers' might had they met Britney Spears.

"Really? You work for Microsoft? Then you must be very smart. They are one of the greatest companies in the world."

"Well, they are good, but there are certainly drawbacks to working there."

"I have heard of Bill Gates. He is a very smart man. You must come see my computer school."

"I would love to. Perhaps later today, or tomorrow," I said, trying to preserve that precious morning time.

"No. Right now! You wait here, and I will be coming back very soon."

He leaped into the air and exited, stage left, with no further explanation. I ordered another cup of coffee, but Vu arrived before it did, roaring onto the patio on a Honda scooter like a Vietnamese version of James Dean. He made an excited "Hop aboard" motion.

"You come, now. We go to my school."

I commented that he had wasted no time getting his *moto.*

"Is not mine. Is my friends. I told him that you are an important visitor who needs to come to the computer school, so he makes us a loan. Come on, let's go."

Concerned that my Vietnamese waiter might wonder why I was "dining and dashing" on my coffee order, I laid 20,000 Vietnamese dong on the table and abandoned my original plan of a leisurely morning. I jumped on the back of the *moto* and felt the life going out of the springs. These bikes were obviously not designed for large American frames. Vu, busy revving the engine, did not notice. We roared off into traffic, and I decided not to contemplate whether Vu was actually old enough to be driving this thing.

WITH DUST FLYING, WE BRAKED TO A SHARP HALT IN FRONT OF THE Computer Academy five minutes later. The school was housed in a single room, with fifteen PCs lining three of the walls. The school was privately run by Professor Than, a kindly man in his early 50s who augmented his university salary by providing private lessons. Vu bragged to Professor Than that "my new friend John from Microsoft is going to teach me how to use Excel." I did not know what to say, as in Vietnamese society the teachers are revered, and I did not want the professor to think I was some young hotshot who thought my lessons would be more valuable than his. But the professor smiled, grabbed my arm, and proudly led me to the best machine in the house. "Here, this one is the only one that can run Windows 95." I winced at the thought that my company's flagship product demanded so much computer memory that over 90 percent of the academy's machines could not use it. I switched the focus of our conversation to Excel.

"Okay, Vu, to start I want to show you how to move a column of numbers from one section of the spreadsheet to another. You just click on the column that you want to move, hit Alt plus Edit plus Cut, then click on the section of the spreadsheet where you want the column to go, and click on Alt plus Enter plus Paste."

"No, it's easier this way," Vu said. Grabbing control of the keyboard, he showed me a way to do the same operation in fewer steps, using "shortcut keys" that I did not know existed.

"Wow, you're good at this, Vu. And Professor Than, you are obviously teaching your students well."

"No, I am not that smart," declared Vu. "You work at Microsoft, you are smarter than me."

I decided that in a pathetic attempt to save face, I would show

Vu a more complicated operation. But again, after I went through a multistep process, Vu showed me a shortcut. At this point, I suggested that we go back to English lessons, where there was perhaps a possibility that I had something to teach. We thanked Professor Than and walked out into the hot morning, with me unclear as to who was teacher and who was pupil.

Back on the bike, Vu asked if he could take me out for a coffee to replace the forfeited one. Interested in learning more about this brilliant young man, I immediately agreed. Before we had even sat down, I began peppering him with questions. Where had he gone to high school? Were his parents well educated? How much time did he have to practice his computer studies, given that he was working a full-time job? He seemed eager to share the details of his life:

"I grew up near Hue. Fifteen miles away, maybe. My parents, they are farmers, and they had no education. But they always told my younger brother—his name is Bang—and I that education is the most important thing. They encouraged us to study. They say 'study English, study computers.' One day I hope to go to college, but now I can't afford, so I work at the hotel and I try to study a little English, a little bit of computers."

I asked him about working at the hotel, and did this allow him enough time to study, and was he going to be able to save enough to afford college.

"I work at the hotel from six p.m. until seven a.m. I am here six days a week. Then I go to computer classes on Monday, Wednesday, and Friday. I know that I must study, or else I will never get a good job. Right now I learn Excel, but I also want to learn Microsoft Access. I like working at hotel because I can practice my English. Also working here means I can study at night while guests are sleeping and not making demands. I know I must study hard. After learning computers, I next want to become good at Japanese."

I asked if there were a lot of Japanese tourists in Vietnam.

"Not today, but in the future it will be important. Japanese companies will invest here, so there will be jobs, and also then there will be tourists from Japan. But now my focus is on computers."

"Can you afford school? Does the hotel pay you enough?"

"I make twenty-three dollars a month. My computer classes

cost fifteen dollars each month. I give five dollars to my parents to help them because they are getting older and I am not there to help them on the farm. So I have three dollars left. For food, I eat two meals a day at the hotel."

"Do you have to pay rent?"

"No, I sleep during the day on a cot in the back room of the hotel. I sleep four or five hours a day, no more. The rest of the time I study."

"But, Vu, certainly three dollars a month does not go far. That's ten cents a day. And you must need things like gas for your friend's *moto* when you borrow it, and other expenses."

"Yes, like taking my friends out for coffee." He smiled as he yelled for the bill in Vietnamese.

"Vu, you are certainly not paying for this coffee."

"Yes, I am," he declared emphatically. "You are my friend. You are not allowed to say no. Besides, I speak Vietnamese and you don't, so the woman will listen to me."

"Okay, thanks. But tell me more. I want to know more about how much you practice on the computer. How did you get so good at Excel?"

"I practice as much as I can. But the academy charges us money for practicing. It costs about one thousand dong per hour. With the money I have left over, I can afford to practice about three hours a week. I wish I could do more."

I did the math in my head several times because I kept arriving at a figure of ten cents per hour, and I simply could not imagine this small amount being the difference between receiving an education and not. So I confirmed the current exchange rate, and my math, with Vu. Yes, ten cents.

"Perhaps I could help you out by paying for some lessons."

"No. If you do that, you are not my friend. Come on, let's go now."

I had hit a nerve. His pride would not allow him to accept a handout. This concerned me, because an amount that was pocket change for me could allow him much more practice time. But I was not about to give up. Vu was stubborn, but I've met few people in life who can match me in this department.

. . .

THAT NIGHT, AS I WALKED OUT TO DINNER, I STOPPED BY THE DESK TO leave my key. Vu was reading a guide to a Casio programmable calculator. "Oh, do you own one of those?" I asked.

"No, some guest left this here at the hotel, so I read it because I want to learn how electronics work. I have read it four times."

My heart skipped a beat. Here was a kid who was so anxious to learn that he would read anything that came into his orbit, no matter how arcane. It made me realize how much I took for granted. I had just recently had to buy a new bookshelf to keep up with my flow of reading. If only Vu could have such "problems" in life.

The next morning on the way to coffee I stopped at the desk and asked Vu to join me as soon as his shift ended. When he sat down, I ordered for him in broken French from the friendly octogenarian running the café. By taking control of the order, I hoped to also take control of the bill. I told Vu that I had run out of books and asked if he knew of any bookstores that carried English books. Before his drink had arrived, he ran off to again borrow his friend's *moto*.

My secret plan was to buy Vu enough technology books that he could continue his self-study. At the store, I kept one eye on the rather thin selection of English books I was perusing, and the other eye on Vu. Sure enough, one book rack over he was leafing through a modern, thick, state-of-the-art Excel guide.

Proud of my cunning, I approached to close the deal.

"That looks like a great study guide for Excel."

Vu slammed the book back on the shelf. "Yes, is nice. Did you find anything in English?"

"No, I had no luck. But how about if we get this for you?" I suggested as I picked up the Excel book.

"No, if you do that, you are not my friend!" He stole the book back, and as one hand thunked it back onto the shelf, his other hand grabbed my arm to lead me out of the store.

How was I going to help him? I was thrilled that he was not begging and that he valued his independence. But I wanted him to achieve his dream of a full education, and he was not making it easy.

. . .

BACK TO THE DRAWING BOARD. THAT NIGHT WAS MY LAST IN HUE; IT was crunch time. I went to my favorite restaurant, a small, family-run place with plastic furniture on the banks of the Perfume River. The sun had set, and the day's heat was all-too-slowly dissipating. I was trying to write in my journal about Vu, but my mind was too busy racing with ideas on how I could best help him with his studies. As soon as I left town, my opportunity to assist would be lost. I ordered an ice-cold 333 beer and let my mind wander in the hope that a solution would come to me.

I recalled my first experience with computers, at the age of 17 as I started my senior year. Our high school had just acquired its first two Commodore PET computers, each with 64K of memory. Mr. Tidlow was also busy teaching calculus and physics but somehow managed to carve out time to allow a limited group of twenty students to begin programming in BASIC. Something in computer coding appealed to the part of me that likes logical structure and mathematical clarity. I became hooked and was soon writing programs to help my father's company plan their investment strategy and to forecast their yields.

Here in Hue was a similarly young and enthusiastic student. For want of a small amount of money, his education was not complete. Maybe I could help him to find a scholarship. Did such things exist and how would I find out?

Suddenly it hit me. Eureka! I had no idea whether there were scholarship programs for Vietnamese students, but that did not matter. It was in my power to create this opportunity. The answer did not need to involve outsiders. I frantically ripped a page out of the journal and grabbed a pen.

Dear Nguyen Thai Vu:

As an employee of Microsoft, I have been financially empowered by Bill Gates to provide scholarship money for promising young students in Vietnam to learn computer science. You are a smart student, so we wish to support your education. Please accept the enclosed cash as a "study grant" that can be used for books and for practice time on computers.

Microsoft and I are proud to support you. The continued development of your country lies in education, and we hope that this grant will help you not only in your studies, but also in your quest to help Vietnam to engage with the rest of the world.

Best of luck to you. Please study hard, and please write to me with reports on your progress.

Smiling at my cunning, I signed my name and put a crisp $20 bill in an air-mail envelope. To celebrate, I ordered a second beer and a steamed fish with rice and contemplated how fun it would be to watch Vu's reaction.

Upon my return to the hotel, I decided on a strategy that would have me several moves down the chessboard, and had Vu at checkmate. At the desk, he gave me the room key, and I handed him the envelope in return. "You have to do me a favor, okay? You're my friend, and I expect you to honor what I am about to ask of you." He nodded slowly, seriously, with a quizzical look. "You cannot open this until I am upstairs, and you are not allowed to talk to me about this until tomorrow morning, okay?" He looked perplexed, but agreed to the terms.

As I walked up the stairs, he said, "You will have coffee with me in the morning before you leave for Hoi An, right?" I agreed and set off to my room to pack.

Five minutes later, there was a knock on my door. There stood Vu. He walked into my room, still reading the certificate. I was worried that he was too proud to accept the scholarship money, until I noticed that he had tears in his eyes. "If you think I am smart, then I must be smart. If Microsoft thinks that I am a good student, then I will study even harder and be a better student. I will send you reports on how I am doing. I am so happy that I will now be able to study harder and spend more time on computers."

With that he did a quick 180-degree turn, assured me that he would wake me up at 7 a.m. for a farewell coffee, and shut the door. At which point I collapsed on my bed and started crying with tears of joy, of hope, of optimism, for forming a connection that transcends words.

He woke me the next morning promptly at seven with a knock

on the door, this being a cheap hotel that did not have phones. Vu walked in as though we were roommates and placed a bag on the bed.

"Here, this is for you."

"Vu, what is this? Water? Why two liters? And why so much 7UP?"

"Yes, it is going to be hot today," he announced, as though it were not hot in Vietnam *every* day.

"Vu, why did you do this?"

"Because today you have a long drive. Five or six hours. And you need water. And I know you like 7UP, because I always see you drinking it."

"But, Vu, you are not allowed to spend your scholarship money on me. You have to spend it on your studies."

"Don't worry."

"Vu, I am going to have to report you to Bill Gates for this."

We laughed and headed downstairs for our farewell coffee. When I reached for my wallet, he informed me that he had prepaid the restaurant owner. Helpless, I shook his hand to seal the deal and sipped my farewell coffee. Vu then handed me a laminated photo of himself, standing ramrod straight next to the hotel's front desk. He had gone to a photography shop the prior afternoon, so that "my friend John will remember what his friend Vu looks like."

As we said good-bye, Vu made me promise that I would stay in touch, and that I would someday return to Hue. "You will be so proud of me. By then, I will be a teacher, and I will be helping Vietnam to develop through education."

I agreed, promising him that I would write back, that I would return to Vietnam, and that we would stay friends throughout our lives. We had known each other for about 48 hours, but as I waved good-bye to him, it felt as if I were parting with my younger brother.

ALTHOUGH I DID NOT KNOW IT AT THE TIME, A PIECE OF THE POST-Microsoft jigsaw puzzle had fallen into place. While I am not certain that the hopes and dreams of one person can represent those of an entire nation, I felt that Vu's zeal for education made a strong argument for keeping on the lookout for other students to whom I could award scholarships.

Because of Vu, my strong preference was to make Vietnam the second country of operations for Room to Read. I had the inspiration, but I had little knowledge of the country. It's naive for a person who has traveled in a foreign land for only a few weeks to assume he now understands its complexities. This is especially true for an American in Vietnam—we did not understand the country when we entered and fought in its civil war in the 1960s any better than we did as I contemplated expanding Room to Read there. So my first goal was to find a smart person with experience in the country who could develop an action plan for Room to Read Vietnam. Hundreds of thousands of young Vus were waiting for us.

VU'S PROGRESS

Vu has made his parents and me proud by continuing his studies. In fact, he has not stopped since our initial meeting back in 1997.

For over a year after my initial Vietnam trip, he would send me reports on his grades at Professor Than's private Computer Academy. A 92 in Word. A 99 on his last Excel exam. A 96 in Windows proficiency. "I promise you to study harder in Microsoft Word," he wrote, as though a grade of 92 were something to be ashamed of.

By 1999, he was ready to tackle Microsoft Access. A friend of mine was visiting Vietnam, and I asked her to meet up with Vu in Hue and transfer some more scholarship money to him. During her first hour in Hue, as she walked along Le Loi Avenue looking for a place to eat lunch, she saw a young man in a T-shirt bearing the slogan www.MICROSOFT.COM.AU (this was a relic from my days running Microsoft's Internet unit in Australia).

"Are you Vu?" she asked.

"No, but I know Vu. I can take you to his hotel."

Five hours before their scheduled meet-up for dinner, she met him, heard all about his studies, and handed over the $50 I had sent to help Vu continue his studies.

Within a year, he was ready for college. In 2000, we were still

continued

exchanging letters by snail mail, as Internet access in Vietnam was sporadic and expensive by local standards. Vu wrote to me to say that he wanted to study English, French, and Japanese. I wrote back to tell him that I'd be willing to support some of his college education, but that he'd also have to pitch in. Next, I inquired about which order he planned to learn the languages in. I should not have been surprised, given his hunger for knowledge, when he replied that he would study all three languages simultaneously.

Upon graduation, Vu took a prestigious job with the Vietnamese National Railway. He trained railroad personnel on conversational French, English, and Japanese. Tourism has grown rapidly in Vietnam and is one of the biggest earners of foreign currency. Because of Vu's studies, I believe that many thousands of travelers today have been pleasantly surprised when being greeted with a friendly *"Bonjour, madame," "Konichiwa,"* or "Good morning" by the Vietnamese railways staff.

He is now married to Yen, a woman equally dedicated to education. She graduated from a local medical college and works as a nurse. Vu tells me that their five-year-old daughter, Thao, has learned how to say "Hello, John," in eager anticipation of my next trip to Hue.

Vu's computer skills continue to pay dividends. He authors a regular column for the *Informatics* newspaper and is now in touch with me weekly via his Gmail account. "I mainly write about the Windows and Office tips, as well as new softwares usage. I like this very well!" The additional $25 per month he makes is being saved for Thao's education.

In the fall of 2005, Vu wrote to tell me that he had decided to pursue a graduate degree in software engineering at the Aptech school in Hue. The cost would run $650 per year. Could I help? His parents had already committed the lion's share of their life savings, 3 million Vietnamese dong (about $200).

My author's advance against royalties for this book was immediately tapped into, and via the miracle of Western Union Vu soon had tuition for both years of study. If you bought this book, you are now one of Vu's benefactors. My dream is to continue to use these funds to help the millions of eager learners who, like Vu, will study so hard if we help them to gain the opportunity of the lifelong gift of education.

CHAPTER 12

A POSTCARD FROM NEPAL

Pᴿᴼᴳᴿᴱˢˢ ɪɴ Nᴇᴘᴀʟ ᴡᴀˢ ʜᴀᴘᴘᴇɴɪɴɢ ˢᴏ ǫᴜɪᴄᴋʟʏ ᴛʜᴀᴛ ᴍᴏˢᴛ ᴏꜰ ᴍʏ time and energy was consumed. Our expansion plans for Vietnam remained on hold. I knew it was only a matter of time before we'd find a way to add more countries, but the time was not right in the spring of 2001.

At Dinesh's invitation, I flew back to Nepal that April to attend the opening ceremonies for five of our new schools. I arrived in the capital, Kathmandu, worn-out from the 38-hour journey from San Francisco. Dinesh met me up at the airport and steered me though the crowd of 100-plus taxi drivers searching for a fare. I was thrilled to be back in Kathmandu. Dinesh dodged cows chomping on garbage, we passed numerous temples of the Buddhist and Hindu faiths, and each stoplight-free intersection jam-packed with honking vehicles was an opportunity for me to have my own spiritual moment to seek favor from the gods.

We had a cup of tea on arrival at my hotel in the tourist district of Thamel. Dinesh told me to spend the afternoon resting up, as we were expected the next day in the rural district of Dhading. As he left, he laughingly told me, "You've traveled for two days, you look tired, but you're still not at your final destination. See you tomorrow at seven."

The next morning broke cold and clear in the Kathmandu Valley. A pure blue sky greeted me, and the smell of wood-fire smoke drifted into my room, making me crave a cup of Nepali *duit chai* (milk tea). The hotel's menu offered several intriguing options:

> *Sweat & sour chicken*
> *Two toast butter jam or honey has brown*
> *Crown crispy fried chicken with salad boneless*
> *Chilly corn corney rice*

As I debated my choices, a Nepali man in his mid-50s approached my table. "Hello, sir. You may not remember me. I believe you were here two years ago. You were with your father. You stayed in rooms 301 and 302." I complimented him on his memory and facial recognition. "May I ask how is your father? Is he in good health? And how is your book project? I hope you are here to continue to help the children of Nepal?"

I pulled some children's books out of my backpack. He smiled, turned the pages and eyed the books with a sense of wonder. He shook my hand and asked if we could have a glass of tea later in the day. With that, he returned to the front desk, and I gave silent thanks for the reaffirmation that our education projects mattered to the people of Nepal.

Dinesh soon appeared, clad in jeans, a black T-shirt, and Ray-Bans. His *topi*, a Nepalese hat that adds at least three inches to his five-foot-four frame, was the only indigenous bit of his outfit.

Dinesh explained that our first stop was Benighat. This village lies only 60 miles, as the crow flies, from Kathmandu. But we were driving on Nepal's notorious roads rather than flying. The twisting, turning, narrow, and slow roads are the downside of the beautiful mountains. The country's economic situation makes expensive earthmoving equipment unavailable. Instead, one sees laborers with picks and shovels clearing landslides, reinforcing walls, and digging boulders out of rivers to use as building materials. It's a miracle that any of these roads, no matter how bad, even exist.

For three hours west out of Kathmandu, we were precariously perched on the sides of vertigo-inducing cliffs. We jockeyed for position with diesel-belching Indian buses and trucks bearing the ubiquitous HORN PLEASE signs. We obliged liberally as we weaved through the slower-moving traffic, as though we were a cross between a slalom skier and a honking goose.

Just after 11 a.m. our minibus pulled off the road and into a small courtyard at the school in Benighat. First dozens, then hundreds, of children ran toward us, excitedly yelling, "Namaste." Beyond the children stood a new whitewashed school building. Red ribbons stretched across each of the five classroom doorways. I felt immense pride in my team, and in our work. Each of these kids, and there now appeared to be several hundred of them crowding around us, would have the benefit of a better education. I had truly found my nirvana. All the work back in San Francisco chasing down donations was indeed worth the long nights and the begging.

I smiled at Dinesh and shook his hand. I told him that he should be proud of his work, and that I found it amazing that this entire school had been built in less than one year, especially using mostly volunteer labor. He did not say much, out of either humility or because he was also overwhelmed with emotion. Instead, he leaned over to let a student slip a welcoming flower garland over his head. He then grabbed my arm and walked me toward the school and the podium that had temporarily been erected for the opening ceremony.

Ceremonies in Nepal tend to be joyous. Incense is lit, red *tikka* powder is applied to portraits of the king and queen of Nepal to honor them, and many (sometimes too many) speeches are made. Local politicians orate, the headmaster then has something to say, teachers and parents are not shy about grabbing the stage, Room to Read team members are asked to speak, and the list goes on and on. Broiling in the sun, I reminded myself that the long list of speakers was a positive sign. Obviously, each community member was proud of the new school and felt some degree of ownership. The more speakers, the better: each of these people would look out for the new school long after Dinesh and I had left town.

As my Nepali language abilities are abysmal, my mind had several opportunities to drift off. I thought about how much my life had changed. Two years ago I had been experiencing my crisis of confidence while working in China. I'd endured tortured intro-spection about whether there would be "life after Microsoft." And now here I sat in a rural village, as happy as I had even been. I did not have any of the trappings of my old Microsoft life and had not collected a paycheck in over a year. But I felt as though I had found my role in the universe. I looked out at the crowd, and several chil-dren smiled and waved at me as soon as we locked eyes. Their faces made every minute of my three-day journey to this remote village in the shadow of the Himalayas worth it.

I also thought of my friend Hilary, who had endowed Room to Read's half of the challenge grant. I was proud to be representing her as the school was opened in honor of her parents. I was still hav-ing a bit of a problem with taking my friend's money, especially since they would not directly benefit from it. Seeing the new school, and the dedication plaque honoring her parents, made me realize that I was merely a conduit. Her money was temporarily entrusted to me as it made its journey to this village, where it was converted to bricks and mortar, and then further transformed into an education for hundreds of kids. An amount of money that for her was a "rounding error" in her investment account had created something permanent that would pay dividends for years to come and would also let her parents know how much she loved and honored them.

My musings were interrupted by the headmaster inviting me to cut one of the red ribbons. I was then asked to say a few words, so I told the school that a friend in America had trekked in Nepal and had been overwhelmed by the kindness of those she'd met during three weeks in remote mountains. This was her way of saying thank you to a country from which she had received such joy. I also sa-luted the community for having donated the land and labor.

The headmaster was the last to speak. I could not follow most of his rapid-fire Nepali, but did recognize that he continually re-peated the number 1,001. I whispered a request for explanation to Dinesh.

"One thousand one is considered a lucky number here in Nepal."

I love palindromes, but decided to leave that observation to myself.

"Why does he keep repeating it?"

"He's reading the names of each family who donated one thousand one rupees to the school construction to honor and thank them for their commitment."

I calculated that 1,001 rupees was $14—a large sum in a country where the average person earns less than a dollar a day.

After the ceremony had concluded, we were invited into the teachers' room for tea. I sat next to the headmaster and told him that I was impressed by the number of families who had donated money. I asked if he knew the exact number of donors. With a look of immense pride and a wide smile full of perfect teeth, he informed me that 183 families had contributed.

It was a wonderful combination. A donor in California had done her part, and the village had done theirs. The amounts donated by each were quite different, but that was inconsequential. Many families—one in Silicon Valley and 183 in Benighat—had proven their commitment to education and had partnered in the construction of a new school.

DURING SUBSEQUENT VISITS TO NEPAL, I WOULD CONTINUE TO HEAR stories about the power of these challenge grants. One of our projects, Himalaya Primary School, was located on the outskirts of Kathmandu, in a poor community whose economy depended on the local brick factories. The local soil was conducive to brickmaking, and six soot-belching factories surrounded the village. On a site visit to check on progress, I met the headmaster. He proudly recounted how he'd visited each factory to ask for support in building a new school. He reminded each factory owner that the workers' wages were so low that parents could not afford to contribute to the challenge grant. But Room to Read required each community to coinvest, so he proposed an innovative solution: each factory owner would donate 10,000 bricks, and Room to Read's money would be used to buy cement, window frames, desks, and to pay for skilled labor to erect the walls. His sales strategy succeeded, and once again I was blown away by the ingenuity of the communities with which we partnered.

Two days after my visit to Himalaya Primary School, Dinesh took me into the foothills of the mountains west of Kathmandu. Our destination was the village of Katrak, which perched on a hillside overlooking verdant rice fields. Dinesh parked our rented truck along the side of the road, and with a head nod and a shout of *"Jhane ho. Orolo"* (Let's go! Uphill), he announced to me that we had a steep hike in front of us.

At 8 a.m. the sun was already burning down on us, and my pace slowed as I stopped for applications of sun cream and gulps from my water bottle. On frequent occasions women with large bags hoisted onto their backs rushed past me, heading up the trail. I could not hope to match their pace, even though I was carrying only my water bottle and a Nikon. I asked Dinesh if they were returning from the market. He laughed and asked whether I realized that these women were carrying cement. I must have looked perplexed, so he explained.

When the local government of the village of Katrak requested Room to Read's help, Dinesh and Yadav (our civil engineer in charge of the School Room program) said that they would provide half the resources if the village could come up with the other half. The head of the village development committee told our team that the village was poor, with more than 95 percent of parents living on subsistence farming. What little economy the village had was simple barter, and as a result few parents could afford to put money into the project.

Yadav explained that contributions other than cash would count toward the challenge grant. As an example, parents could prove their commitment to education and the new school by donating labor.

The women we saw this morning had responded to the call. Each morning, a group of them would wake up before sunrise, walk an hour downhill to the roadside where the cement bags were being stored, and then walk 90 minutes back up to the village. The bags weighed 50 kilos—110 pounds—and some mothers were making the trip twice in one day. Dinesh reminded me that this was a farming village, and that the women would still have to spend their day in the fields.

We crested the hill and on the building site saw 20 men, presumably the fathers, digging the foundation and beginning to put up the walls. I asked one of the mothers if I could try picking up her bag of cement. I nearly threw my back out as I struggled to get the bag above my waist. The mothers were greatly entertained, and the group around me grew larger as I failed to impress them as Hercules.

I outweighed these women by at least 50 pounds. Most of them probably survived on two bowls of rice and lentils per day. Such was their belief in the power of education to provide their children with a brighter future that they were willing to make any sacrifice. I felt inspired and vowed to work even harder to find the funding to enable more of these challenge grants. I also vowed that I'd get to the gym to lift weights a bit more often.

BACK IN THE SPRING OF 2001 THE POWER OF THESE COMMUNITY PART-nerships was becoming clear to me. At each ceremony, a proud headmaster or teacher would tell me a unique story about how their community had rallied around the challenge grant. As I listened to the recitation of the story, I would sneak furtive and proud glances at the school building, decorated in prayer flags and with red ribbons stretched across the doors. It quickly became obvious that the model designed by Dinesh and the local team was not just an ivory-tower theory. It was paying everyday dividends across the country.

Dinesh was so excited to show me every Room to Read project that he insisted we squeeze in a site visit on the way to my departing flight. A group of parents were mixing cement as their children played nearby. Without enough resources for even a soccer ball, the kids had filled an empty water bottle with stones and were kicking it toward their makeshift goal with the zeal of a young Pelé.

I shot photos. Soon, every child was hamming it up, competing with his or her friends to occupy the camera's lens. As Dinesh ushered me back into our car to drive to the airport, my eager young subjects ran after us with shouts of "Thank you" and "Bye-bye."

As we made slow progress over the rutted road, the students had no problem keeping up; indeed, some even passed us. As they continued to smile and wave, and as I finished off the 15th roll of film from the trip, I had a feeling in my gut, one approaching pure certainty, that I had made the right decision as to how I would spend the rest of my life.

YOU SAY YOU WANT A REVOLUTION? ADVICE ON CHANGING THE WORLD

Think Big from Day One

When I started Room to Read, I declared immediately that our goal was to help 10 million children to gain the lifelong gift of education. Some people told me that this was hubris—how could a guy who had established only a few libraries set such a brazen goal?

I did not allow myself to be talked out of this, as I believe that it's important to think big. There was a saying at Microsoft—"Go big or go home"—and this lies at the heart of my advice to anyone who wants to create change. The problems facing the world today are immense. This is not a time for incremental thinking. If a cause is worth devoting your time to, then you owe it to yourself—and those you will serve—to think in a big way.

The side benefit is that thinking big can be a self-fulfilling prophecy, because bold goals will attract bold people. Let's say, for example, that your cause is to bring clean water to villages in Africa where children are dying of diseases that nobody should be killed by in this modern world. Below are two statements that you could make while talking to a potential donor or board member about aiding your nascent organization:

STATEMENT #1: My dream is to bring new wells and clean water to at least 25 villages in Kenya over the next three years.

STATEMENT #2: The scale of the water problem in Africa requires bold solutions, because millions of people die of diseases that they would not contract if they had clean water. So I want to help at least 10,000 villages, throughout Africa, to have clean water within ten years.*

The latter statement is probably going to scare some people away. This is fine—after all, you don't want people who think small or who are afraid of big challenges. The second statement will also attract the attention of potential donors. One of the biggest frustrations that funders have is that "we are spending all this money, yet so little seems to change as a result." Therefore, when they meet someone who declares a bold set of goals, they are likely to take notice and you'll be in a position to "get the meeting."

My favorite "poster child" for this advice is actually from the private sector—Amazon. When Jeff Bezos launched the company in 1995, the home page boldly declared Amazon to be "Earth's Biggest Bookstore" even though they had yet to sell a single title. He was referring, of course, to the breadth of selection they would be able to offer via a virtual store, so the claim was at least plausible. Many naysayers were of course on hand to point out that Amazon's first-year revenues were less than what a single Barnes & Noble outlet in Manhattan might do during a slow week. I can imagine that his lawyers tried to talk him out of it, but Jeff was bold, and his claim to be building earth's biggest bookstore got him a lot of attention from investors, the media, and customers. They talked about the company, and the buzz led to publicity and sales. Amazon is a classic case of a self-fulfilling prophecy. It not only became earth's best-selling bookstore, but also its biggest record store.

* When setting bold goals, it is important to allow yourself more time.

CHAPTER 13

WHAT EVERY ENTREPRENEUR NEEDS:

A STRONG SECOND-IN-COMMAND

Bᵧ JUNE OF 2001 I WAS FRUSTRATED WITH MY INABILITY TO FIGURE out how to expand into a second country. I was thrilled with the progress in Nepal, but well aware that we were missing so many children in Cambodia and Vietnam, our next expansion targets. Raising funds for our work in Nepal was such a big job that I could not find the time to visit either of the two countries. My goal was to go global, and yet we were still only in one country. I felt like a charlatan—talking a good game but not able to deliver.

Thankfully, the universe sometimes conspires to solve one's problems without prior notice. One perfect summer afternoon I was walking into a coffee shop on San Francisco's Fillmore Street to meet with a potential donor. The dot-com bubble was in the middle of bursting, but a lot of people who had timed their stock sales right had a pile of funds to deploy. I was using every connection I had in the technology world to get meetings with anyone who had been at Yahoo!, eBay, PayPal, or any of the other success stories—those companies that had not gone down in flames.

As I walked into the coffee shop, crowded with laptop surfers, I answered my cell phone. Erin introduced herself. She was calling because a mutual friend had mentioned our work in Nepal and desire to expand into Vietnam. "I really want to meet you. I looked at your Web site and I think that the work your team is doing, and the approach they take in enlisting the communities, could be replicated in Vietnam. Can we meet up?"

Two days later, we introduced ourselves at Betelnut, a hip pan-Asian eatery on trendy Union Street. Over steaming-hot spring rolls and noodle soup, Erin talked of her desire to return to Vietnam:

"I spent two years working for Unilever, setting up their ice cream business. This was one of the best periods of my life. The people welcomed me into their homes and into their lives. Everything was an adventure—from taking trips to rural villages on the back of underpowered motorbikes to eating from sidewalk food stands run by entrepreneural women. The whole country had such an appeal to me. I've been back in America for a few years and I miss Vietnam. Working in the dot-com economy does not do it for me. I always thought it would be so great to join a tech start-up. But I miss Vietnam and want to find a way to have it be part of my life again."

I asked if she had any ideas on how she would make that happen.

"I've been offered a job by a company here in San Francisco that imports furniture from Vietnam. But what I really want to do is to work in some capacity that helps children rather than a company's bottom line. When I was working for Unilever, my favorite project was a community outreach program to help a village near our ice cream factory to build a new school. That was the best part of my time in Vietnam. So when Verna and I were talking earlier this week, and I told her about my goals, she immediately turned into a yenta. She said that you have the desire to go into Vietnam but lack the expertise. Here I am with some knowledge and experience but there is no charity I know of with which I can work."

I was impressed with her passion, but explained that I could not pay her. She said that was all right—that she was willing to volunteer. She simply wanted to do something, anything, to help Vietnamese children gain an education. She was going back to Vietnam for a friend's wedding and was willing to spend a few extra weeks, or a few months if that's what it took, to investigate whether Room to Read could start operations.

The organization was being built by dozens of people like Erin who offered themselves up without preconditions. I immediately accepted her offer. She was leaving soon, so we dedicated the next two days to a thorough tutorial on the organization's business model.

In advance of her trip, she e-mailed friends in Vietnam with an overview of Room to Read. She asked them to start translating our marketing materials into Vietnamese. She requested meetings with officials in the Ministry of Education. I was impressed with how quickly she moved.

SIX WEEKS LATER, ERIN RETURNED TO SAN FRANCISCO. SHE WAS EX-hausted from the 22-hour journey, but phoned immediately. "We need to talk as soon as possible. The Vietnamese government is excited about the potential of working with us. I have a plan."

The next morning, it was back to our favorite coffee shop. The Chestnut Street Coffee Roastery had replaced my home office as the world headquarters of Room to Read, which was fitting, as it was run by Sam and Rose, who had come to America from Cambodia. They encouraged me to continue our expansion to help their country to rebuild in the post–Khmer Rouge era.

The Vietnamese are fond of gift giving. Erin showed the genes of her adopted country; she presented a photo album with a lacquered wood cover. As I sipped my latte, I opened to the first page, on which an adorable young Vietnamese girl was reading a book. Erin had written, in gold pen, the proclamation "Announcing Our Launch in Vietnam."

I laughed. "So, uh, it's decided? We're opening in Vietnam? That was quick!"

"Well, it's obviously your decision, but I think we should. There is so much need in the country right now. The last decade has been relatively stable after years of war with France, the U.S., and China. That stability has led to a baby boom, because during times of peace and economic growth people tend to have more children. As a result, half the population is under the age of twenty. But there is a flip side to this. The rural communities are too poor to build adequate schools and libraries. So basically you have many more kids, without having enough capacity for all of them to go to school.

"Vietnam may not have enough money, but the parents have so much enthusiasm for education. Teaching is one of the most respected professions. There is a Confucian belief in the power of learning. So when I told people about all the great work you have done in Nepal, their first reaction was to ask when we could start work in Vietnam."

"I'm totally into the idea," I replied. "But there are practical considerations. This year, 2001, our entire budget is $150,000. That is barely enough to pay for our work in Nepal, and Vietnam has four times the population."

"That's all right—I will help you fund-raise so that we have more money coming in."

"But how can I afford to hire you? It's one thing to hire program officers in Nepal because they can afford to live on $200 per month. In this town, that will pay your rent for all of three days."

"I've talked to my roommate about this, and also my mom. They both know that helping kids in Vietnam is my dream. My roommate works at Goldman Sachs and does quite well financially. She offered to pay my rent for the next month. My mother thought that was a good idea, and she offered to fund a second month. So my biggest expense is taken care of. I can fund my day-to-day living expenses from savings. So if you want to have me join you, you've got me for two months."

I was glad that Erin had thought this through and was also willing to make a personal sacrifice to make it happen. That her mother was also willing to invest in Erin's dream spoke volumes.

I immediately decided to emulate these positive examples.

"Actually, you can work with me for four months."

"Why four?"

"Because tomorrow we should get to work. When we meet up, I will give you $1,000, freshly withdrawn from the ATM. I hope you can make it last for a month. Next month I will give you the same amount. That will be my contribution to making this happen.

Within four months, you and I collectively will have to find a way to get you on the payroll. One of the things I learned at Microsoft is that if you find a good person, you should hire them, and they will more than pay for themselves.

"But here is my 'Welcome to Room to Read' speech. You have four months during which you need to help me bring in some serious bucks, or else you won't have a job. We have no time to waste. Let's get to the phones and start smiling and dialing!"

ERIN PLUNGED INTO HER ROLE. TWO MONTHS INTO HER TENURE, I walked into the office on a Monday morning and noticed that she was grinning as if she'd won Wimbledon. She asked if I wanted to hear some good news, and I replied that it was better than the alternative. We had just received word of a $32,000 grant from the Global Catalyst Foundation. At our first meeting, a month prior, they had told us they really liked our work and in particular thought that our Computer Room program in Nepal had real potential. Thankfully, they had made a quick decision, and we now had 32,000 fewer reasons to feel financial pressure.

The next day, as I walked into the office, it was like a scene from the film *Groundhog Day,* where each and every day is a repeat of the prior one. Erin asked me if I wanted to hear good news, I quickly assented, and she told me that Microsoft had just called. They had approved our $30,000 grant proposal. We could set up our first two computer labs in Vietnam. We hugged, then got back to e-mails and the phones in hopes of continuing the momentum.

On Wednesday, a grant arrived from the Tibet Fund to establish computer labs in predominantly Tibetan refugee communities in Nepal. On Thursday, a couple in Silicon Valley called to say that they had hosted a Room to Read party and raised $10,000. They planned to visit Nepal that year and wanted to see our work. But they did not want to be just tourists and thought it would be fun to help finance a project. My mind raced with thoughts of what would be possible if we could convince thousands of global travelers to follow this example.

We had raised $80,000 in a week! The organization was starting to fire on all cylinders. Best of all, we were attracting money from multiple sources. This was true to my goal of never being overly dependent on any one donor. Too often in the charity world an organization would have all its eggs in one basket, and the decision of one funder to pull out or scale back significantly could unravel the entire organization. We were still young, but in just this week we had attracted money from two foundations, a corporation, and two well-connected white-collar executives.

With our literacy war chest filling, we decided that it was time to approve our first Vietnam projects. Erin again crossed the Pacific Ocean on short notice. This was a habit that neither of us would break for years to come. Her goal was to visit the communities in southern Vietnam and meet the people who had asked for Room to Read's help. I would hold down the fort in San Francisco, continue to fund-raise, and eagerly await her reports from the Mekong Delta.

FOUR DAYS AFTER HER DEPARTURE, I WAS IN THE OFFICE PREPARING A slide show that I would be presenting at a fund-raising event in Seattle later that week. My e-mail chimed with a missive from Erin.

Hi John:

Writing to you from a cybercafé in Saigon. I just returned from a day in Can Gio District, a two-hour drive from here. I spent the day with the guys from the local Education Ministry. They have proposed several school construction projects to us.

Can Gio is the poorest part of Ho Chi Minh Province and in much need of assistance. The main industries are salt mining and shrimp farming, both of which are owned by rich city businesses, leaving the locals working hard for next to nothing.

The local school was built as a small primary school. However, it is being used for a kindergarten, primary, and middle school because the other schools are too far away for the children to travel to. In fact, the school is so crowded—over 500 children— that they have to teach in two shifts. This means that the children only get four hours of school a day instead of the normal seven hours in Vietnam. The unfortunate result is most of the primary-school children don't pass the exam to enter middle school, thus ending their opportunity for education at the tender age of nine or ten!

We are working with Can Gio on a challenge grant to expand the school, thus helping to give the children in this area the hope for a brighter future. I was touched by the sincerity and depth of need of the people in Can Gio during my visit. The profound impact we can have on this community is real and immediate and is what makes our work so worthwhile!

Bye from Vietnam,

Erin

I closed my eyes and tried to imagine what this village looked like. I visualized the overcrowded classrooms that I know all too well from Nepal, but substituted Vietnamese children's faces for the Nepali ones. A thought came to mind of a teacher-to-student ratio that was probably 50:1. And I became sad thinking of those children who were told at age ten that they had failed to advance to secondary school. With only half the normal school hours, they were fighting this battle with one arm tied behind their back. It was not their fault, and I knew that we had it in our power to do something about it.

Immediately, my Monday had clarity—my only goal was to find a donor to support the school project in Can Gio. I combed my Rolodex and began making a prospect list. Someone was going to adopt this project—I knew that in my heart. It's not often that we are given an opportunity to forever change the lives of 500 children. How could anyone say no to this? If I couldn't close this deal, I didn't deserve to be in the business.

So I brewed myself a cup of coffee, put on my headphones, cranked Talking Heads to loud volume, and began firing off an edited version of Erin's e-mail to prospective donors. Over 500 children in Can Gio District needed me to find a donor. So I really had no choice but to ask and was confident that someone would feel that they had no choice but to say yes.

Within 48 hours, we had not one yes, but two. One was from a senior executive at Microsoft, and the other from a venture capitalist in Silicon Valley. I punched the air like a bad rock singer. Firing up my e-mail, I sent a short note to Erin:

> Good news. The eagle has landed. Don't stop at one school. I have already sold two. Find a few more projects if you can—I know from what Vu and you have both told me that they are needed. We can get funding, as donors love this model of adopting an entire school for $10,000–12,000, and knowing exactly where their money goes.
>
> One guy said to me today that when he gives money to a big charity, he has no idea of whether the money goes to pay the light bill, the rent, or finds its way to the programs the charity runs. He likes our model so much that he's going to try to convince a few of his friends to also endow a school. This model works, and donors will get behind it. I know that Room to Read is still young and that there are only two of us right now, but let's think big!
>
> And while you are over there, buy a digital camera for the Vietnam team, so that we can get photos of the finished schools to these donors. They will probably share them with friends, and who knows how many of them might decide to also endow a school. If we have our donors doing our marketing for us, the result could be huge!

EVERYDAY HEROES: THE NAME GAME

By late 2001, we were working in Vietnam and Nepal, with plans to expand into Cambodia. We were setting up schools, libraries, and computer labs and funding long-term scholarships for girls. Yet our organization's name was Books for Nepal. Erin recalled for me with horror her experience trying to convince Vietnamese Communist Party officials to give permission for "Books for Nepal" to build schools in Vietnam.

Obviously, I had chosen a name that did not scale.

continued

Erin and I struggled to come up with a new name. It was one of the biggest challenges we've faced. Two months into brainstorming, we had not found one we were enthused about. It seemed as though all of the good brands were taken.

One night I arrived late at my friend Paul and Susan's house for a dinner party. I apologized to the group, explaining that I'd been caught in a meeting related to our Vietnam expansion.

"How are you expanding into Vietnam if your name is Books for Nepal?" Paul immediately challenged. Susan, playing a more welcoming version of host, poured me a glass of Shiraz.

I explained that we were currently struggling with this problem and that we were looking at alternatives.

"One of our ideas was to call the organization Literacy for Life," I offered tentatively.

Several loud guffaws came from around the table. "That's the worst brand I've ever heard," my friend Chris offered. "I'd never give money to an organization with such a terrible name."

"Okay, well, if you guys are so smart, then let's see you come up with something better," I challenged. "What you probably don't realize is that coming up with a brand is a lot harder than it looks. As they say in the song about dating, "All of the good ones are taken." Every time I think I've come up with something I like, I go to the Internet and learn that it's already been claimed."

More wine was poured. The risotto was served. Ideas flew around the table. *The International Literacy Initiative.* Nah, too dry. *Reading Is Global.* Too vague. *Kids Need to Read.* Too didactic. *Global Readers.* What the heck was a Global Reader?

Finally, I had it. I waited for a moment of silence.

"Wait! I've got it. How about . . . *Books Ahoy*?"

Martina nearly spit out her wine. Between coughs, she managed to laugh and ask, "What are you talking about? *Books Ahoy*? Like Chips Ahoy? Only with books?"

"Well," I began lamely, air already leaking from the tire, "we ship books overseas, and they go by boat, so you can picture all of us on the dock waving good-bye to . . . uh, never mind."

More laughter at my expense. Another bottle of wine was opened. Paul meanwhile had moved his laptop out of his home office and onto the table so that he could be ready to test the domain-name availability of the next brand we actually liked.

As the wine flowed, so did the ideas. All of them bad. *Books and Schools for Nepal and Vietnam.* Too verbose. *World Schoolhouse.* This brought up images of *Schoolhouse Rock! Partners in Learning. Read the World* (a play on the "feed the world" lyrics by Band Aid). *Global Students.* Lame, lame, lame.

And then, I had it. This time I knew. I threw it out over the din.

"How about *Room to Read*?"

Silence.

Martina: "That's it!"

Chris: "Perfect. It's literal, and it's metaphorical."

Susan: "It's also really aspirational."

Mike: "I like the *R, t, R* pattern. Four letters, two letters, four letters. Simple. Easy to remember."

Paul brought us crashing down to earth. "It's way too good of a name. It's most likely taken."

He went to the browser. The room was silent. I crossed my fingers, even though I am not superstitious. The seconds ticked by in slow motion.

"It's ours!"

"Really?!"

"Yes, both www.roomtoread.org and www.roomtoread.com are available. I'm going to buy them right now, and, John, tomorrow I will sell them to you for quadruple the price."

Our group cheered. Some high fives were exchanged and I hugged Martina and Susan, who were seated on either side of me. We'd found the perfect brand. It had taken over two hours and a few bottles of wine, but our informal group had succeeded.

Martina, the marketing whiz, kept the momentum going. "Tomorrow, let's start working on designing a logo." Chris, a software engineer and Web designer, volunteered to help. As usual, nobody on the extended Room to Read volunteer team was content to rest on his or her laurels. Tomorrow was another day for action.

CHAPTER 14

SEPTEMBER 11

B Y THE FALL OF 2001, I WAS CONVINCED THAT WE WERE ON THE right growth trajectory. Several more foundations had committed funding. We had hired a development director to bring in more capital. Our teams in Nepal and Vietnam were finding dozens of communities that wanted to work with Room to Read to set up new schools and libraries. Scholastic continued to give us regular donations, each one containing at least 30,000 new children's books. We opened our 100th library and several press stories were written about our work. Some old friends from Chicago were starting a Room to Read fund-raising chapter and had convinced Erin and me to fly out to speak at their first event. There was also interest in starting chapters in New York, London, and Paris. As our goal was to eventually do fund-raising in every major "money center" city in the world, my globe-trotting continued at its usual pace.

On that fateful day of September 11, 2001, I was in France. My former Microsoft coworker Clarissa and I were taking a long weekend cycling through Bordeaux. She was on the phone, trying to arrange for me to meet with some moneyed friends in Paris, when one of them said, "If you're with an American, you had better get to a television immediately." We pedaled as fast as we could to a friend's cottage, not knowing what to expect. The image of the Twin Towers on fire was shocking, but before I had even fully mentally processed what had happened, the first tower fell, then the second. The world changed in that instant. My only desire was to be home, immediately, in my country.

SHORTLY AFTER MY RETURN TO SAN FRANCISCO, ERIN AND I DEBATED what these events meant for our organization. We faced great uncertainty. We knew that the world had changed in fundamental ways. But nobody could comprehend exactly how it had changed. We debated whether our mission to educate children in the developing world would still seem relevant to donors.

We also questioned whether we'd be able to raise sufficient capital to fund our ambitious growth plans. We needed to increase our annual fund-raising from $150,000 to over $500,000. Could we triple the size of the organization during a forecast recession?

As we watched airlines laying off tens of thousands of employees, and economists predicting gloom for the economy, we questioned our ability to remain in hypergrowth mode. We also worried about Americans turning inward, or possibly xenophobic. Nevertheless, we immediately assured our teams in Nepal and Vietnam that there would be no layoffs and that their positions were secure.

Thankfully, we would soon have an opportunity to gain market feedback on these issues. Our new Chicago chapter had planned their first fund-raising event for September 23. On a call with the event's host committee, we debated canceling the event. America was still a shell-shocked nation in catatonic gloom. This wasn't really a good time to be hosting a cocktail party and asking people to donate money to a cause halfway around the world, especially given the charity world's current focus on raising money for the families of the deceased.

I recommended that we stick with our plan:

"By September 23, people will have had two weeks of staring at the television in a state of disbelief. They may need an excuse to turn off CNN and get out of the house to socialize. Let's give people at least a small dose of optimism and let them feel that even at a very sad time, we can still look out for our fellow man, especially those who are different from us."

One week later, we convened at the Tavern Club, a somewhat stuffy old-money men's club high above Michigan Avenue. We nervously wondered whether there would be any guests. Decades of cigar smoke clung to the curtains, and the walls were lined with old English hunting prints full of dogs, red-suited men on horseback, and fox carcasses. The location seemed somewhat incongruous with our organization's image, but we were never ones to refuse the offer of a free venue. Room to Read could be "cheap and cheerful" in its approach, even while perched at an expensive club 37 floors above the city.

As I was setting up the projector and wondering how the crowd would respond to our slide show, I was interrupted by my old friend John Flynn. He was the club member who had secured the venue. He introduced me to his friend Ben Shapiro. Ben immediately gave me confidence that the evening would go well:

"I looked at your Web site and was really impressed. I plan to write you guys a check that is relatively large, at least for me. This work is exactly what America should be doing more of in the Third World. We are the richest nation on earth, and we want to sell everyone our products like Coca-Cola and we want to benefit from the cheap labor that makes Wal-Mart's low prices possible. But we don't do that much in return, especially for the poorest countries. We're doing globalization on the cheap. As one example, we should have been building schools in Afghanistan over the last decade, because we'd have a lot fewer terrorists running around right now if we had only made an effort to set up an education system there. Do you know the story behind the madrassa schools in Afghanistan?"

John Flynn and I both admitted that we did not, so Ben explained. Afghanistan had been invaded by the Soviet Union in 1979. The United States, fearful of a further expansion of Soviet influence, provided weapons and large amounts of cash to the Afghan resistance fighters. After tens of thousands of deaths and years of warfare, the Soviets realized that they were not going to win control of this fiercely independent country. It marked the end of eight decades of Soviet expansion, and the beginning of the implosion of an empire that had reached too far and stretched itself too thin.

"The United States watched the withdrawal and decided that with the Soviets vanquished, America's job was done. The U.S. could pull out immediately and leave the Afghani people, amongst the poorest in the world, to live amongst their piles of bombed rubble. The American government did not so much as buy them some brooms to help start the cleaning."

Ben's voice rose, and his delivery quickened:

"This was such a major strategic error on the part of our government. Because guess what came next? There was the need to rebuild the destroyed buildings, including the hospitals and the schools. The Soviets had been merciless in their attempts to intimidate the Afghani people by bombing them back to the Stone Age. The U.S. did not stick around long enough to help in the rebuilding, because our reason for being there was not pro-Afghani, but rather anti-Soviet. So the Afghan government needed help in rebuilding, and the Iranians and the Saudis were only too eager to help.

"Both countries, neighbors to Afghanistan, wanted to fill the vacuum that had been left by the departure of the two superpowers. They each made a big commitment to constructing schools. The only problem is that these were not secular schools. They were madrassas, or religious schools, that taught a very hate-filled version of Islam. The Saudi schools taught their own anti-Western Wahhabi version, while the Iranians built schools that taught their students to curse 'the Great Satan' of America. The only difference between the Saudi schools and the Iranian ones was the degree of anti-Westernism in their curriculum.

"The CIA estimates that between them, the governments of Iran and Saudi Arabia sponsored the opening of over ten thousand madrassas in Afghanistan. And you know the rest of the story, because we've been living it for the last two weeks. A large percentage of the terrorists at large today were trained in these schools. Can you imagine how different the world would look today if those students had been more focused on one-two-threes and ABCs instead of being taught to chant 'Death to America'? We lost our opportunity to rebuild those schools, and we will be paying the price for decades to come. You can continue to count on me to support you guys. I don't want our country to keep repeating the same mistakes."

TWO YEARS LATER, WHILE READING ASNE SEIERSTAD'S MOVING POR-trayal of Afghan life, *The Bookseller of Kabul,* I was reminded of Ben's comment by a particularly chilling passage in which Sultan, the protagonist, journeys over bumpy roads from Kabul to Pakistan on a mission to help his war-torn country educate its children:

"He sits in the back row of the bus, squashed between other travelers, his suitcase under his feet. In it is his life's undertaking, written on a scrap of paper. He wants to print Afghanistan's new schoolbooks. When the schools open this spring there will be hardly any textbooks. Books printed by the Mujahedeen government and the Taliban are useless. This is how first-year schoolchildren learn the alphabet: '*J* is for Jihad, our aim in life, *I* is for Israel, our enemy, *K* is for Kalashnikov, we will overcome, *M* is for Mujahedeen our heroes, *T* is for Taliban . . . '

"War was the central theme in math books too. School-boys . . . did not calculate in apples and cakes, but in bullets and Kalashnikovs. Something like this: 'Little Omar has a Kalashnikov with three magazines. There are twenty bullets in each magazine. He uses two-thirds of the bullets and kills sixty infidels. How many infidels does he kill with each bullet?' "

Seierstad's book raised the question, how could we hope for a world at peace when these were the lessons being drilled into the heads of millions of children throughout their formative years?

BACK IN CHICAGO, A FEW DOZEN GUESTS WERE STREAMING INTO THE club prior to the event's 7:30 start. As I conversed with old friends and new, I noticed that the crowd was less somber than I'd antici-pated. People were obviously saddened and furious over the events in New York. They were also in a mood to take action. One woman told me that she had come because she felt insulted by President Bush's advice that the way to help America was to go shopping. She and her roommate felt the need to do something more tangible to begin changing the world. Building a school or two seemed a great place to start.

This feedback buoyed me, as did the sight of over 100 people gathered for our slide show. A large contingent of young Chicagoans had come out in search of positive change. Many said it was the first time they had done anything social since September 11. Erin and I delivered a brief slide show highlighting the need for schools in rural villages in Vietnam and Nepal. We explained our challenge-grant model and our low overhead. I then went for the close:

"The events of September eleventh remind us that we live in a very confused world. I think that how we respond says a lot about our capacity as human beings to be optimistic in the face of nihilism, and to prove that light can win out over darkness. I am not saying that education is going to solve all the world's problems. But it's something direct, and tangible. We can do it right now. You can go home tonight knowing that within a year, a few new schools will be open. I hope you'll choose to support our work."

There was an encouraging round of applause, and more important, the heartening sight of checkbooks and credit cards being pulled out of pockets. The donation table had a line forming.

The energy in the room was overwhelmingly positive. We raised enough money to fund two schools. The crowd stayed so late that the club management had to kick us out. A small group moved next door to a grotty Irish pub to debrief.

Everyone was thrilled we'd exceeded our financial goal. We were also proud of our fellow citizens. Even in our darkest hour, Americans have a willingness to help people halfway around the world, even former "enemy nations" like Vietnam. It would have been easy for this group of Chicagoans to justify turning inward and adopting an us-versus-them mentality. They instead displayed resilience and generosity of spirit. These values are so deeply ingrained in the American psyche that no terrorist could ever hope to wipe them out.

The positive and proactive forces in this universe will always defeat the dark and nihilistic ones. We simply must create the spaces in which concerned citizens are offered a way to take action.

. . .

THE ENHANCED AIRPORT SECURITY AFTER SEPTEMBER 11 MADE IT ALL the more difficult to be a road warrior. Two weeks after the Chicago event I was in New York's JFK Airport feeling bleary-eyed. The airlines were recommending that travelers show up two hours before their scheduled departure. To assure that I could catch my 7:30 a.m. flight, I had been awake since 5 a.m. and at the airport since 5:30.

The check-in line moved all too slowly. After twenty minutes my magical moment arrived. Next to me, a clearly exasperated man was having a tense discussion with a JetBlue check-in clerk. The exchange was loud; I had no choice but to listen in.

In his heavy New York accent, the man was telling the clerk, "Your solution will not work. This is simply too small to be shipped as checked luggage, and I will never see it again."

The clerk insisted that "sending it as checked luggage" was the only solution.

I could not figure out what "it" was, as the man had no bags with him; indeed, he looked to be traveling as empty-handed as Bill Gates did when his clothing was sent ahead for him.

The man insisted that his family was already at the gate, and that he had to go back to security immediately or he would miss his flight and his weekend away with his wife and kids. The clerk advised one more time that he could either "check *it* in as baggage, or throw *it* away, but they are not going to let you through security with *it*. The rules are very clear that no sharp objects are allowed."

Only then did I realize that they were referring to the man's key chain, on which was attached a tiny letter opener whose blade could be popped open with the push of a button. He had been turned back at security and had sent his family through while he searched for a solution. To the clerk he insisted, "But this is a family heirloom; it belonged to my grandfather and I cannot throw it out. It's so small that if you stick a baggage tag on it there is no way I will see it again as it will get lost amongst the suitcases. It would be like sticking a baggage tag on a grain of rice, sending it to London Heathrow, and hoping that I could find it amongst a crush of several hundred bags on the carousel."

At this point I intervened and told him that I might be able to solve his problem. If he could give me the letter opener, and a business card, I could put the letter opener in the bag I was checking. When I got home to San Francisco, I could drop the family heirloom in the mail to him.

His jaw dropped. Native New Yorkers may not be used to strangers going out of their way to offer favors. He removed the letter opener from the key chain and took a card from his wallet, saying, "I don't know who you are, but thank you."

With that, he dashed off, exit stage right, toward his waiting family and hopefully a short line at security.

The JetBlue clerk handling my check-in remarked that this had been a kind thing to do. In my own mind it seemed like something quite simple—just trying to help a stressed-out traveler at a time the nation was tense.

She insisted that I was a good guy. I smiled as I thought that maybe she'd upgrade me to first class as a reward. The six-hour flight to SFO would be much better in the front of the plane. My bubble burst as I remembered that JetBlue did not actually *have* a first class.

Instead of rewarding me, the clerk had a few questions:

"Has anyone unknown to you asked you to carry anything?"

"No. Except, that is, for my new buddy"—I looked at his business card—Brent Erensel," I replied with a laugh.

"Sir, I have to warn you that this is not funny. You have to be very careful about accepting packages from strangers."

"But . . . but . . . you were here the whole time and told me that I was a good guy for helping him. So how can you be chastising me three minutes later?"

She shrugged and handed over my boarding pass.

The country was definitely in a strange state.

. . .

TWO WEEKS LATER, I RECEIVED A LETTER IN THE MAIL FROM MY NEW best friend, Brent Erensel.

> Dear John,
>
> Thank you for sending me back my letter opener, which as you know from our conversation has been in my family for seven decades. After receiving the package from you along with your business card, I went online to look up what Room to Read does. As I viewed the photos of the kids you are helping, I decided that both you and Erin must be angels. That would be the only explanation for what I have witnessed from meeting you briefly at JFK, and then viewing the slide shows on your site.
>
> Enclosed please find a little something to keep the positive energy flowing.
>
> With warm regards,
> Brent

He had written Room to Read a check for $1,000. I shook my head in disbelief. My intention in helping Brent was not to gain a funder, but as a result of our chance encounter we had just gained half of what was needed to set up a school library serving several hundred children. If only those kids could know the story of how a random meet-up, combined with heightened airport security, had been turned from a negative into a positive.

Brent's donation, combined with the success of our Chicago event, convinced me that we could continue to grow, even in the post–September 11 era. People seemed more eager than ever to find ways to bring some positive energy back to the world. I was grateful to all the donors who were sending us a signal not to shrink, but to continue to expand our work.

CHAPTER 15

BUILDING "THE MICROSOFT

OF NONPROFITS"

EVEN THOUGH MY LAST MONTHS AT MICROSOFT WERE PAINFUL, I feel lucky to have worked at the company for so long. Not only was it a financially lucrative period in which to be an employee, but I met amazingly smart people and learned valuable lessons about running a business. When I started Room to Read, I wrote down the core principles I had learned at "The Soft" and that I would try to emulate.

Bill Gates was most certainly an inspiration to me, despite my experiences with him in China. I have the utmost respect not only for the company he built, but also for the bold effort he and Melinda have made to use their wealth to immunize millions of children against diseases from which no child should have to die in this modern age. But the majority of the lessons I learned were from the firm's #2, Steve Ballmer. Bill gets most of the press, but Steve is arguably as important to the company's success. Bill is the technologist, whereas Steve is the businessman. Any great technology company needs both.

Many of the highlights of my years at Microsoft were the times I spent learning from Steve.

Steve lives, eats, breathes, and sleeps results, results, results. Like a dog with a chew toy, he is manically focused and not willing to let anything distract him from performance. It was a lesson I kept top of mind as I began building Room to Read and sought to differentiate us from the thousands of other nonprofit organizations out there.

One of my most interesting set of experiences with Steve was in early 1996, when he visited the Asia-Pacific region. In my role as marketing director for the region, I attended all of his meetings during the weeklong visit. His first stop was at a review meeting for all of our Southeast Asian subsidiaries, in Kuala Lumpur, Malaysia. The Vietnam team drew the short straw and had to go first.

Vietnam was a brand-new business for the company. The subsidiary faced a formidable challenge. Piracy rates were insanely high—around 99 percent. It was actually easier to measure *legal* software sales than it was to measure illegal sales. The local managers were in a difficult position because it was nearly impossible to convince a company or an individual to pay $300 for an official version of Microsoft Office when they could buy a pirated version for less than $1 in the local market.

The campaign to convince Vietnamese consumers to buy legal versions was not exactly making the cash register ring. In its first year the local team had badly missed its revenue budget. I was worried that it would be a "lamb to the slaughter" meeting.

Steve was impatient for results and wasted no time letting the team know it:

"Everything I read tells me that a lot of foreign companies are investing in Vietnam. So forget these excuses about Vietnamese consumers not being able to afford our product. Focus on the multinational companies that are opening up offices here. They can afford to buy legal.

"Why have you not sold to Shell? Or BP? They're investing in Vietnam. Why not Unilever? Or Honda or Toyota or Hyundai or the other car companies? Go to each embassy and get a list of the biggest investors from their country. Holland, Germany, France, Korea, Japan, the U.S., Canada. Those are all countries where business managers are used to buying legal software. I want you to visit all of those embassies. Tomorrow—as soon as I leave.

ABOVE: During the summer of 2000, the walls went up on one of the first Room to Read schools in Nepal.

RIGHT: Nepali boys settling in at a new school, 2001.

BELOW: As we gained early momentum in Nepal in 2001, I had the pleasure of seeing our ideas become reality.

श्री बुद्धि बिकास प्रान्वि

घुषा, चरौंदी, घादिङ्

उद्घाटन समारोह

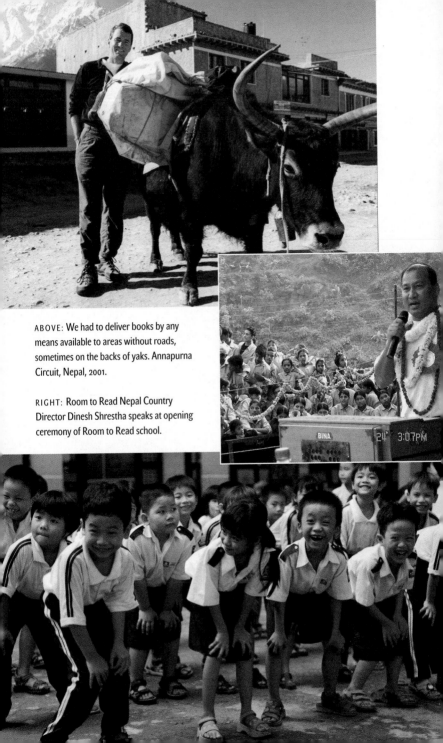

ABOVE: We had to deliver books by any means available to areas without roads, sometimes on the backs of yaks. Annapurna Circuit, Nepal, 2001.

RIGHT: Room to Read Nepal Country Director Dinesh Shrestha speaks at opening ceremony of Room to Read school.

ABOVE: From the beginning we've welcomed donors to view the projects they funded. Here, Room to Read Singapore chapter member Kurt Messersmith visits a new Computer Room in Vietnam.

RIGHT: Our Room to Grow girls scholarship program was launched in 2001. These Nepalese girls were among the first to join the program.

FACING PAGE BOTTOM: Our first projects in Vietnam broke ground in 2001. Here, Vietnamese children are performing morning calisthenics in the Mekong Delta.

ABOVE: Vietnamese students at a new Room to Read school ham it up for the camera.

BELOW: Room to Read's Chief Operating Officer Erin Keown Ganju returns to Vietnam and begins planning a new round of school construction projects.

ABOVE RIGHT: These Vietnamese girls are at an opening ceremony for a new Computer Room. Computer literacy is one of the largest unmet educational needs in Vietnam.

ABOVE LEFT: Students enjoy their first computer experience in rural Vietnam. Room to Read began building Computer Rooms in 2001.

RIGHT: Erin and I met this eager student during our study trip to Cambodia in 2002.

Room to Read's first libraries in Cambodia opened by the end of 2002, reversing losses incurred by the Khmer Rouge's destruction of schools and libraries.

Crossing the Throng La Pass in Nepal, at 17,769 feet elevation, requires a ten-day trek uphill, followed by seven days downhill. On the left is Room to Read volunteer Angela Hanke.

ABOVE: Cambodian students attend the opening ceremony of their new Computer Room. With each new Computer Room, local teachers are provided with computer literacy training.

RIGHT: A Room to Grow scholar in Vietnam: girls should not be afraid to be extraordinary.

BELOW: Nepali students respond positively to books relevant to their culture. We addressed this need by getting into the publishing business and creating books the children could relate to.

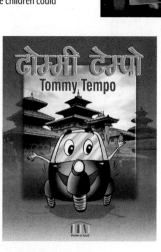

ABOVE: Our publishing program extended to Cambodia. Here's a Cambodian boy enjoying a new Khmer-language book.

LEFT: Backpacks await their new owners on the day of a Room to Grow scholarship initiation ceremony in rural Cambodia.

BELOW: In addition to backpacks, each new scholar is given a bike. Schools in rural Cambodia can be up to three hours walk from some villages.

Room to Read Chicago chapter leader Tina Sciabica visits some of the Nepali Room to Read scholars benefiting from the funds she has raised.

On this night, Netscape co-founder Marc Andreessen made a $250,000 gift in honor of Room to Read's five year anniversary.

ABOVE: Many rural Laotians never have the opportunity for a formal education. With the goal of reversing this trend, Room to Read began operations in Laos in 2005.

LEFT: I talk with the headmaster of Harihar School, Uday Kharki, in Pokhara, Nepal, during a visit to open the school's new Computer Room in 2003.

BELOW: This new Language Room in Vietnam will teach 300 kids per day a foreign language. English speakers in Vietnam can earn up to three times as much money as those who are not bilingual.

ABOVE: In November of 2005, I helped inaugurate a new school in rural Nepal. With an illiteracy rate of 70%, Nepal is in urgent need of educational resources.

BELOW: Room to Read Cambodia staff and chapter leaders from around the world enjoy the opening of the 2,000th library funded by Room to Read, September 2005. This school stands in the shadows of the legendary temples of Angkor Wat.

ABOVE: After the tsunami devastated Southeast Asia in 2004, we received a deluge of donations to build schools in Sri Lanka. Many Sri Lankan students, like this preschooler, attend new Room to Read Schools.

LEFT: Room to Read is grateful for the hard work of volunteers, and so is Congress! Ten-year-old Jacob Rasch of Maryland was honored by the Congressional Human Rights Committee for selling more than 70,000 wristbands to aid tsunami-impacted villages in Sri Lanka.

BELOW: These female students are at a Room to Read–sponsored library in the desert state of Rajasthan, India.

Jacob Rasch
Student Activist

This is one of the nearly 2,000 girls on long-term scholarships through the Room to Grow program. Only $250 per year can put a girl in school in the developing world.

Room to Read celebrated the donation of its 1 millionth book in Nepal, November 2005.

After a warm reception with marigold garlands made by students, I congratulated all the volunteers who made this amazing milestone possible.

I'm Sok peou and I am a student in grade 10.

I Live in Svay Pork Village. Batheay Commune Batheay District.

kampong chen Province.

I Love Computer. because when I was a little I never think that, what's the Computer? but now I know and want to Learn it. I am studying about it.

It's my job and it my good future.

thank you for brought the sixteen Computer for me.

this is my dream in the future.

ABOVE: Students in rural Nepal wasted no time in learning how to make welcome signs in PowerPoint!

MIDDLE: This Nepali girl is proud to show off her computer skills. The sign she made read, "Welcome John Wood."

LEFT: A Cambodian student illustrates his dream of growing up to become a businessman, thanks in part to the new computer lab established in his village.

ABOVE: Ethiopian boys at a library in the capital city of Addis Ababa. This photo was taken during a study trip in 2004 as we prepared to launch Room to Read Africa.

RIGHT: Who knew that an Amharic-language version of Harry Potter was available in Ethiopia?

ABOVE: Here, I am with a shepherd boy in the Simien Mountains of northern Ethiopia—November 2004. We plan to bring library access to millions of children like him across the African continent.

RIGHT: Still partners after all these years—John Wood and Dinesh Shrestha enjoy an opening ceremony in Dhading Province, Nepal.

"Once you have those lists, you have your sales prospects for the next year. And if they won't buy, then tell them that they're at risk of being busted. The last thing any expatriate wants is for his cushy all-expense-paid life to be interrupted because head office in Amsterdam or New York comes down on him for giving his company a black eye.

"And enough of this bullshit calling it 'software piracy.' It makes it sound like something almost romantic and swashbuckling, like the perpetrators are wearing eye patches and drinking rum with a parrot on their shoulder. Call it what it is—call it theft.

"You were supposed to do $500,000 in revenue this year. You've barely hit $100,000. I'll expect that by the next time we meet you'll have closed some big deals with multinationals. Four deals, $100,000 each, and you are there. Bang! Done!"

With that, he slammed his big, meaty fist on the desk, jolting several of the Vietnamese teacups an inch into the air. It was classic Ballmer—he cut straight to the heart of the matter with no time for excuses or small talk. And since the team had not given him a solution to their problem, he came up with one and gave them their marching orders to go implement it. If they had a better idea, then great, they could propose it. But in the absence of such, then Steve was not going to sit idly in the conference room brainstorming. His bias was toward action, not talk.

THIS INTENSE FOCUS ON RESULTS WAS THE FIRST PART OF MICROSOFT'S culture that I wanted to emulate within Room to Read. As part of my research, I had talked to a number of people about their charitable-giving history and preferences. From many I heard a derivation of the comment "It's frustrating, because I give money to various groups, but I never know if they are achieving anything. I keep hearing stories about how the world is a terrible place with lots of problems, and I wonder what they've been doing with all the money I've given them over the years. Few groups report to me on tangible progress. Mostly what I hear from them are repeated requests for more donations."

I decided that one way I could differentiate Room to Read was by talking about, and frequently updating, our results. Rather than talking about what we were *going to do,* I would instead talk about what we had done. Tangible stuff: the number of schools opened; the number of books donated; the number of girls on scholarship. I'd think of it as the Ballmer test. What if I had to do an update for him every quarter? I'd have to show progress or, just like the Microsoft Vietnam team, I'd get my head handed to me.

In 2001 I came up with an idea that is still used today. I set my e-mail signature file to list our results at the bottom of each and every mail that I sent out. It was kind of like a stock-ticker symbol that scrolls across the bottom of the screen on CNBC, with constantly updated numbers. Here is my current e-mail signature file:

> John J. Wood
> Founder and CEO
> Room to Read
> World Change Starts with Educated Children
> www.roomtoread.org.
> "We're all about results. 200 schools built, over 2,500 bi-lingual libraries established, 1.2 million books donated, and over 1,800 girls on long-term scholarships. Join us in the quest for universal education."

I discussed with our team that all day, every day, we were now accountable for results. If we collectively sent 300 mails a day, we had 300 opportunities to tell people what we had, or had not, accomplished. Few other charities are so accountable, and we knew it would be a great point of differentiation as we competed for scarce funds.

"We should be really clear that if our donors do not see those numbers going up, they are going to wonder why, and possibly stop investing in us. They have thousands of charities to choose from. We need to give them every reason to pick Room to Read."

I believe that if every charity held itself similarly accountable, the dollars invested in the social sector would skyrocket. I think that every organization, be it for-profit or not-for-profit, should decide what to measure and put those results at the bottom of their e-mails. Be it the number of meals served to the homeless, the number of students they've helped to get into college, or the number of people who've had cholesterol screenings, nothing focuses the mind quite like having to broadcast your results hundreds of times per day.

On my frequent travels, I noticed a reminder of this from the private sector. United Airlines touted their number one on-time performance record on each and every napkin. Tens of thousands of times per day, they were telling their customers (and their employees) that this metric mattered. Within a few weeks, I noticed that their flight attendants were much more focused on helping people with their overhead bags so that we could "push back for an on-time departure." Knowing that they would be measured each month, and having bragged about it, the entire organization was focused on not losing their number one ranking.

DURING HIS EXCHANGE WITH THE VIETNAM TEAM, I NOTED THAT STEVE had treated them with tact and respect. He did not yell at them or cut down their character. He was more than willing to tear into their mediocre results, but he did not attack them personally.

There is a saying within Microsoft that "you cannot attack a person, but you can attack an idea." Employees had carte blanche to argue with anyone, about anything, regardless of where each person sat in the corporate food chain. Steve was the ultimate personification of this adage, and his example inspired me to encourage vigorous debate within Room to Read as our team grew. At times it could be difficult, as I was used to the early days when I was making every decision. I was sometimes taken aback when new team members challenged me. But I reminded myself that we had hired smart people, and that any decision arrived at after vigorous debate would be better than one decided by simple fiat of the top dog.

For me, the hardest times to accept defeat were when my team argued with me either to grow slower, or to spend more money on overhead to keep up with our growth. I had, unrealistically, thought that we could run the organization on 5 percent overhead and continue to add countries to the mix at an insane pace. But this was

easier for me, as I was the guy at the top who did not have to implement daily with too few resources. Thankfully, we had created a
culture where anyone could question the CEO. I was not only
questioned, I was quite often gang-tackled on these issues. We had
an internal joke that I was working the accelerator while other team
members were stomping on the brake. In the end, we found a compromise pace of expansion that was unanimously signed off on.

We also hired employees at a faster pace than I had thought necessary. To this day, I don't regret creating a single one of those positions. I have my team to thank for helping me to see the light of day
on these important issues. I plan to continue this tradition of encouraging employees to challenge my thinking.

A THIRD ASPECT OF MICROSOFT THAT I WANTED TO EMULATE WAS BASED
on an example Bill and Steve set every day: being data-driven. The
belief that everything should be measured, and that every business
manager should study every bit of data available about his or her
business, permeated Microsoft. It was not enough to know how
your Windows NT sales were tracking against budget. You also had
to know how they compared to last year, and the year before that,
and be able to recite your YOY (year-on-year) growth rate off the
top of your head. You also had to know how your revenue compared to everyone of your competitors', and you were also expected
to be able to benchmark yourself against other Microsoft subsidiaries. My team could have had a barn burner of a year, but when we
then compared ourselves to Microsoft Switzerland's growth rate,
we realized that we could do better still.

Many late nights were therefore spent studying the numbers.
Because my team covered multiple product lines, in eight countries
of the Asia-Pacific region, "knowing your numbers" was akin to
preparing for an MCAT or an LSAT examination. Or perhaps both,
simultaneously. No amount of preparation could ever be thorough
enough, but knowing that Steve's expectations were high, we were
ready to die trying.

The hardest of Steve's visits came in early January of 1996. His
arrival date of January 3 meant that I spent most of my Christmas

holiday preparing. It was painful to drive into work each day, in our gloomy office park in the faceless suburbs north of Sydney, knowing that most everyone else was at the beach. As the Australian sun was stoking itself for another day of body-bronzing weather, I'd arrive at the office by 8 a.m. to continue our preparation.

The Ballmerism that caused your heart to leap into your throat was "You don't know your numbers." Before our annual review with him, I used to have nightmares of his big, bald head yelling these words at me as I clumsily tore through a pile of papers looking for a statistic he had asked for.

The studying, thankfully, paid off in one of the first meetings I had with Steve during this trip to the Asia-Pacific region. He was grilling Paul, the country manager for Thailand, about the business there. Paul mentioned that one of my team members had helped the subsidiary by arranging for all Windows NT certification exams to be translated into the Thai language. Paul said that this had dramatically improved the "pass rate."

Steve: "So, what are the numbers? What percent of people passed the new Thai version of the test?"

Paul: Silence.

John: "It actually improved the pass rate to eighty percent."

Steve: "So what? Is that good or bad? I don't know, because I don't know the worldwide pass rate, so I have no basis of comparison."

John: "The worldwide pass rate is fifty-two percent. So in six months we've gone from one of the worst pass rates in the world to having one of the highest and being twenty-eight points above the worldwide average. The result is that we've gone from less than a hundred people in all of Thailand being certified on Windows NT to over a thousand."

Steve smiled at me. He nodded to Paul. That was his signal to go on. I hoped this meant his cameo appearances in my nightmares would soon end.

ALTHOUGH STEVE'S QUIZZES ON THE NUMBERS COULD BE TOUGH, I knew that he did it for a reason. He wanted to test how much the manager's cared about their business. If they were not passionate enough to have studied every facet of their operations, to such a degree that the numbers were seared into their brains, then these managers were not going to make it in Steve's data- and performance-driven world.

I've often thought of Steve while interviewing job candidates at Room to Read. I want to know whether they are passionate and hardworking enough to have studied our organization in thorough detail before interviewing with me. When Erin and I were hiring the first staff to help us run the San Francisco office, my initial interview questions aimed to establish how well they had done their research. Did they have passion? Did they know their numbers?

I was once interviewing a promising candidate for the position of development director. Marcie had years of fund-raising experience and I envisioned having another employee working the phones and securing donations. I wanted this interview to work out. But it quickly became obvious that for Marcie, this was just another job. There was no passion.

"To start, can you tell me how many schools Room to Read has built?"

"I'm not sure. Ten?"

"No. Thirty so far, and we're building thirty more this year."

"I did not know that."

"Do you know how many libraries we have established?"

"No, I don't know that either. How would I?"

"Well, our results are posted on our Web site, and in our annual report, and also at the bottom of each of my e-mails. Anyway, no worries. Let's move on to the next question. Can you name the three countries we're working in?"

"I know you're in Nepal, and I think you are going into Cambodia," she said, her voice trailing off at the end.

I knew right away that the interview was over. How the heck could she possibly sell Room to Read to our donors if she was not able to tell them about our results and business model? The candidate we ultimately hired had studied our annual report and our Web site in detail. She had passion. She knew her facts, figures, and, yes, her numbers.

Any new organization will die unless every person it hires has passion for the mission. This is especially critical with the early hires because they will pass along the corporate culture to new employees. Any entrepreneur therefore has to "ding" a lot of job candidates. Hiring only people who have passion, and who know their numbers, is one of many ways I continue to emulate Steve.

ANOTHER LESSON I LEARNED FROM MICROSOFT, AND THAT I WANTED TO implant firmly in Room to Read, was loyalty. And like much else that I took out of Microsoft, I learned this lesson from Ballmer.

Although Steve can be demanding, he is also intensely loyal to his people. Steve could care less where somebody is in the hierarchy. He will talk to everyone within the company if it means he can gather more information and data. On two occasions I learned just how loyal he was to those who worked for him.

On one of Steve's trips to the Asia-Pacific region, we took the red-eye from Singapore to Sydney for a morning meeting with the Australian subsidiary. We landed just before 6 a.m. I was groggy on four hours' sleep. Steve, however, looked fresh as a newly laundered shirt. When I told him that our first meeting was not until eight, he clapped his hands together and his voice boomed, "Let's head out for a run!" It seemed more of an order than a suggestion. Fortunately, one of my favorite running routes was close to his hotel.

Sydney's Botanical Gardens are squeezed between the central business district and the inner harbor. The hilly terrain provides fabulous views of the Opera House, the city's skyscrapers, and its famous bridge, from which flies one of the world's largest Australian flags. Hundreds of trees provide needed shade and a resting place for kookaburras and other native birds. It seemed the perfect place to give Steve an hour's break from the frantic pace of our week.

The heat of the southern hemisphere's summer peaks in January. The intense sun, combined with the hills, had both of us sweating hard early in the run. Since I carry about forty fewer pounds than Steve, he was struggling behind me. But I could not escape his booming voice, which shattered the morning calm of the gardens.

He regaled me with complaints about areas of the business that were underperforming, and ideas on how we could do better. So much for my theory of the run being a peaceful respite from work. I picked up my pace, in the futile hope that he would then concentrate on his breathing. It didn't work—as he fell farther behind, he simply yelled louder.

After five miles, we returned to the hotel. As we stood dripping sweat on the polished marble floors, the concierge eyed us with suspicion. I pointed Steve toward the elevators and told him that we had twenty minutes until our first meeting. He wasted no time and began marching across the lobby. But after five paces he stopped, whirled in a quick 180-degree turn, and filled the lobby with his booming voice.

"Hey, wait a second."

Uh-oh, I thought. He wants to get in one more rant about our dismal sales rate of Microsoft Office in the Philippines.

"You live here in Sydney, right?"

"Yes."

"Then how are you going to get home in time to change? Do you need to use my shower?"

I thanked him and said that my secretary had thought ahead and booked me a room at the special day rate so that I could freshen up after the red-eye. Before I had finished my sentence, Steve was marching on ahead, not willing to waste a second on chitchat.

As I walked back to the bell desk to get my bag, I was thankful for a small glimpse into Steve's personality. Here was a guy worth over $10 billion, but he had not lost his human element or his willingness to look out for his team members. He's a man who demands intense loyalty from his team. He more than reciprocates. In my head, I filed away yet another management lesson.

After two days of meetings in Sydney, we flew to Auckland, New Zealand. The two-hour time-zone change worked against us and guaranteed another night of too little sleep as part of Ballmer's Traveling Circus. Upon arrival at the hotel at 1 a.m., Steve asked if we were going to run in the morning.

"I know a great route, but our first meeting is at seven a.m., so there won't be time."

"So what? Let's go early."

"How early? We'd have to go at five thirty, which is exactly four and a half hours from now. Don't you want to sleep?"

"No, I want to run! Five-thirty it is."

I gave him a stunned look. Where did this guy get his energy? He quickly sealed the deal by loudly declaring, "I'm running tomorrow morning at five thirty. Either you're going with me, or I'm going alone. Your decision!"

I could not desert him. Loyalty was a two-way street. Sleep would have to wait for another day.

I arrived in the lobby at 5:33. It was empty except for an impatient Steve looking at his watch, shaking his head, and walking out the door. I vowed to punish him by running even harder than I had on our Sydney run.

Early morning is a beautiful time in one of the world's most picturesque cities. Like Sydney, Auckland sits on a beautiful natural harbor. Sailboats bobbed in the clear blue water, and the sun began to rise for one of its 18-hour days at this far-southern latitude.

The morning tranquility was soon shattered. Steve was delivering a tirade on how "completely screwed up" the Mac Office marketing team was. Since I was not part of that team, I did not know why, exactly, this subject was germane. I ran faster, which caused Steve to ask me why I was going out of the gate like a jackrabbit. I couldn't admit that I was trying to escape, and even if I had, he would probably have pointed out that his tirade was like a black hole—a force that cannot be escaped.

I told Steve I was training for the Boston Marathon, and that speed work was essential. He commanded a compromise pace and immediately switched the conversation back to business. As we jogged along the harbor, I noted the curious glances of Kiwis checking out the Human Bullhorn.

THE NEXT TIME I SAW STEVE WAS THE DAY AFTER THE BOSTON MARAthon. In April, Microsoft had its annual Worldwide Sales and Marketing meeting, and Steve's keynote speech was always the highlight.

I lucked out, as the meeting was slated to start the day after the race. It would be a tight squeeze, necessitating catching flights from Sydney to Boston, running the race, and then jumping on a 6 a.m. nonstop flight from Boston to Seattle. But this meant one less trans-Pacific flight during a year that had been full of them.

I was sore and exhausted after the race, and the 4 a.m. wake-up call made me regret my usual habit of trying to be in two places at once. Limping to my gate, I debated asking for one of those beeping carts on which you see elderly travelers. Once we were airborne, the pilot told us that due to swift headwinds, we would be half an hour late arriving in Seattle. I was worried about missing Steve's keynote speech. His "call to arms" is a legendary annual ritual that is one part General Patton, one part old-time Southern preacher, and one part Anthony Robbins–inspired "awaken the giant within" motivational speech.

I rushed from the Seattle airport to the downtown Sheraton and walked into the meeting ten minutes into Steve's presentation. Over 1,000 people were in the room, so I was not worried about anyone noticing my late arrival. Steve's speech was, as usual, a loud and passionate call to arms. "Push hard to get Windows 95 adopted by our corporate accounts. Grow the Office business by at least thirty percent this year. Take the Netscape threat seriously, and don't let them gain traction." Fight them on the beaches, fight them on the sand.

After an hour of Steve's fiery oratory, the crowd of employees gave him a two-minute standing O. We then walked out of the main ballroom for a break. As I was talking to colleagues, I noticed out of the corner of my eye an entourage moving at warp speed in our direction. It was Steve, with twelve disciples trailing in his wake. As he passed us, he stopped, spun 90 degrees on his heels, and stared me in the eye. Holy shit, I thought, did he actually notice me walk in late? A maniacal grin crossed his face, he raised his right arm (to hit me?), and bellowed out in his inimitable style:

"Three hours and four minutes in the Boston Marathon. Great time! Well run!"

He gave me a high five of incredible force, spun back in his original direction, and resumed his progress. The entourage followed.

"Wait. Stop! How did you know that?"

Another abrupt halt. He grinned and with gusto boomed, "I know everything about my people!"

That loyalty, more than anything else, explains why so many people who have worked for Steve are, to this day, intensely loyal to him. He demands much of his people, but he also lets them know that he's got their back.

MY HOPE IS THAT EVERY ROOM TO READ TEAM MEMBER FEELS THAT I AM just as loyal to them as Steve was to me. Too many executives demand allegiance from their employees without making the effort to determine how best to earn it. They often remind me of a quote from Thomas Edison: "Opportunity is missed by most people because it is dressed in overalls and looks like hard work."

My own ways of showing loyalty to employees are simple and straightforward and will never win me any awards for innovation. I believe that collectively, however, they show everyone working for Room to Read that I am looking out for them.

At Room to Read, it all starts with a positive work environment. Our walls are lined with photographs of the students we are helping. Laughter permeates the building, as we will not hire people who lack a sense of humor. We have team lunches with the menu rotating between different Room to Read countries—Vietnamese spring rolls and noodle soup one month, followed by Nepalese chili chicken, then Lao fish curry. I strongly encourage people to take time to exercise. In fact, we opened our office near the Presidio YMCA and its amazing gym and pool.

Does this mean that employees are distracted and don't work hard? Not at all. We only hire people who have a proven track record of hard work, focus on results, and passion. They work long hours and travel to the ends of the earth to further our mission. My firm conviction is that in return for this dedication, they deserve a positive environment.

It's also important to emphasize that every victory is a team victory. As the spokesperson for Room to Read, I do most of the speeches and press interviews. I always say, "I am very fortunate to be surrounded by great people who make me look good." One of our chapter leaders, after hearing me say this to a donor, told me that this reminded her of Lance Armstrong. "When Lance gives an interview after winning a stage of the Tour, he always begins with the words 'The team was great today.' "

We also show loyalty to our employees through our benefits package. I hesitate even to call them "benefits," as it makes it sounds as though we think we are doing the employee a favor by providing them. To me, nothing is as straightforward as the idea that an employer should provide health care for its employees.

We recently took a team survey to ask what they thought was lacking, and dental insurance got the highest number of votes. We added it, along with a 401(k) plan. Our CFO's belief is that by offering a tax-efficient retirement program, and providing a 5 percent employer match, we send the signal that we want our team to be together for the long term and will be their partner in setting aside sufficient funds for retirement. The employer match was an unintentional echo of our challenge grants, in that we'd help employees save for the future if they were also willing to do so.

Of course, we will never let our costs get out of control. We therefore added these benefits incrementally over time. Rather than starting with the King Midas package, our management team decided that as long as we could keep our overhead below 10 percent, we could layer additional benefits on over time. To date it has been a success, and we've added new morale-enhancing features to employment at Room to Read each and every year.

Finally, I try to show loyalty through a large number of small acts. It might be dropping by an employee's birthday party, or surprising Emily, a fellow wine nut, with a great bottle of South African Pinotage. Writing an anniversary card. Buying books that team members might enjoy.

I hope that my gang knows that I am thinking about them, and paying attention to their satisfaction in working at Room to Read. Steve Ballmer's lesson—that loyalty is a two-way street—will permeate Room to Read for as long as I run it, and hopefully even after I hand over the reins. We have firmly embedded this Ballmerism into our own company culture. The 5:30 a.m. runs, however, I leave to Steve.

CHAPTER 16

BUILDING THE NETWORK

WITH EARLY SUCCESSES LIKE THE CHICAGO EVENT, IT WAS APPAR- ent that we had potential to seriously expand the number of fund-raising chapters around the world. My vision was to create a powerful network of volunteers, who would, collectively, raise millions of dollars. Ideally Room to Read could raise money wherever there were wealthy people, from Austin to Boston to Vancouver.

It would be a relatively new way of creating large-scale social change. In the old days, large-scale philanthropy was practiced only by the rich. If one wanted to change the world, it helped to have a large fortune. A man like John D. Rockefeller could take on numerous infectious diseases. Brahmin families in New England would start universities. My own personal hero, Andrew Carnegie, could visualize a network of 2,000 libraries and actually have the financial might to fund all of them. One man, one swipe of a pen across a check—that was the way things were done in the corridors of power, wealth, and privilege.

There are, however, a few problems with this model. First, there simply are not enough billionaires out there to solve all of the world's problems. True change requires mass participation, because one person writing a large check is never enough. He could change his mind about the cause, or make bad investment decisions that deplete his capital, or die and leave his money to his heirs rather than to charity. To rely on just one person is quite risky, especially when the future of millions of people is at stake.

The larger problem is that too many of the truly rich are loath to give away their fortune in any meaningful way. We live in a world where the megarich think nothing of spending $50–100 million on a yacht, complete with helicopter landing pad. They forget the Talmudic principle that "there are no pockets in the burial shroud," and upon their death half of their fortune goes to the government (which will likely squander it), and the other half goes to his or her heirs (who hopefully won't, but then again many of them do).

From the beginning of Room to Read's existence, I have thought that hoping for billionaires to solve the world's problems is like waiting for Godot. It's also the surest way to perpetuate the status quo. I greatly respect men like Carnegie in his day for building libraries, and modern philanthropists like Bill and Melinda Gates for taking on so many "overlooked" diseases that kill millions. I just wish there were more of them.

But my bias is not toward dreaming; it's about doing. When I set out to establish at least as many libraries in the developing world as Carnegie did in North America, I was well aware of my limited, and declining, bank balance. It was therefore necessary to update the model and enlist an army of volunteers. One cold and foggy San Francisco night, curled up in a large reading chair in front of a blazing fire, I pulled out my journal to brainstorm on how to raise the funding we'd need. The opening thought that popped into my head was simple, clear, and would provide direction over the coming years:

The Andrew Carnegie of the 21st century will not be a rich white male. It will be a network of concerned global citizens, and we will create it.

None of us could, alone, accomplish what Carnegie had. But together, with the power of dozens (and eventually hundreds, then thousands) of high-energy people working together, we knew that it was possible to think even bigger than Carnegie had.

. . .

ONE OF THE FIRST "NODES" IN THE NETWORK I SET OUT TO BUILD WAS A
Chicago-based entrepreneur named Michael Lindenmayer. He had
attended one of our first slide shows. Afterward during the social
hour he pulled me aside to compliment our work and to say that he
had a myriad of ideas for how he could help us to reach our auda-
cious goals. He had been involved early on in Grameen Bank, and
what he said was music to my ears.

"A decade ago, few people had heard of, or understood, micro-
credit. But today millions of people knew how much good it could
do to lend small amounts of money to help people start businesses,
and how income from those micro-enterprises could help to lift
people out of poverty. Most importantly, the model recognized that
the poor are capable of helping themselves and could earn their way
into self-sufficiency instead of relying on the traditional model of
aid."

In Michael's view, Room to Read circa 2001 was no different
from Grameen Bank circa 1991.

"Both organizations are doing something that in the early days
is considered difficult and a bit revolutionary. But one day it will be
'obvious,' and people will wish that they had thought of your idea
first. Both organizations have brilliant and dynamic leaders who
can make a persuasive case for their cause.* And both organizations
expect the people they help to be willing to also help themselves.
You both demand the best out of human nature—the willingness to
think long term, to invest for the future, and to use one's brain-
power. This is just so different from traditional notions of aid, which
'give charity' rather than 'invest in people.' The main reason Grameen was able to expand its awareness was that they were brilliant
at energizing volunteers around the world to help them make the
case for microfinance. I'd like to help you do the same with Room
to Read."

* I was flattered by this comparison, as Muhammad Yunus was one of my
heroes.

Never one to refuse an offer of assistance from a bright person, I immediately booked time with Michael during my next swing through Chicago.

TWO WEEKS LATER, ON A BRILLIANT, CRISP SPRING DAY THAT MAKES A Cubs fan's thoughts turn to opening day at Wrigley Field, Michael and I grabbed a coffee at the Barnes & Noble Bookstore just off Michigan Avenue. As we have done dozens of times since that day, we both began talking at a mile a minute.

I started by explaining my overall goals. Even though we were proud of having set up 500 school libraries, I felt as if I were still in the first mile of a marathon. The organization was only two years old. There were whole regions of Asia in which we had no presence, including poor countries near and dear to my heart like Burma and Bhutan. Of all the countries in Africa, we were in zero. On America's doorstep, we had neighbors like Haiti and El Salvador with perpetually high poverty and a shocking lack of educational opportunities for their children:

"I love what Carnegie did, but the weakness of his model is that he only thought about one country. The need for education, and children's love of reading, are both forces that are universal. Did you know that in Niger, eight out of ten children do not get past fifth grade? That seventy percent of women in Ethiopia cannot read? I think of my friend Vu, in Vietnam, and how little it took, resource-wise, to help him to complete his education. I had the easy part—I just had to find him some money. All the hard work was done by him—working long hours at the hotel, sacrificing his sleep, and all for the love of learning.

"So then I visualize all the Vu's who live in India and South Africa and dozens of other countries. I'd like to help all of those kids, and I don't want to be limited in my thinking, either in geographic scope, or in terms of having a huge goal. Why is it not possible to set up five thousand, or ten thousand, or twenty thousand schools and libraries? We know that there are at least that many villages that need help. The biggest missing ingredients are building out our team and of course attracting the capital that will be needed to fund this many projects. That's where the network comes in."

Michael succinctly concluded, "Okay, you need capital. Let's talk about where we are going to find it. Let's make a list of the richest cities—let's go where the money is. What we will need to do is find the people in each of those cities who know how to get things done, make things happen. Not everyone in the world wants to 'pull a John Wood' and quit their job to go save the world. But there are thousands, maybe millions, of people who are making good money and want something more from life than career success. They're the people Thomas Friedman refers to as super-empowered individuals. They will be willing to give this cause some of their time. Rather than ten more of you, we need a few thousand people who can each devote a few hours a week. We'll tie them all together into a fund-raising network that will be so powerful that your teams overseas can double, and then double again, the number of projects they can take on. Okay, let's make a list of the cities where we need to build these chapters of zealots."

New York was obvious. All those billions on Wall Street— maybe we could redeploy a small percent of it to the developing world. Boston was obviously a target, as was Washington, D.C. Michael had lived for years in London and thought we should start a chapter there. I replied that two of our first in-country volunteers were a British couple, Frances and Douglas, who were passionately devoted to Nepal. We would unite Michael's friends with mine.

Too excited to not begin acting immediately, I pulled out my laptop and began firing off e-mails: first to Frances and Douglas, then to Scott, my old friend from Microsoft Australia who was now working for the company in Hong Kong. Next I wrote to Jason, a PR exec who had recently moved from Silicon Valley to Singapore.

Michael, meanwhile, was on his cell phone with an old friend in Atlanta, and by the end of the call Raj had agreed to start our first Southeastern chapter. Our table at Barnes & Noble resembled an international airport, with flights (of fancy) taking off at supersonic speeds in all directions. By the time we had finished our brainstorm, I felt exhausted and jet-lagged, but also exhilarated by the bold vision we had formulated and embraced. In my notebook, I wrote down the proclamation we had made, which was simple, but potentially world-changing: everywhere on the globe where there are people with money, Room to Read would be pitching them to help fund our goal of universal education.

There was just one risk, but it could bring our fantasy crashing down—would people respond and offer to take part in our vision? After all, we were asking people who held down demanding jobs to carve out scarce hours to devote to a new and unproven cause.

THE RESPONSE, FROM NEW YORK AT LEAST, WAS IMMEDIATE. MY PHONE rang the next day, and I heard the enthused voice of my friend Nancy. We were old friends from Sydney, and she had recently moved back to her native New York. As I walked through the bustling United terminal at O'Hare with one finger jammed into my ear to block out the loud boarding announcements, Nancy machine-gun-blasted me with a torrent of ideas for starting a New York chapter:

"Give me some dates that you can be out here and I'll throw you a fund-raising party. I'll host it at my apartment so that we don't have to pay for a venue, and I will cover the costs like sushi and beer. My place can only hold fifty people, but that's all right, it will be cozy like a Nepali teahouse on a cold night. Put me in touch with any friends you have here, and we'll get them involved and invite their networks. We'll tell people at the event that there are only two calls to action: donate, or help us to build a chapter. Preferably both.

"I have only one request, though, and, John, you're not going to like it."

"Yes?"

"You know how much I loved living in India, right? You also know how desperately that country needs programs like your library initiative and your fund for girls' scholarships. You have to promise me that you'll consider expanding Room to Read to India. I know you had a bad experience traveling there because you are a wimp who hates crowds, and who can't deal with heat or constant haggling. Put that aside. Get over it. The country needs you."

I promised that I would consider her offer, despite the unprovoked commentary on my weaknesses. But my brain was weighted down with the thought of taking on yet another country. We could barely keep up with our existing slate of projects. I was continuing to help our anemic cash flow by not taking a salary, and with Microsoft stock having dropped from $40 a share to $22, half of my savings had disappeared. Boarding the plane, I suddenly realized that within Nancy lay both the challenge and the solution. The challenge was to continue to expand our educational programs into new countries. The solution to our funding problems was to build out this network of fund-raising volunteers. I told her that this only upped the pressure on her to deliver a successful party.

Five days later, I fumbled for the ringing phone in my backpack and nearly fell off my bike. It was a cool morning in the Presidio, with the scent of recently departed fog. From 3,000 miles away, I could hear Nancy, calling as usual from the dog-walk pen at her Upper East Side park. In between yelling at Nathan the Wonder Mutt to stop harassing the other dogs, she gave me an update:

"Hey, can you stay in New York for an extra night? We already have eighty RSVPs, and my place can only hold fifty people. So I'm thinking about adding a second 'spillover' night. We can still use my place, refresh the sushi supply, and serve the leftover drinks. It's better than turning people away. So many people have called me and told me their travel stories. You know, the same thing you and I have experienced, being in a magical and remote place and loving it, but also being appalled by the poverty. The Room to Read solution really resonates. I think we'll have a good crowd. Or two of them. And they will donate.

"Oh, yeah, and my father called this morning. He's going to show up with a $1,000 check from our family foundation. But just to warn you—he asked me to tell you that his strong preference is that the money be spent in India."

. . .

THE NETWORK OF ROOM TO READ CHAPTERS GREW AT AN EVEN FASTER pace than Michael and I had visualized. By the end of 2002, we had active fund-raising teams in New York, Chicago, the San Francisco Bay Area, and Seattle, and embryonic teams starting up in a few other cities. Although most of the chapters were being started by old friends of mine who wanted to support the organization's ambitious goals, each of them was also proving savvy at recruiting additional volunteers and leaders. In New York, as an example, I was surprised upon walking into Nancy's first event to be introduced to the "host committee" of five women. Each had traveled in the developing world and been touched by the poverty and lack of opportunities for children. I asked one of them, a media executive named Jen, what motivated her to get involved.

"This is an easy cause to get behind. The result of what you do is so tangible. Nancy told me that if we raise $8,000, you can build a school, and that if we raise $10,000, that would mean a school plus a library. The causal link between what gets donated and what gets built is really compelling. I've volunteered for other organizations and have never really known where the money goes. So when Nancy told me about this, and that we might even be able to travel to Vietnam or Nepal to visit the school, I was hooked. And when I told my parents, my father gave me a check for $2,000. He got off easy, as he could give much more than that, but when I pressed him for more, he said I was the one getting off easy as I was already one-quarter of the way to a school. He told me to quit while I was ahead and count him in for the same amount next year."

She continued, "Look, New York can sometimes be a cynical place. People can come up with all kinds of reasons to not give. You have hit on something that will cut through that negativity. So this event will be a huge success. Everyone who will be here tonight has had a great education, be it college or grad school. Every one of them will understand that this is a powerful model. How often in life can you go to a cocktail party, have fun while meeting great people, and fund a school or two in the process? That direct correlation between what we give, and what gets done, makes me think we're going to do really well."

Jen's prophecy proved correct, not only in New York, but in

other cities as well. Our two nights of events at Nancy's apartment netted over $20,000. Our Bay Area team planned an event that in one night underwrote over 100 years of girls' scholarships. A strong team was being built in Chicago under the leadership of an enthusiastic lawyer. Tina Sciabica had just returned from a trip to Asia and had read an article about Room to Read in the *Chicago Tribune*. "I knew immediately that this was my cause," she told me upon our initial meeting. "Once I read that you are doing scholarships for girls, that's all I could talk to my clients about. I decided that I might as well raise money for you. My business will probably suffer a bit since I am so focused on Room to Read right now, but I want to see you go from one hundred girls on scholarship to one thousand."

NOT EVERY FUND-RAISING EVENT WENT AS WELL AS WE'D HOPED. IN-deed, a few of them were such failures that I found myself going back and forth on whether this chapter structure was worth the investment of my time and energy.

In the spring of 2002, a woman who was planning to start a Room to Read chapter in Boston called to ask if I could fly out to present at their initial fund-raising event. I knew that the city was full of young people, and old money. This seemed a potent combination. I therefore rationalized the $900 round-trip fare on American, the only airline then flying the SFO-to-Boston route nonstop.

It seemed like a good idea at the time, but not so good when the alarm went off at 4:30 a.m. There are days when I wish I could simply drive ten minutes to work and punch the clock rather than dashing to the airport for a 6 a.m. flight. This would be one of them.

I arrived at SFO on time. American Airlines did not return the favor. They had canceled the early-morning nonstop to Boston. As a poor substitute, they gave me an itinerary that would have me cooling my heels for two hours, then catching a flight to Dallas, where I would have some more dead airport time before connecting with a Boston flight. I'd arrive four hours later than planned. So much for paying a premium to fly nonstop.

After a long day in transit, I was not in the best of moods upon arrival at Boston's overcrowded and run-down Logan Airport.

Things only got worse as I waited outside in the exhaust-enhanced afternoon heat of the airport's pickup area. Our new chapter leader had insisted on picking me up, and I now regretted not sticking to my original plan of the ten-minute cab ride into the city. Repeated calls to her cell phone went unanswered. After a half hour of frustration, I decided to brave the taxi queue.

Building a team of volunteers requires a founder to take many leaps of faith. Some work out brilliantly. Others leave you wondering. As I schlepped my bags toward the cab stand, my phone rang. Our new chapter leader was "only" ten minutes away, and so again I went into wait mode.

She finally arrives. I hop into the car and eagerly throw out questions about the next night's fund-raiser.

She quickly corrects me.

"Well, it's not exactly a fund-raiser."

"What do you mean? Isn't that why I am here?"

"I think of it as more of an 'awareness raiser.' We need to get people first to know about your cause, and then later, maybe in a year, we can ask them for financial support."

At this point I want to say that one can't pay salaries or buy bricks using "awareness." It is not a universally accepted currency. I bite my tongue. I don't know this person well enough to be a smart-ass. Yet.

Instead, I make the case for requesting at least a small amount of money. I don't get very far.

"I'm willing to ask people to pay $10 at the door, but will also tell them that if they can't afford it, then that's okay too."

"How many people are you expecting? And can't most people afford $10? I mean, if we have the right demographic . . ."

She ignores the latter question and answers the former.

"Probably 40–50."

"I thought you told me on the phone last week that you were expecting 125–150."

"That was my goal, but I did not really have time to publicize your speech."

In my head I do the math. Even if we hit fifty, and even if all of them give (despite our basically inviting them not to) we'll only cover half the cost of my flight. The CPA working his adding machine in my head is interrupted.

"Of course, I'll need to use some of that take at the door to cover the catering costs. Those ran about $400."

Ugh! I wish I were home in bed. I wish I were *anywhere* besides here. Have I really just flown cross country to attend an event that was going to have no cost of admittance, free food and drink, and no call to action asking people to donate? This is no way to run a railroad! I had made several leaps of faith in building out the chapter structure, and apparently this one had been a leap into the abyss.

THE NEXT AFTERNOON I TOOK A LONG RUN ALONG THE CHARLES RIVER. As eight-man crews whizzed by with each rower in perfect unison, and the Hancock Building shimmered in the afternoon sun, I convinced myself that regardless of the event's bad economics I should simply have fun with it and drop my obsession with revenue. Heck, maybe I'd meet some fun people and have a good time.

An hour later, I was testing my presentation on the floor-to-ceiling screen at the Swiss House, the Cambridge-located liaison office of the government of Switzerland. I had no idea why they were hosting us, but was too busy playing with all the whizzy high-tech gadgets to spend time worrying about it. Our Yak Mobile, delivering books to kids in the mountains of Nepal, had never looked cooler than on this twelve-foot screen. I was excited to start the slide show and tell the crowd about our work.

As fifty to sixty people ate cheese and crackers and sipped chardonnay from plastic tumblers, I projected images of children devouring books in our new libraries in Nepal, toddlers in Vietnam attending our new kindergartens, and our newest group of scholarship girls. It felt that I had nailed the presentation. Yet at the end not a single person clapped. Odd. Our work had always drawn vocal and positive feedback.

Staring out at a sea of skeptical faces, I paused, wondering what was going on. I filled the void by asking if anyone had questions.

"Yes, I have one." A young woman in horn-rimmed glasses, short-cropped hair, and a blue Patagonia fleece threw me a zinger. "Can you explain your pedagogical theory?"

Ped-a-gog-i-cal theory. Do I have one? "Uh, sure. Kids need to grow up learning, reading, and going to school, and in the developing world a lot of them currently don't. We help to fill that void with new schools, teachers, libraries and books."

She pointed out that this was not really a unified pedagogical theory. I could not argue with her on this one. I made a mental note to ask someone smarter than me whether Room to Read had a UPT.

I changed the subject by calling on a young kid who looked like the quintessential "smart kid in the first row," the one who spent all of third grade being the fastest to have his hand in the air.

"How can you guarantee that these kids will have jobs when they finish school?"

"Quite honestly, I can't. Then again, neither could my parents when they sent me to school. The goal of our programs is not to guarantee a job. Our raison d'être"—maybe a French phrase could impress this hypersmart crowd—"is to give children opportunities that they would not have otherwise had. To develop their brains from a young age. To become lifelong learners. To have better health. To pass on knowledge to the next generation."

"So," he said in his best Perry Mason voice, "what you are saying is that you can't guar-an-tee that your students will have jobs." With that, he tossed me his best frown.

Time for me to make another deflection. I called on a 30-ish woman who was almost raising the roof as she thrust her hand in the air.

"It says in your bio that you went to MBA school. How can you do this work without having a Ph.D. in education?"

Could this trip possibly get any worse? I felt as though we had invited the Harvard Debating Society, the MIT Curmudgeon Club, and the Cambridge Chapter of Youth United in Skepticism to our event. I wanted to scream from the stage, "Look, people, I don't have all the answers. I am simply trying to do what little I can."

Question time was abruptly curtailed by administrative fiat of the CEO. Demoralized, I packed up my notebook computer. A few of the event's attendees came up to tell me that they really liked Room to Read's projects and invited me out for a beer.

We found a small pub and chatted over a highlight reel of '80s music. A Coloradan named Pam, who had recently moved to Boston, told me that she felt badly about the Q&A session. "This is the problem with Cambridge. So many people here have gone to elite schools all their lives and have several advanced degrees. They are eager to prove that they are smarter than everyone else in the room. Your host let you down. Rather than treating this as a fund-raising event, she let it degenerate into an academic debating society."

I told Pam that the crowd had brought to mind one of my favorite Chinese proverbs:

"Those who say it cannot be done should not criticize those who are doing it."

She laughed and clinked glasses. "Come back this fall. I'll rally some friends who aren't afraid to ask people to give money. I met a great woman tonight named Jen who wants to get involved. We'll throw you a real event. All checkbook, no curmudgeon."

DESPITE THE SETBACKS, I KNEW THAT WE WERE ONTO SOMETHING BIG with the chapter model. Not everyone could quit his or her job to try to change the world, as I had. However, millions of white-collar professionals were contemplating how they could focus some of their talent and energy on the social sector. My in-box was living proof of this. Every time our work was featured in *Fast Company, Forbes,* or *Time,* hundreds of people would e-mail me with a derivation of the simple question "How can I help?"

With so much progress happening in the United States, we made the internationalization of our network a main focus for 2003. London was first. My cell phone rang one blustery morning in New York as I was dashing to catch a subway to meet with a foundation that donated millions of dollars to education projects in India. Dean Chan introduced himself succinctly and got straight to the point. He was a fellow Kellogg graduate who had read an article in our alumni magazine about Room to Read's progress. He saw serious fund-raising potential in Great Britain and was ready and willing to set up Room to Read as a public charity.

Dean laid out the business case. The country had over 60 million people and one of the strongest economies and incomes per capita in the world. The average citizen was well aware of the global condition, partly as a result of the glory days of the British Empire. There was a strong history of citizens donating to causes beyond the borders.

I agreed that the British market was tempting, but asked whether it wouldn't be logistically and bureaucratically complex to set up a charitable entity. Dean replied that he had already contacted the charity commission, studied the application process, and believed it was possible to get set up in less than two months. Besides, his business was consulting. He was good at dealing with complexity and process.

I was impressed that he had already done his homework, rather than calling me with a pie-in-the-sky idea that had not been thought through. I asked next about his motivation for wanting to get involved with Room to Read. He explained that education had made a big difference in his life, and now that he was a successful adult he wanted to devote some part of his energy to helping others to gain that same advantage.

As I descended the steps to catch the no. 9 train, I shouted above the din that he had my approval to get started with the process. I suggested that we talk again in a week to iron out the logistical details.

He asked if I could come to London to speak at his first fundraising event. Yes, yes, count me in. The train was approaching and I needed to catch this one if I was to avoid being hopelessly late for the foundation meeting. But was I really agreeing, in an initial five-minute "nice to meet you" phone call, to start up a UK chapter, and to fly over there for a total stranger? Isn't that the same mistake I had made in Boston?

Something in my gut trusted Dean. He seemed genuine, smart, and focused. The Kellogg connection was there. We needed capital and the Brits had quite a lot of it. The pound was a strong currency. This felt right. Dean said he would "ring off" so that I could catch my train and offered a "Cheerio." As I rushed past the closing doors, I marveled that our pace of growth would continue to accelerate if we opened Room to Read up to the millions of globally minded individuals outside the United States.

Two weeks later I had a surprisingly similar phone call from Vancouver. Anja Haman, like Dean, was a consultant, and she had read a *Fast Company* story on Room to Read. She was motivated to start a Canadian arm. She explained that she wanted to have a "service hobby" to go alongside her obsession with ultimate Frisbee.

"Why Room to Read?" I asked.

"The organization has a way of motivating people who are looking to do more with their lives. You reach a certain level of business success and you realize that this is not enough. You start to look for something more meaningful. This is the best thing I've found, and I have been searching for a long time."

I asked why Canada would be a good market.

In an extremely high-energy and rapid burst she overwhelmed me with her sales pitch:

"Vancouver is the most international city in Canada. We have very deep ties to Asia; over thirty percent of citizens here are originally from there. Every year I throw myself a birthday party, and a few hundred people show up. This year I'd like for the party to be not about me, but instead have it benefit kids who need education. I could do the party as a one-off event, but the businessperson in me thinks that this could be much bigger and more sustainable if we set up some structure around it. I'm thinking about a Canadian board of directors, getting tax status so that donations are deductible, and having an annual event that grows and grows in both number of attendees and money raised. This could become one of the best parties in Vancouver. I've already talked to a bunch of artist friends, and all of them are willing to create pieces that we can auction at the first event. And I've found a perfect venue. I know I should have waited to talk to you first, but once I read the article, I got so excited that I got to work immediately. I'm the kind of person who does things and then asks for permission later!"

Like Dean, she had already done her homework and estimated

that it would cost about $1,000 to set ourselves up as a Canadian charity. She could get it done in a month. She then gave me her unique version of a challenge grant—she'd pay for half the incorporation costs if I'd fund the other half. I liked her closing skills and continued the negotiation with my own counteroffer. We had an event in San Francisco in two weeks' time. Could she fly down for it, meet the team, and give us the opportunity to get to know her better? She agreed. I offered up my guest room and promised to send a $500 check.

Before hanging up, she extracted a promise that I'd come to Vancouver to speak at her first event. I visualized a one-way round-the-world ticket connecting all of our new international chapters, in London, Hong Kong, Singapore, and Vancouver. My old travel schedule as a Microsoft exec was going to look wimpy in comparison to what lay ahead.

FROM SEATTLE TO THE HIMALAYAS (SEE BOX), FROM HONG KONG TO New York, our network of fund-raising volunteers and chapters was working like a well-oiled machine. It amazed me that I could walk into a small cocktail party in a distant city like Chicago or London and see over 100 people who were passionate about our cause. I believed in Room to Read, of course, but to see so many other people who had made a conscious decision to spend a night of their life hearing about our work meant a lot to me. It gave me faith, during the early years, that maybe we were onto something and that we'd succeed in building a mass movement. The early results were promising, but they were only a slim indication of what lay ahead.

EVERYDAY HEROES: FUND-RAISING ON MOUNT EVEREST

Not every fund-raising event took place in a major city like Vancouver, New York, or London. In the spring of 2002, one of our volunteers threw an impromptu fund-raising event at a base camp at Mount Everest.

An amazing group of women had decided to form the first all-American women's Everest expedition. It had been less than thirty years since the first woman had reached the summit of Everest, and less than fifteen since the first American woman had. This group of five women decided that they wanted to show the world what a group of American women could do when they put their minds to it.

My friend Alison Levine was serving as the team captain. I wanted to ask her if she would be willing to use the expedition as a "platform" to raise money to build schools in Nepal, but was cognizant of her already insane schedule. In addition to working full-time at Goldman Sachs, she was also trying to raise $250,000 in corporate sponsorship for the climb, and undergoing rigorous physical training to prepare for several weeks at high altitude. In addition, she was attempting to raise $100,000 to endow a cancer research grant at the V Foundation, named after the legendary North Carolina State basketball coach Jim Valvano. Any one of those things could have been a full-time job on its own. Since she was, in effect, holding down all four of these roles simultaneously, I decided that I should focus on being her running and snowshoeing partner and hold off on asking what she could do for Room to Read.

One day, during a trail run in the beautiful hills of Marin County, Alison asked me what was new at work. I told her that we had recently approved four new school construction projects, and that my challenge for the next month was to find donors willing to sponsor them.

"I'll find two of them," she said in midstride.

"How are you going to do that, given everything else you have going on?"

"I have no idea. But I'll find a way. I always do. I want some part of this climb to be about helping Nepal, rather than just attaining the top of the mountain."

That's the kind of amazing person Alison is. She had a million reasons not to take on an additional task in the frantic lead-up to her Everest ascent. But she does not like saying *no*. *Yes* leaves a much more positive ring in her ears. It's the reason she had al-

continued

ready reached the summit of mountains like Alaska's Denali and Antarctica's Mount Vinson.

Two days later, my cell phone rang.

"Hey, it's Alison. I'm so excited. I just found a sponsor who agreed to fund both the schools I adopted: 85 Broads said they'd do it."

"Eighty-five who?"

"85 Broads. It's a group of female employees and alumni of Goldman Sachs. Goldman is headquartered at 85 Broad Street in New York, so they call the group 85 Broads. Cute, huh? Anyway, 85 Broads is run by the most amazing woman named Janet Hanson, and when I told her about the climb and my goal of funding two schools in Nepal, she immediately agreed to fund them. She's sending you a check tomorrow. And then an hour later this flower guy comes to my desk with a huge bouquet of flowers, and I am wondering who the heck they're from because my dating life is a disaster, and they're from Janet. The card wishes me luck on Everest. And I'm thinking that it's supposed to be *me* sending *her* flowers."

I loved life. Two more schools. Two more villages we could say yes to. And another amazing example of members of our network doing everything in their power to help Room to Read get more schools built.

I congratulated Alison.

"Wait, hold on, there's more. She wants you and me to come to the 85 Broads annual dinner and present our story. They don't usually allow men to attend, but they're going to make an exception for you. There will be at least two hundred people there."

"Wow! You, me, and two hundred female investment bankers. Karma exists!"

"Good one. Gotta run. Bye."

As is usual with Alison, the conversation had lasted for less than thirty seconds. Lots of info, lots of good news, all downloaded quickly. Therein lay at least some of the secret as to how she was simultaneously holding down the equivalent of four full-time jobs.

Two months later, Alison was at Everest base camp. During a long period of waiting for the weather to clear, she was visiting another climbing team's mess tent. A Swiss-Italian climber, Bruno Rodi, was suffering from bronchitis and was bemoaning that he had not gotten higher on the mountain than camp two.

"All my life it's been my dream to climb Everest. And I didn't get to the top."

Alison tried to change his mind-set.

"Bruno, at the end of the day, it doesn't really matter whether or not you tag the top of Everest. What matters is whether you do something to help the people of Nepal. Look around you, and what do you see? Crushing poverty, and one of the poorest countries on this earth. You should do what I did and find a way to endow some schools. Even if I never leave base camp, I'll still be happy that there is a positive legacy from this trip."

A few hours later, half a world away, and 17,600 feet closer to sea level, an e-mail arrived in my in-box.

From: Bruno Rodi
To: John Wood
Re: New Schools in Nepal
Hello, John:

This is Bruno Rodi, writing to you from the only e-mail account at Everest Base Camp. It is not possible to send large messages from here. We are using very old equipment, hooked to a satellite. So this will be short. I met Alison. I want to be like her and endow two schools in Nepal. Please send to me wiring instructions for your bank. I will then tell my office in Switzerland to donate the money to Room to Read.

Thank you, John, for the work that you do. From what little I have seen of Nepal, it is needed. I will be in touch when I am back down from the mountain.

I read the mail several times and tried to convince myself that it was not a hoax.

A week later, the money miraculously hit our account. The information flow started in Nepal, came to San Francisco, went back to Nepal, then to his office in Switzerland, and then back to San Francisco. And soon we'd be wiring the money over to our

continued

account in Nepal to get the schools started, closing the circle. The bits of information traveled over 35,000 miles. Within a month this data stream would be turned into bricks, mortar, chalkboards, and desks. It was one of those moments that made me thankful for technology, in addition to the amazing worldwide network of volunteers who were every bit as passionate about Room to Read as the founder.

CHAPTER 17

YOUR LIFE IS A MESS

THE EARLY DAYS OF STARTING ROOM TO READ EXACTED A TOLL. While my business card read CEO, in actuality the organization had so few staff that this was just one of many roles I played. I was also the head of fund-raising, the VP of human resources, the guy who walked the deposit to the bank, the stamp-licker when we sent out receipts, the receptionist who answered the phone, and the janitor who took the trash to the Dumpster in the empty parking lot after a 14-hour day.

The constant travel only exacerbated the feeling that life was spinning out of control. As the number of chapters and planned events grew, and as we investigated new countries for expansion, there was pressure on me to be everywhere to present the Room to Read story and to close the sale.

Unfortunately, there was little backup. I wanted to avoid the trap many charities fall into—that of hiring a huge staff in their first year, and therefore having a high overhead ratio from day one. Erin and I were both willing to wear many hats, given that a lean and mean payroll would allow us to tell donors that their money was going to programs, not to bureaucracy. Many people told us that our overhead was too low, but those people did not have to sell, sell,

sell. Erin and I had to personally pitch donors on every school we needed funding for, and every computer lab and language lab and library. Low overhead was one of our key points of differentiation, and an important one given that many of our early donors were technology entrepreneurs who preached the gospel of economic efficiency in a way that would make Alan Greenspan proud.

Unfortunately, this also exacted a toll, as we worked insane hours to keep up with our growth. My idea of a weekend was to take either Saturday or Sunday morning off, but certainly not both. On Sunday, I might leave the office at 8 p.m. rather than the usual 10 p.m.

These hours did not usually bother me. In fact, I felt lucky. I saw nothing wrong with loving your work so much that you were willing to devote extreme hours to it. Better to do that than to work at a job you hate and watch the clock while praying for 5 p.m. to hurry up and arrive.

There were downsides. I saw my family less frequently than I would have preferred. My skis rarely made it out of the garage. Our board of directors said that they were worried about my burning out. But the biggest downside kept rearing its ugly head: the long hours were absolute hell on my relationships.

At times I would begin dating a woman, and then, within a month, she would get extremely frustrated with how little time I had to devote to the burgeoning relationship. One frustrated woman opined that Room to Read was "your wife, your mistress, your child, your family dog, and your career." She then told me that nodding vigorously in agreement while grinning was *not* the proper response. I apologized for being so emotionally tone-deaf, but explained, "I have found the one thing I always wanted—a career with meaning and about which I feel passion. I wake up eager to jump out of bed and head to the office, excited for whatever it is that the day holds. That is a rare luxury in this world."

Alas, this monomaniacal focus meant that I was not the most accessible bachelor in San Francisco.

. . .

ON A WARM SPRING DAY IN 2003, I WAS LATE GETTING TO THE OFFICE for a meeting with two potential donors. The couple had met our staff during a recent fact-finding trip to Vietnam and were interested in funding new computer labs at schools in the Mekong Delta. I had four minutes to go, and 15 blocks of Lombard Street in front of me. I stomped on the accelerator in hopes of getting a good run of green lights.

The only lights I saw were accompanied by a siren. Oops, cancel that meeting.

The cop is twenty pounds overweight and wearing mirrored sunglasses, as though he's straight out of central casting. I roll down the window and flash him my best smile. "Hey, how's it going?" I ask lamely.

"I'm fine, but I'm a little bit concerned about how fast you're driving. Are you late for something?"

Realizing, of course, that this is a rhetorical question, I nevertheless begin to explain that actually, yes, I am late for a meeting. I pause with the vague hope that maybe he'll suggest that, well, in that case, we'll skip this whole ticket thing. Heck, maybe he'll tell me to pull behind him, and we'll race down Lombard Street toward the Room to Read office with siren blaring, lights flashing—an official escort, just like President Bush gets when he visits town!

"I'll need to see your registration and proof of insurance," he drawls, bursting my fantasy bubble.

"Okay, I think they're in here somewhere," I say as I dig frantically through the glove compartment. "Here's my proof of insurance. Oh, wait, that's the old one. Here it is. Shoot, that one's expired too. Hang on, sorry, sir, I know it's in here. Aha, here we go."

"Thank you. Now, how about your driver's license? Do you think you can find that for me, maybe at some point today?"

I search through my wallet, the glove compartment, and finally locate it in the auxiliary storage area between the two front seats. Attached are two Post-it notes with numbers for phone messages I have yet to return. The officer looks annoyed.

"Washington State? Your car is registered in California."

"Yes, I used to live in Washington."

"And when did you move to California?"

I have no idea how to answer this question. I left Washington State in 1995, eight years ago. Since then I have lived in Australia and China and now San Francisco. Technically, one is supposed to renew one's driver's license within thirty days of moving. I'm slightly overdue. So I tell him vaguely, "A few months ago," and hope that we can move on.

Thankfully, we do.

"Okay, now one more step in the process. I assume you know that your registration is expired?"

"Uh, yes, sir, I do. I was traveling for most of the last month so I am way behind on paperwork. But I have the new registration documents in my briefcase, along with the check. I was going to send it in today. It's in the trunk. Can I grab it and show it to you?"

He nods yes. His patience is close to the breaking point.

"Officer, can I point out to you that this is not any kind of funny business on my part?"

"What exactly do you mean?"

"Like in the movies, where the guy is hiding something in the trunk, like a weapon or an explosive device. I just want to assure you that the only thing I'm going to pull out of my trunk is my briefcase."

"Sir, you don't look like a hardened criminal. I am not intimidated. Just . . . get . . . the . . . registration . . . papers . . . out . . . of . . . the . . . briefcase . . . please."

The trunk is a visual cacophony. Boxes of children's books, packaging tape, random papers that should be filed but aren't, empty water bottles, tennis racquet with broken string, running shoes, dry cleaning that I've yet to drop off, a still-loaded-with-dirty-clothes duffel bag from my last New York trip, bank statements that are unopened because I do not want to face the reality of my dwindling savings, and somewhere beneath it all, a briefcase.

The officer gives me a look of pity and shakes his head. He then sums up my existence in one sentence.

"Your life is a mess."

More images flash through my mind. The 2001 taxes that I have yet to file. And the 2002 taxes. Boxes that are still unpacked from my move over two years ago. I nod sadly in agreement with the officer. "Yes, sir, it is. Sorry."

He realizes that I have bigger problems to deal with. "How about if I let you off with a warning?"

I give him a goofy grin. "Really? Do you mean that? That would be so cool!" I offer him a handshake, as though I have just sold him a used car. I jump into mine before he can change his mind, vowing to drive the required 45 mph to the office.

Of course, I know exactly what will happen. Despite my vow to spend the rest of the day dealing with my license, taxes, dry cleaning, and empty refrigerator, there will be Room to Read issues that I'll find to be more urgent, and more interesting, than the mundane tasks that I should be doing. If the trade-off is between getting funding for a school versus standing in line at the DMV, I will choose the former.

Maybe that's why Bill Gates doesn't always have the best haircut in the world. He simply finds building the company to be more interesting than visiting the hairstylist. And he's 22 years further into his entrepreneurial gig than I am.

MY FINANCIAL LIFE WAS ALSO A BIT OF A MESS. LIKE MANY PEOPLE WHO had made good money during the technology boom, I had naively assumed that these stocks moved only upward. I thought that if Microsoft stock advanced a "mere" 10 percent per year, and I then sold off enough each year to harvest that gain, I'd be able to survive quite well without taking a paycheck from Room to Read.

In retrospect, it's always easy to tell how obvious our mistakes should have appeared at the time. By 2003, Microsoft stock was down nearly 50 percent from its peak. Not only was my asset base cut in half, but I was in the third year of living without a regular salary. Like an ostrich burying its head in the sand, I would let financial statements pile up, unopened, delaying the inevitable glance at my deteriorating situation. This reality was especially difficult for me because I had been raised by my parents to always be a saver. To now be in the third year of a declining bank balance felt unnatural, and if the headlong downward rush continued, it was doubtful that I'd be able to keep pursuing my dream.

The reality hit home one day as I was taking a Sunday-afternoon run along the water at San Francisco's outdoor sports mecca, Crissy Field. The sun-drenched day had brought out every slim and buff triathlete and marathoner the city had to offer. As I left the water after a fast five miles and headed home through the Marina District for a Gatorade and a cold shower, I noticed a FOR SALE sign on a beautiful Italian Renaissance home. "That's my house!" I almost shouted upon realizing that this was one of those homes I had always run by and thought that maybe, someday, I too could have a balcony with a view of the Palace of Fine Arts and the Golden Gate Bridge.

As luck would have it, there was an open house that day. Wiping the sweat off my Timex Ironman, I realized that the house was actually open, but only for ten more minutes. Knowing that gems like this were not bound to stay available for long in the hot San Francisco real estate market, I decided to take a quick tour despite my sweaty clothes.

I did not get far. Upon entering the home, I noticed a table at the base of the stairs on which were stacked up marketing materials prepared by the Realtor. My eyes gazed adoringly on a photo of their bridge view, the marble floors, and the bookcases surrounding the fireplace. As I pictured moving *my* beloved books onto *my* beloved new shelves around *my* beloved new fireplace, my eyes caught the price listing.

Gulp. There. Is. Just. No. Way. I did a quick 180-degree turn and walked back to my rental.

Later that night, over a chicken curry with my friend Laura, I went into a rant about how much I hated that I could not afford a decent house in this city. Here I was about to turn 40, and I was still renting. What kind of success was a person if he was a tenant this late in life? Wasn't it the American dream to own your own home, to live in a place that you loved and knew would be yours for decades to come?

I explained my dilemma. I could afford a nice house in a place that was less expensive than San Francisco, but I felt pressure to stay in this city. So many wealthy people were here that it would be suboptimal for Room to Read to have me live somewhere else. I could certainly afford a house in a city like Topeka, but I would not be spending time with venture capitalists and technology entrepreneurs if I lived there, and our budget would suffer.

But what worked for the charity did not work for me. My life would continue to be lived as a renter, who was flushing money down the toilet and not building equity in anything. My brow was sweating as the curry magnified the intensity of my griping. On the way home I again passed my dream house.

The next morning I received an e-mail from Laura. She quickly set the record straight for me:

"John, your role in life is not to live in a fabulous house overlooking the water. You are never home anyway. You need to keep doing what you do, because not enough progress is being made in the world, especially for the poorest countries. Don't think about real estate as being what matters. You have something that few other people have—the certainty that comes with knowing you are doing, every day, exactly what you should be doing. To sacrifice that to chase a big home would be a disaster and a huge mistake."

I knew she was right and felt foolish that I had lost sight of this reality. However, a change in attitude would not be enough to solve my financial dilemma or help me determine what the long-term plan for financial sustainability would be.

PART 3

HITTING OUR STRIDE

CHAPTER 18

PUTTING GIRLS

IN THEIR PLACE–SCHOOL!

IN MUCH OF THE DEVELOPING WORLD, LIFE IS EXCEEDINGLY DIFFICULT for men, but even more difficult for women. Due to cultural bias, and a history of men being in charge and making the key decisions, women are often treated as second-class citizens. Most of society's, and the family's, choices are optimized for the men. The women's voices are not heard, and their opinions (and often their lives) are treated as expendable.

I believe that much of this bias starts from a young age, when the boys are sent off to school and the girls remain at home to work or to take care of their younger siblings. The message sent to the boys is that they are superior, and that their parents are willing to make the long-term investment in their education. The girls receive the exact opposite message. It should therefore not be a surprise when men exhibit biased attitudes, and when uneducated women show a profound lack of self-confidence. What we learn at age five or age ten stays with us for life.

There are, of course, other cultural issues and biases that create this inequality. Disparity in access to education is both a promulgator and a reflection of the problem. Closing this gap is a powerful way to plant the seeds for a more equitable society. Girls who are educated know their own worth. Boys who go to school alongside girls are more likely to treat the other gender as being equal.

Proof of these vast gender gaps is provided by the education statistics. In Nepal, as just one of many stark examples, adult male illiteracy is a staggering 39 percent. But for Nepali women, the situation is even worse, with 75 percent of adult women unable to read or write a simple sentence.

It's a pattern repeated throughout the developing world. The United Nations estimates that two-thirds of the 850 million illiterate people in the world are female. This problem perpetuates itself, since an uneducated mother will have less knowledge to pass down to the next generation. The effect is felt by every child a woman bears. My friend Usha, who helps run a wonderful girls' education program in Nepal, always says, "When you educate a boy, you educate just the boy. But when you educate a girl, you educate the whole family, and the next generation."

It has always seemed apparent to our team that if we want to create lasting social change in the developing world, the best thing we can do is to get girls in school from a young age and help keep them there through the end of secondary school. They will grow up empowered and self-confident and will have increased earning power and economic independence. Room to Read set up the Room to Grow girls' scholarship program in the hopes of changing lives, one girl, then one family, at a time.

INDIA IS A COUNTRY WHERE GIRLS TOO OFTEN SUFFER FROM BIAS against women. A common wish to a bride is "May you be the mother of a hundred sons." Favoritism toward boys is shown by another quote: "To give birth to a son is like witnessing a sunrise in heaven. A daughter is like having an uninvited guest at the banquet."

Anita, a 15-year-old girl from an underprivileged family in New Delhi, was introduced to Room to Read's local staff during her brave fight to gain an education. It was an uphill battle. Her parents together earned less than $400 per year and were struggling to support themselves and their four children. Perpetually short on cash, they frequently pressured Anita to drop out of school so that they could avoid the monthly fees. For many years she was able to argue successfully to continue her education. One day, as she prepared to enter ninth grade, she was given the bad news: Her parents told her that this time they were firm in their decision to no longer pay her school fees. She was 15, and it was time to get married.

Anita argued that a complete education would allow for many more opportunities than would marriage at a young age. But her parents were just as stubborn at arguing their point of view—it was time for her to leave school and get married so that a husband could have the burden of providing for her.

Anita discussed her plight with a local teacher, breaking down in tears as she talked about her love of school. How could she be forced out when she had not even started grade nine? The sympathetic teacher said that she had one possible salvation: the Room to Grow girls' scholarship program.

Anita was excited as she visualized her return to school. She told her parents about the opportunity and gained their commitment that she could stay in school as long as Room to Read paid her school fees.

With her teacher friend in tow, Anita confidently approached a member of the local selection committee to make her case. But before she could even get started, she was dismayed to hear the news: the committee had already finalized their choices for scholarship recipients and the program was full for the year. Anita had missed her opportunity.

She protested vehemently and made a strong case for support. "If you do not help me to stay in school, I will be married within a year and will be stuck at an eighth-grade level of education. My husband will have more schooling that I have, and he will use that to rule over me. How can you tell me that you will not help me to avoid this?"

Her persistence and heartfelt desire to gain an education impressed the member of the selection committee. He promised to talk to the other committee members about whether they could make an exception and allow Anita to join the program.

Two days later a nervous Anita heard the news: extra funding had been promised by Room to Read to pay her school fees. In addition, a small stipend was budgeted to allow her to have a tutor. The team was concerned that since her parents were not wholeheartedly supportive of education, it would be best if Anita had a mentor dedicated to helping her study during the after-school hours.

Today, Anita beams with joy as she walks to school. At her side is her younger sister, for whom Anita has become a role model. Sunisha, a charming sixth-grader, has vowed to follow Anita's example and stay in school through age 18 so that she also can gain a complete education. Anita has not only raised the bar for her younger sister, but will do the same when she eventually has children of her own.

As much as I like having rules and structure at Room to Read, I encourage our selection committees everywhere to keep making exceptions like this one! Fortunately, in each country Room to Read has strong female program officers on staff who reach out to local communities to find girls who would benefit from long-term scholarships.

FOUR HUNDRED MILES EAST OF ANITA AND HER SCHOOL IN NEW DELHI, nine-year-old Sujina Tuladhar is a direct beneficiary of the female program officers who run Room to Grow in each country in which Room to Read operates. In Nepal, the program has been run by two strong local women—Shilpi and Nebedita. Both grew up in families that stressed the importance of education for women, and they attended university as a result. They are now working to provide these same opportunities to girls in Nepal. When they run into a girl like Sujina, they work long hours to learn her story and find a way to get her in school.

Sujina is nine years old and in the third grade. Neither of her parents finished high school. When she was eight years old, her father died tragically in a motorcycle accident. Her mother, a housewife, had never held a full-time job.

Sujina and her mother did not have any family willing to help. The marriage had been between different castes, and both sides of the family shunned the couple and their charming young daughter. The mother has had no luck finding a job, due to her own lack of education, and Nepal's anemic economy. As happens too often in the world, short-term economic hardship would mean the loss of the long-term opportunity inherent in education. Sujina would have to drop out of school.

During one of their outreach trips to talk to headmasters and local government officials, Shilpi and Nebedita were told this sad story. They visited the family to learn about their living conditions. The family owned no property and had moved in with the maternal grandmother. In Sujina's eyes, the Room to Read team members saw a zeal for education. They interviewed her mother separately. She expressed hope that "my daughter be educated, so that she can handle difficult situations and not suffer like I have."

Within a month, Sujina was one of the newest Room to Grow scholars in Nepal. As with all of our girls, we have budgeted to allow her to continue to study through the end of high school.

SOME PEOPLE MAY ASK, "WHY, AS A MAN, DO YOU CARE SO MUCH ABOUT education for girls? Isn't this more of a women's issue?" Absolutely not.

I have faced those questions on numerous occasions. Indeed, groups have sometimes asked us to present slide shows on our girls' scholarship program, but have inquired whether . . . er . . . well . . . could we have a female staff member make the presentation instead of me? I have politely replied that this request felt like misguided political correctness. Can only women be concerned with the future of young girls? Didn't it benefit the civil rights movement to have all races of people fighting for equality?

My concern is that if we cordon off the issue of education for girls in the developing world as a "women's issue," we will make far less progress than if we enlist both genders in the drive for full equality. I hope that this is not only a *women's* issue, but also a *men's* issue.

I have three strong women in my life who showed me, from a young age, the importance of education. My grandmother, mother, and older sister were all educated. They spent countless hours reading to me and then, later in my life, having me read to them. My earliest memories are of one of these strong and opinionated women teaching me to color with crayons, cheering me on as I counted to ten with Ernie and Bert, and reading me bedtime stories. I remember my mother giving me a pile of coins and teaching me how to count. My grandmother would always tell me, "If you have a book, you will never be lonely." And my sister would tease me by speaking French, a language I did not understand, but which I vowed to study once I was old enough.*

I am certain that I would not be where I am today were it not for these three educated women in my life. They provided constant mental stimulus and created a lifelong learner. To provide education to girls throughout the developing world feels, in a sense, like karmic payback.

EDUCATING GIRLS IS ALSO A SMART INVESTMENT. FOR A RELATIVELY small amount of money, one can change the future of a girl in the developing world through the lifelong gift of education. Room to Read's program, as an example, supports a girl by paying her school fees, buying her two school uniforms, two pairs of shoes, a book bag, and school supplies. She is also given health insurance, a bicycle (schools tend to be sparse in the developing world, so travel times are long), and a strong female mentor to look after the group of young scholars. The all-in cost of this wide-ranging package: only $250 per year. It's not often in life that one is given the opportunity to change another person's life for such a small amount of money.

Beyond the impact for each individual girl, countless studies have shown that increased female participation in the education system has benefits for the society as a whole. These include:

- improved maternal health
- lower infant-mortality rates

* Anyone who has heard me attempt to speak French can attest that I failed miserably at this goal!

- combating the spread of HIV/AIDS and other prevent-
able diseases
- decrease in hunger and poverty

The United Nations has consistently advocated that educating girls has a larger impact on the developing world than any other initiative. If girls do not have the opportunity to attend school, we cannot hope to make lasting progress in the fight to eliminate global poverty.

For me, educating girls is an easy choice, both at an emotional level and from the pragmatic standpoint of providing a high return on investment. Whether you use your heart or your brain, you quickly realize that there are few better ways to change the course of the world than getting girls into school and keeping them there.

Of course, I need look no further than around our San Francisco office to see the power of smart, educated, and well-informed females. Women comprise the majority of our staff. They have attended great schools, worked and studied hard, and now help me to lead our organization to new heights. As of early 2006, four of our six country directors are women. We see the benefit of educating women every day, and we hope to successfully share this message with communities around the world.

IN THE SPRING OF 2005, I WAS HIT WITH AN UNEXPECTED REMINDER OF the importance of the scholarships for girls in the developing world.

I was invited to San Diego to make a speech at a software conference. The organizers had suggested that I frame my slide show around the theme "life after Microsoft" and focus on how I was applying lessons learned in the business world to the nonprofit sector. They had offered me a $10,000 speaking fee, which I suggested they donate to Room to Read. We then had a brainstorm and decided to challenge the audience. At the end of my slide show, the event organizers would present me with a check and announce that the funds would be used to endow forty years of girls' scholarships. They'd encourage the members of the audience to donate enough money to double this amount and allow eighty "girl years" of education.

My fifteen-minute slide show received an enthusiastic round of applause, and I returned to my table pleased with the response. Within seconds, many of the 400-plus conference participants were coming over with checkbooks and credit cards in hand. As I chatted with these new donors, a CEO from the audience grabbed the microphone and announced that his company was donating $20,000 on the spot. The room erupted in wild cheers, and many more attendees followed his example by coming over with checks. Two more speakers were slated next, so the MC asked people to return to their seats and shift their focus back to software.

As the next speaker began to talk about strategies for effective customer service, I leaned back in my chair and smiled at the thought of how much we could accomplish with the money that had been donated. In our first year as an organization, we had brought in only $51,000, and fully 20 percent of that money was from me! Now we had made $35,000 in under an hour, and 140 years of scholarships were now possible.

My thoughts were interrupted by a woman refilling my water glass. She said something to me in a voice so quiet that I had to ask her twice to repeat herself. Obviously she did not want to interfere with our table's enjoyment of the presentation, but she clearly had something to say.

"I wish we had been able to have Room to Read in the town where I grew up," she repeated. Without waiting for me to respond, she dove into her story. She had lived her youth in a farming village in Sonora, northern Mexico. As a young girl, she loved going to school and was shocked at age 12 to be told by her parents that she needed to drop out. Money being tight, they wanted her to start working. She helped out on a neighboring farm for ten hours a day, receiving eight cents for each hour of backbreaking labor under a scorching sun. At age 16, she had been smuggled across *el norte*—the U.S. border—and worked as a dishwasher and floor mopper. She had never had the opportunity to resume her education.

"If you had been there, maybe I could have stayed in school," she said with a voice that was so sweet and full of dreams that I could not take it as an accusation. But she was roughly my age, and to compare my own life to hers made me feel as though the world did not always work in ways that were fair. I had been born a white male in middle-class America, and she was the daughter of poor Mexican parents. Our fates had been decided for us at a young age. It was as though I had been given a winning ticket in the lottery of life, whereas hers had simply said, "Sorry, better luck next time."

She was not bitter. Her face wore a look of pride as she told me of her life in San Diego. "Now, I have two daughters. I work here [at the Hyatt], and I make a union wage. My two daughters, they both go to good private schools run by our Catholic church. They study, and they earn excellent grades. They will have the opportunities in life that I missed. Thank you for doing your work, because there are many girls out there who are just like I used to be in my little village, and they are waiting for you. Don't forget about Mexico."

My brain was overwhelmed with thoughts running everywhere and bouncing off each other. First, I thought of how proud this woman should be for having worked hard and for carving out a better life for her family. The odds had been stacked against her, and one could only speculate on what hardships she had overcome to have arrived at her current life. I also felt a sense of meaning, because this woman's comments had reminded me just how important these scholarships were to young girls. Third, I wanted to put her up onstage at next year's conference, as she had made a more eloquent case for the Room to Grow program than I ever could.

My last thoughts were a bit melancholy. Clearly, there were thousands of villages in the developing world in which girls lacked educational opportunities, and where Room to Read did not operate (including Mexico). How could we get these girls in school more quickly? What if we failed, or did not set high enough goals for the Room to Grow program?

I knew that we needed to accelerate growth. There was no shortage of girls in the developing world who wanted to be in school. We just needed to find the funding and hire more great program officers in each country to identify and mentor the girls. As I sipped the water that had been poured by this kindred spirit with a different life path, I began thinking about other speaking engagements that might present opportunities for us to raise money for the Room to Grow program. As a multitude of possibilities crashed through my brain, I vowed to speak whenever possible about the importance of girl's education, in hopes of enlisting an army of volunteers to help us raise more funds and reach more girls.

EVERYDAY HEROES: TINA AND THE ROOM TO GROW PROGRAM

In response to the need, Room to Read's scholarship program has continued to expand. Over 2,000 girls were recipients of long-term scholarships by the middle of 2006. Our chapter leaders were true heroes in making this happen. They rallied behind the program and raised funding to underwrite our aggressive growth plans.

The most enthusiastic advocate was Tina Sciabica, the head of our Chicago chapter. When we first met in the fall of 2002, she asked if I'd be willing to come back to Chicago in February to speak at a fund-raising event geared toward the Room to Grow program. I had learned enough from some of our fund-raising disasters to ask questions first, and then only to say yes if the event organizer had fire in the belly. Tina so overachieved in this area that we were potentially in need of an extinguisher.

"I have traveled in the developing world, and doing so has given me a new appreciation for the huge difference that education makes in the life of a woman. I am lucky because my parents valued education. One of my father's greatest priorities was to make sure that he could pay for me to go to college. I did that, plus law school. Since then, I have had financial opportunities that my parents never dreamed would be possible for me. As an educated woman in the United States, I have unlimited freedom. I have a career, own my home, and I will only get married if I want to—not because I need someone to provide for me. Were my situation reversed, and I had been an uneducated woman in the developing world, I would probably not have these freedoms."

I told Tina that she did not need me to fly out for the event, as she spoke more eloquently on the subject than I did. She insisted.

I was still haunted by that night in Cambridge. I needed to learn more. What was Tina's motivation, and would she devote time to making the event a success? I asked more questions.

"I will be able to sell this to my friends and work colleagues," she replied. "The model is so simple. You know that running costs are low, so donations are translated into a direct and tangible result. There is no barrier to getting involved, or giving, because there is a straight correlation: if you give X dollars, then we do thing Y. In my case, I'm going to tell everyone that if they attend, I am going to ask them to fund one year, for one girl. That is $250. Simple. Hand over your credit card."

She had the right stuff!

We made a deal. I would fly out to speak at her fund-raiser, but in the future she would present solo to women's groups throughout Chicago.

The February event started a winning streak of a dozen fundraisers that Tina and the Chicago chapter threw over the next four years. At the first one, she borrowed a party room at a friend's condo and convinced two friends who owned Monsoon, a hip Indian eatery, to underwrite the food and drinks. As I munched down vegetable *pakoras* and noted her shared passion for low overhead, Tina welcomed the crowd. She spoke eloquently and with passion on her belief in helping girls to get into school. She introduced me, and I did my best slide show and pitch for the Room to Grow program. At the end, Tina surprised all of us with an announcement:

"As John mentioned, Room to Read can put a girl in school, and keep her there, for only $250 a year. This is such a small amount of money. As a legal headhunter, I know what all of my clients in this room make each year." Nervous chuckles. "I want to give you an incentive. For any donation you make at the $250 or higher level, I will match you, dollar-for-dollar. My business is having a good year. I would not be a successful entrepreneur had I not been educated. Tonight is about giving that same opportunity to a lot of girls. I'd like to help Room to Read to add one hundred

continued

girls to the program this year. That's $25,000. You know what to do."

With that, I popped up a photo of a Vietnamese girl, with a thought balloon above her head reading, "All Major Credit Cards Accepted." That elicited some laughs, and a stampede toward the donation table.

Tina hit, then exceeded, her event goal. Over the next three years, she traveled at her own expense to visit Room to Grow scholars in Cambodia, India, Nepal, and Vietnam. She returned from each trip even more energized and continues to host parties and strong-arm her friends into doing the same. Chicago remains our number one fund-raising chapter in the United States, and hundreds of girls are the beneficiaries.

CHAPTER 19

"COUNT ME IN, DON"

DURING 2002 AND 2003 WE RECEIVED REQUESTS TO START ROOM TO Read programs in over a dozen countries, ranging from Cameroon to Nicaragua to Pakistan. The demand for our programs seemed to be limitless. Personnel and finances, however, were not. Each time I had to write an e-mail to explain, calmly and rationally, to a mother in rural Bangladesh why we could not help her children, it burned me up. I was a rookie at this. Who was I to be making these decisions that would result in a kid in Vietnam gaining access to a school, while we told this mother in Bangladesh that our best answer was "not yet."

We made plans to add at least two more countries in 2002 and 2003. Several of our funders told me that we were crazy. "You have barely launched in two countries, you are only a few years old, and now you're thinking about additional countries?" One donor even threatened to withdraw his funding if we did not "stick to our knitting" and remain in just Nepal and Vietnam. I tried to explain: "With all due respect, three years ago we knew next to nothing about working in Vietnam and Nepal, and now you are not only praising our work, you are writing an annual check for $20,000 to fund it. I need to ask you if you'll give us a similar vote of confidence to go into other countries that need Room to Read. I promise you that we will study each opportunity carefully and that we won't make any capricious decisions. But the world needs these programs. These kids do not get a second chance. If I follow your advice to wait five more years before launching any other Room to Read countries, then the kids who are now five years old will be ten. They may have missed their entire primary education. Please, can you trust me? Erin and I know what we are doing, we are hiring smart staff, and we spend money wisely." He agreed and pulled out his checkbook.

In 2002, we launched Cambodia as our third country. The nation had a desperate need to rebuild educational infrastructure that had been decimated by the Khmer Rouge. Cambodia's genocidal murderers had burned down 80 percent of the schools and killed 90 percent of the teachers. Getting children back into school would be one way to help life return to some semblance of normalcy.

Despite Room to Read's limited resources, Erin and I decided to leap in. We both knew the horrors of Cambodia's past from travels there and were both passionate about playing a role in the country's redevelopment back from the Pol Pot–imposed "Year Zero." We were concerned whether donors would show up with their checkbooks to help finance our aggressive growth plan, but took the philosophy of Boxer the horse, from *Animal Farm,* that all things were possible if the protagonist vows, "I will work harder."

As if launching in a third country were not enough, we were also being encouraged by numerous businessmen of Indian descent to launch Room to Read India. Sabeer Bhatia, a man famous in the "nonresident Indian" (NRI) community for having been a co-founder of Hotmail and then selling it to Microsoft for $425 million, challenged me one day over lunch. As we drank tea and enjoyed the view of San Francisco Bay from his lofty Pacific Heights terrace, he threw out a scary statistic: "The United Nations estimates that by the year 2020, half the world's illiterate population will live in India. So unless you have an India strategy, you don't really have a strategy for world education."

All of these ambitious growth plans would, of course, come to nothing without capital. Thankfully, we had quite a few rainmakers helping to connect us to wealthy donors. This included Hilary Valentine, who had decided that in addition to being a school donor in Nepal, she would become a fund-raiser for us. This was part of the power of the Adopt-a-Project model. Once someone like Hilary saw how much good could be done for so little money, and had proof that we'd deployed her money wisely, she wanted to introduce her friends to the opportunity.

She started by hosting a fund-raising event on a Friday evening in early 2003, shortly after our Cambodia launch. The venue, the Alpine Hills Tennis and Swim Club, lies amid the sun-scorched hills of Silicon Valley. It's an understated club, but as I walked in, I could not help but think that the cost of each German luxury car in the parking lot could probably finance five schools in Nepal. I had to remind myself that my newest little mental game—fantasizing about turning luxury items into Third World educational projects—was quite annoying to others. A friend of mine put it best: "I could show up in a hot new pair of Manolo Blahniks and you would not say that I looked cute. You'd be too busy thinking about how the price of my shoes would fund two years of a girl's scholarship."

We had high hopes for the evening. Hilary and two of her friends on the host committee had invited a moneyed crowd with a strong philanthropic bent. They had identified the heavy hitters and sent me briefing notes in advance. During the cocktail hour, I was walked around the room and introduced to the biggest fish.

Shortly before I started my presentation, Hilary gave me a pep talk, "Okay, I've done my part. Now it's up to you. If your slide show and talk are good, you'll easily make $20,000 or $30,000 from this crowd. Don't screw it up!" she said with a sly smile.

This made me a bit nervous, but also gave me a surge of energy. If I could nail this, we would be able to say yes to many more villages and hopefully make strides in getting Room to Read Cambodia off the ground. Showtime!

I began my slide show talking about why I had left Microsoft and what I had experienced during the transition. Many people in the business world have a fantasy about leaving their job to do something that is more meaningful to them personally, but there can be huge constraints, from financial to societal. I said that even though I was living on far less money, there was a "karmic payback," at which point I brought up slides of Nepalese and Vietnamese students eagerly reading books, of several of our newest school projects, including three new kindergartens in Vietnam, and of smiling girls the day they started school on Room to Read–sponsored scholarships. I used the shots of the girls to transition to our dreams for expansion.

"We currently run the Room to Grow girls' scholarship program in Nepal and Vietnam. We are hoping to expand it to Cambodia. There is a huge problem with girls orphaned by the Khmer Rouge being sold into prostitution. Our hope is to instead keep teenagers in school so that they develop self-confidence and an opportunity to work in a good job. We have identified one hundred girls whom we would like to put on scholarship, but we lack the funds. I have three months to raise the money before the school year starts. If we succeed, it means that these girls' destiny will be forever changed by the lifelong gift of education."

"How much do you need?" a voice boomed from the back of the room.

Don Listwin, a Silicon Valley legend, had thrown out the question. Dressed nattily in blue blazer, jeans, and loafers without socks, he looked like a cross between *Wired* magazine, *Esquire,* and the J.Crew catalog. He had been the number two executive at Cisco, then left to become CEO of Openwave, a company he took public. As though one fortune by age 45 had not been enough, he now had a second. He was known as a generous investor in areas ranging from education to cancer research. I'm not used to being interrupted in the middle of presentations, so I asked him to repeat the question.

"I said that I want to know *exactly* how much money you need to get all one hundred girls in school."

This, after all, is Silicon Valley, where deals are made quickly, and Don didn't want to focus on the concept; he wanted to move straight to the practical execution.

I answered that it took $250 per year to put a girl in Cambodia on scholarship. In total, we needed $25,000 per year, or $150,000 over the life of the scholarships.

"Great, thanks," Don roared. "I'm going to interrupt our regularly scheduled slide show with an announcement, and a challenge. There are more than fifty of you here tonight. For every one of you who sponsor a scholarship, and you have to write the check tonight, I will match you, dollar-for-dollar, girl-for-girl, year-for-year. You fund fifty and I will fund fifty. We need to do this. No excuses."

There were audible gasps, and some chuckles from people who knew Don well. He was known to be generous and also for challenging others to match his example.

Don was not yet done throwing down gauntlets.

"Furthermore, there are some people here who used to work for me at Cisco, and a few who work for me now at Openwave. I want them to pay attention to this next part. For every school that one of you underwrites tonight, I will match you school-for-school."

Dramatic pause.

"How about it, Mark?"

Mark, sitting one row in front of Don, emits a nervous laugh. He pauses, probably doing the math on how much money he's made while working for Don through some flush years in Silicon Valley. Realizing that $8,000 is probably a rounding error, he replies, "Count me in, Don!"

"Great. And how about you, Bill?" Don's eyes are laser-locked on his next target.

Poor Bill. He not only has Don's pressure on him, but also Mark's example.

"Count me in too, Don."

With that, Don smiles at his ability to close deals and nods in my direction to say that I may continue.

My mouth is agape. My brain is running the numbers. I think that in less than two minutes we've received over $150,000 of commitments. I want to bottle this moment, place it on dry ice, and preserve it forever. It's not all that often that someone you barely know not only does your job for you, but does it better.

"Okay, Don, but before I go on, let me repeat what I think you just committed to."

"Don't repeat it—that will only depress me."

He gets his laugh, and I resume the slide show completely relaxed that there is no pressure on me to close the deal. All I need to

do is finish quickly so that fifty people can rush to the donation table and sponsor scholarships.

Thankfully, they do. Don's challenge is met, then exceeded.
Dina, who had worked for Don at Cisco, writes a check that is
"much larger than I had planned, just to stick it to Don." Another
donor quietly and without fanfare hands me a $20,000 check and
tells me to allocate it wherever we need it most.

It's the most successful night in our young history. Eager to celebrate, the host committee and I head out for a late dinner. My head
is spinning as I crunch the numbers. I feel as though our little charity has just stepped up to a new level. Hilary orders champagne, and
we toast what, to us, feels like one of the best deals in the history of
Silicon Valley.

POSTSCRIPT: HILARY AND DON, THOUGH NOT DATING AT THE TIME OF
the event, soon were. They were married in June 2005.

In honor of their wedding, I endowed a girl's scholarship. I did
not, however, ask Don to match me.

CHAPTER 20

THE STUDENTS OF CAMBODIA

Shortly after the most successful fund-raising event in our history, I had the pleasure of journeying to Cambodia to see our programs at work. I was excited to make the connection between the money that had come in, and the students and communities that were benefiting from these fund-raising events.

Friends have asked me many times how I keep up the insane pace of travel, public speaking, and fund-raising events. I remember a particular week when I spoke at events on four successive nights in Washington, D.C., New York, Boston, and Vancouver. After too many late nights catching up on e-mail before spending the day traveling, I arrived in Vancouver. It quickly became apparent that the grueling pace was taking its toll. There was one chapter volunteer, Lynda Brown, whom I had always thought of as a rare combination of beauty, sincerity, and intelligence. So it was exciting to run into her, and having just made what I thought was a decent speech, I confidently asked her to join me on the dance floor. She smiled and asked in a concerned tone, "You look pretty tired, especially in the eyes; are you sure you'll be able to stay awake through an entire dance?"

Why do I work these long hours and put so much of my

personal life on hold to focus so intently on Room to Read? Some people may not understand it and may wonder if I'm simply one-dimensional. I don't believe that is the case. Throughout life, I have always had hobbies and a lot of friends. I still try to make time for each, but over the years of building this organization I'll admit that I've devoted less time to nonwork activities. It's made some friends mad at me, and my work hours and travel schedule have hijacked some otherwise-promising romantic relationships. At times, the long hours and the constant feeling of being behind have made me less enthusiastic about life than I'd like to be as I struggle through yet another morning on little sleep.

So why do it? Every time I ask myself that question, or lose faith in my life choices, I book myself on a flight to one of the countries where Room to Read works. Seeing the villages we are helping provides an adrenaline rush and a quick end to my existential angst. Shortly after Lynda's comment, I decided it was time to visit Cambodia and catch up on our progress.

HISTORY AND FATE HAVE NOT BEEN KIND TO THE PEOPLE OF CAMBODIA. The threats to their well-being seem to have come in waves over the last fifty years—exploitation by their French colonizers, collateral bombing by U.S. forces during the war in Vietnam, and the brutal regime of the Khmer Rouge. The genocide perpetrated by this nihilistic force eliminated nearly 2 million of the country's 15 million citizens. Picture New York City without Manhattan and that approximates what happened to this desperately poor nation.

The survivors faced a reality that must have made them question how lucky they were—the country had a ruined economy, little infrastructure, over a million orphans, and no functioning government. This scene may sound like something out of ancient history, but it actually describes the situation in the early 1990s, when I made my first trip to the country. I was, as expected, saddened by the situation, but also impressed with the spirit of the Cambodian people. That first trip started my lifelong love affair with the people of this ravaged nation.

The Cambodian spirit is resilient. Life has thrown at them most of the bad experiences one can dream up, and many that I'd rather not imagine. Yet they still work hard, rising each day before the sun to plant or harvest their rice fields, to attend school, or to run small businesses. On my first trip to Cambodia's capital, Phnom Penh, I sat on my hotel's small front balcony eating fried eggs and toast and was immediately surrounded by young children hoping to make some money. One boy offered to shine my shoes, while another presented me with an array of foreign newspapers ranging from the *Süddeutsche Zeitung* to *USA Today* to the *Financial Times.* How he had gotten his hands on these were beyond me. Always one to encourage entrepreneurship, I paid one boy for three newspapers including an Italian one that I could not read, while the other boy happily shined my flip-flops.

I thought of these boys several years later, in 2001, when Erin and I were researching possibilities for further expansion. Cambodia seemed a natural place for us to work, given the lack of educational infrastructure, the strong work ethic, and the Confucian- and Buddhist-influenced respect for education. The Khmer Rouge had burned down the majority of the schools and killed 90 percent of the teachers in their war against the educated. One could be branded an intellectual, and murdered, simply for wearing glasses. Erin and I decided that our response to this must be one of forward-thinking optimism: we would help Cambodian communities to build schools and libraries. That which had been destroyed needed to be replaced. We spent little time talking about it. As usual, we just dove in.

By the spring of 2003 we had hired a local team and opened an office in Phnom Penh. I made my third trip to the country to see our first projects in the company of the new team.

My first few days were spent peacefully in the capital city of Phnom Penh with its wide, French-influenced boulevards. As in my previous trips, microbusinessmen hung out in front of my guesthouse. This time, rather than offering shoeshines or newspapers, the boys were cajoling me into taking a ride on their *motos.*

During my five days in Phnom Penh, I had a morning routine with these young entrepreneurs. As I walked onto the front porch of the Renaksi Guest House along the river, I would smile and wave to the group, look at my watch, and count from the second hand . . . one, two, three, four, five . . . at which point a gaggle of *motos* would screech to a stop in a cloud of dust, just inches from my feet. "Where are you going?" "Are you going for coffee?" "I will take you." "I took you yesterday, you remember me?" The shouts went up, each boy smiling while also negotiating hard to be the victor for my meager $1 fare. The five-minute ride to the aptly named Java coffeehouse and art gallery, where I spent the first hour of each day beneath an underachieving ceiling fan writing in my journal, might be their only business of the day.

I felt bad choosing only one driver. Each clearly wanted the business, and there were more *motos* out front than guests at the hotel. So each day I chose a different driver and wondered at what point they would catch on and no longer say, "You remember me? I took you yesterday."

One morning, as the sun rose and began to heat the city toward the expected high of 101 degrees, I asked my driver about his background. What were his dreams for his life and his business?

"Before 1995, I speak no English. I speak a little bit of French only, but no English. But now every day I learn. Every day I drive *moto,* I learn English."

I told him that his English was impressive. I asked if he had a family.

"Yes, I have two children. Eleven years old and seven. Both are boys. I tell them that they must study and learn more than their father learned. My education was interrupted by the Pol Pot regime. My sons, they have opportunity for education. I tell them to keep studying. I tell my oldest son, 'You work hard and I will buy you a nice watch.' He did well at school, so he got a watch. Now the younger brother, he is jealous, and he is studying hard, so now I want to also give him one because his grades are also good. Someday they will have a better life than me, maybe work for the government or in the office of a business. But they will only do that if they study."

We pulled up in front of the Java coffeehouse. I wanted to turn my wallet over to the guy so that his sons could have the best education possible. I remembered my friend Vu in Vietnam, and his pride, and counseled myself not to do anything obnoxious. I told the driver that he was a smart man to have learned English so thoroughly, and that his sons were lucky to have such a good father. I doubled his fare, to $2, and asked him to apply the extra dollar toward his younger son's watch.

The hope that comes through education, the belief that in schooling lies the key to a brighter tomorrow—those are ubiquitous throughout so much of the developing world. When I observe Cambodian parents smile and look wistful as they talk about the life they hope their children will have, I am driven to continue to work insane hours and do whatever it takes to help them achieve this dream.

THE NEXT MORNING I HAD TO BREAK THE NEWS TO THE GANG OF *MOTO* drivers that I was leaving town for a few days. The Room to Read Cambodia team was taking me to the opening ceremonies of our first two computer rooms in the remote province of Kompong Cham.

We left Phnom Penh at 7:30 to begin the long drive three hours to the northeast. An hour into the journey, Dim Boramy, our country director, treated me to a breakfast of noodle soup at a roadside stand. Dozens of Cambodians squatted on small plastic stools, steam rising from the large bowls that cost 40 cents with meat, 30 cents without. Nobody talked, and the air was filled with a chorus of slurping noises. I recalled my mother's loud protestations at this mealtime offense during my childhood, thought, 'What the heck, I'm an adult now,' and slurped more loudly than was necessary. Boramy then topped me, so I one-upped him. As far as breakfast conversation, it was not overly mature, but it made Boramy much less intimidated by his first road trip with the CEO.

Two hours later we arrived at Tong Slek Secondary School, where a dozen teachers and several hundred students were waiting to initiate the first computer lab ever built in this part of Cambodia. During the preceremony tour, I noted that every monitor, keyboard, and mouse was covered in protective wrappings against the dust. I caught Boramy's eye and nodded toward a cot and blanket set up in the corner. He asked the group of teachers clustered around us about this. A dark-haired teacher in his late 20s explained that the school was waiting for a lock for the door, and bars for the window. Until this security was in place, the teachers were each spending a night sleeping in the lab. I was impressed and made a mental note to share the story with Bill Draper, who had told me that the only aid projects that worked were the ones where the local people felt ownership.

My musings were interrupted by a small boy. He approached boldly and announced to me in perfect English, "Thank you for Room to Read. My dream is to be a businessman." With that, he handed me a drawing (see photo insert).

I thanked him and asked if I could keep the drawing. He nodded, shook my hand like the businessman he dreamed of becoming, and melted back into the crowd. My thoughts quickly turned 3,000 miles northwest, to Nepal, where a seventh-grade girl had written a note about *her* new computer room: "Thank you for this wonderful machine inside which the world is hidden." These labs held such promise for students who had previously had no connection from their remote villages to the outside world. These schools were now becoming, through our work, a powerful combination of low-tech libraries where students could fall in love with books and high-tech computer labs that would eventually allow them access to all of the world's knowledge.

The headmaster interrupted my musings. The ceremony was about to start. In the schoolyard were crowded hundreds of children, including 25 girls who were receiving scholarships from Room to Read. After warmly welcoming the village elders and the Room to Read team, the headmaster spoke:

"It is unheard of for a rural area to receive an investment like this. It's always the city people who have these opportunities. Please tell your donors that we are so very happy today, because now our children can compete with any other students and don't have to leave our village to have a good education. We tell the parents, especially those with girls—don't let your daughters become prostitutes or drop out of school. If they stay until grade nine, they will learn English, they will learn computers, and they will have a better life and more opportunity."

A female teacher then stood up. It's rare for women in these rural communities to speak in public. It appeared to be spontaneous on her part, as the headmaster looked a bit startled. With intense passion, she spoke about the lab from the women's perspective:

"The girls are always overlooked in our society. But Room to Read has trained female teachers like me to understand computers. You did not just train the male teachers. So now we women who have learned computers have shown that we are also deserving, and that we can teach the children these new skills.

"Also, you have required that girls have to have the same access to this lab as the boys. That is going to change how girls in this province view themselves, and how they are treated by others. I have only one request for you, Mr. John. The trainer you sent here to teach the teachers is good and helpful, but we do not yet feel that we know enough. We would like to ask if he can stay for one more month."

I asked the trainer, a 19-year-old whiz kid we had hired from a computer training center in the city, if he was okay with this idea. He nodded excitedly and gazed at the teachers as though they were family. I then asked Boramy, quietly, how much we were paying the trainer. The sum: $25 per month. I told the teacher that this was something I was unable to decide, and that Boramy was the country director in charge of all decisions. Boramy was trying to look serious, but a smile was breaking across his face. He said yes, in both Khmer and English. Twice. The teachers applauded, and I felt a strong conviction in my gut that we had made the right decision to launch our programs in this country.

With that, we all walked over to cut the red ribbon on the door to the computer lab that was part of a brighter future for Cambodia. The students, without wasting a nanosecond, ran into the room, eager to start learning this new technology.

I wanted to learn more about our scholarship girls. The headmaster introduced me to Nam Sreyny. A tender and shy 16, her early education was cut short due to financial hardships at home. Her father had died two years earlier while serving in the army. The government had offered neither explanation for his death nor any compensation. Nam and her mother were now scratching out a meager existence on a small plot of rented farmland.

There were two obstacles to Nam attending school, both economic. Her mother could not afford the $5 monthly fee, and the nearest secondary school was 20 miles from their home. Even a bicycle would not solve this problem (unless we taught Nam to "be like Lance"), so she was forced to drop out after grade six.

Fortunately, the Room to Read Cambodia team had learned about her situation during a routine visit with the village's teachers. She had always gotten good grades and enjoyed her studies. She was described as being shy in public, but not at all reserved when attacking a book or her math homework. The local team offered her a scholarship. In addition to paying for her school uniform, shoes, a book bag, and school supplies, a stipend was paid to one of the teachers to allow Nam Sreyny to board with her during the week. And Nam Sreyny did get her bicycle and on weekends goes home to help her mother tend to the farm and its animals.

CHAPTER 21

THE NETWORK GOES INTO OVERDRIVE

F ORTUNATELY, ROOM TO READ'S NETWORK OF VOLUNTEERS CONTIN- ued to grow in lockstep with our programs. By 2005, we had added chapters in Atlanta, San Diego, and Washington, D.C. International chapters had started in Milan, Paris, and Sydney.

A spirited competition sprang up to be the chapter raising the most funding. It started gradually, when Chicago raised $75,000 in an evening, and the New York chapter vowed to beat them. They did, upping the ante to $82,000. A few weeks later, in November of 2004, the San Francisco team planted their flag by generating over $90,000 at a "Reading Room" event with facsimiles of four libraries (from Nepal, Cambodia, Vietnam, and India), one in each corner of the room. Within weeks, the London chapter hosted a private dinner for high-net-worth individuals who collectively pledged over $100,000. It was all done in a spirit of friendly competition, and it was fun to watch the mails fly around the world as the bar continued to be raised.

The Hong Kong chapter treated the British record as though it were made to be broken. Our chapter leaders jokingly told me, "The Brits take forever to make decisions. Here in Hong Kong, we move quickly. We'll definitely get the crowd to donate more than $100,000 at our next event."

I asked when their next event would be, and they replied with a casual "When can you be here?"

Within six weeks, I was once again on a trans-Pacific flight, wondering when this pace of travel would kill me. As with our initial Boston event, I was taking this one on faith. The only difference was that the flight was more than twice as long. Our previous Hong Kong chapter leader had moved to Singapore, and we had an almost entirely new team. I had met two of the chapter leaders, Robin and Robert, for breakfast. Grand total of time spent together: two hours. The third chapter leader, Fiona, I had met the previous summer in a café in Louangphrabang, Laos. After she'd asked what I did for a living, she'd signed on to do whatever she could to help raise money for our impending Laos expansion. Grand total of time spent together: one dinner.

I was, quite literally, living on a wing and a prayer.

The Hong Kong event was held at One Bar and Grill, a trendy open space of wood floors and polished marble. After presenting my slide show, I announced that the Hong Kong team wanted to beat the Brits, who currently held the fund-raising record. The target was $125,000. Who was willing to help us?

Three people yelled out to me that they would donate immediately. "I'll endow a school for $10,000." "I'll do $2,500 for a ten-year girl's scholarship." "I'll give $1,000, and my employer matches charity donations." Three more people shouted that they would endow long-term scholarships. A guy I'd briefly met earlier held up five fingers and mouthed, "Five."

"Five hundred?" I asked.

"No, five thousand."

As our guests yelled out their numbers, my mental calculator put us at over $75,000. Just then, Jacques Kemp, the CEO of ING's Asia Pacific headquarters, announced that they would donate $70,000. Yes, we had beaten our goal!

But there was no way to announce this, and to do so would have been counterproductive. People were still yelling out numbers. Two more offered to endow schools, and another said that his family foundation would donate $15,000. It was as if we had a hundred versions of Don Listwin ("Count Me In, Don") in the room. All of them had traveled in developing Asia, had seen the poverty, and had wanted to do something. Tonight, they responded to our solution.

Other guests who were more diffident about their philanthropic giving made their way to the donation tables. The final tally: $330,000! It had been a philanthropic feeding frenzy. The team took a photo to share with the other chapters to let them know that Hong Kong was now "wearing the crown."

OVER THE YEARS WE'D HEAR FROM DONORS AND VOLUNTEERS WHO stayed abreast of our progress via our Web site (www.roomtoread .org) and quarterly newsletters. My phone would ring with updates from the open road from the global travelers who supported Room to Read. I'd hear at least annually from Bruno Rodi, the Italian Swiss climber who'd decided at Everest base camp to endow two schools in Nepal. He'd be on a business trip to India, or at his home in Montreal, or cross-country skiing to the north pole with his two sons. He was like a philanthropic version of Where's Waldo?

One night in June of 2003, about a year after Bruno had originally made contact with me, I was having dinner with friends. I usually have a cardinal rule: never answer a phone call during a social meal. But on this evening, when my phone rang, something told me that I had to take this call, even though I could not tell from caller ID who it was. I excused myself and left the table.

"Hello, John, it's Bruno Rodi. I'm calling you from Kathmandu."

"Hi, Bruno. It's nice to hear from you. To what do I owe the pleasure of a phone call from Nepal?"

"Well, three days ago I was standing on the summit of Everest. John, this year I made it. Last year I was very disappointed, and the only thing that made me feel better about not summiting was that Alison talked me into building two schools. And now, to celebrate being on top of Everest, I want to endow two more schools in Nepal. Can you send me the same information as last year, and I will have the money wired to you?"

Amazing. Bruno kept pushing the limits, both in life and in giving. Despite my lack of a pop-chart voice, I wanted to sing and shout on this one. Smiling, I returned to the dinner table, eager to explain to my friends that this had been a call worth taking.

NOT EVERYONE IN THE ROOM TO READ NETWORK WAS A SUCCESSFUL global industrialist. During the same month that Bruno called me from Kathmandu, I received an e-mail from Tennessee outlining how a slightly younger donor wanted to get involved:

To: john@roomtoread.org
From: Kapila Devkota
Re: We Want to Build a School

June 19, 2003

John Wood
Chairman, Room to Read
The Presidio
P.O. Box 29127
San Francisco, CA 94129
Dear John:

We read about your Room to Read project in Suskera (a Web site for Nepali-Americans) last October and were very impressed. We have a daughter named Kripali who is eight years old. She loves to read. She just completed second grade, and so far, she has read over 500 books. She wants to buy books all the time. After knowing about your project, we informed Kripali about it. We suggested her not to buy as many books as she would want for herself, instead save the money to create more meaningful and long-lasting opportunity to other less privileged children in Nepal to read. As Kripali has access to computers and good libraries, she could easily do so without compromising her desire to read. Since then she has been saving her "pocket money" for a Room to Read project. It is very exciting to see our daughter engaged in such a good cause.

This year, during her summer break, we have asked Kripali to focus on raising funds from our friends and families. We are helping her, in every possible way, to get the initial funds for the project, prior to her returning to school for another session. In our understanding, we have to raise $8,000 for one school. We are optimist[ic] about collecting that amount by the end of August 2003.

We therefore request you to educate, and advise us as to whether we are moving in the right direction, and if there is anything specific that you expect us to do or to focus on. Please let us know.

Hoping to hear from you soon, and looking forward to working with you for this cause.

Thank you.

Sincerely,

Kapila Devkota

Girija Gautam

I was amazed and in awe when I read this mail. "This girl has seriously cool parents," I thought, as I pictured them being actively engaged in helping her learn the joy of reading, and the satisfaction of service to others.

I forwarded the mail to a dozen of our most dedicated volunteers to let them share in a heartwarming story. And then it dawned on me how lucky I am, to be working in a role that provides so many examples of basic human kindness. I have a near constant interaction with people who believe that in education lies independence, self-sufficiency, a better life, and progress for humanity. Best of all, they are willing to take action, rather than sitting around talking about the problem. Sometimes I get so caught up in the day-to-day parts of running the organization that I forget how extraordinary this network of supporters and volunteers is. To Kripali and her parents, I wanted to simply say thank you for the reminder.

EVERYDAY HEROES:
KRIPALI'S NEXT SCHOOL

The school in Nepal sponsored by Kripali was finished in 2003. We sent photos of the students and teachers standing proudly in front of the new building to the family. Her parents e-mailed me back immediately to say how happy they were to see the results of Kripali's read-a-thon. They also asked if I could call them in order to speak with Kripali. "You are her hero," they said, "and it would mean so much if she could talk to you. Also, she has an idea that she wants to share with you."

I was quite nervous about calling. If a small child views you as a hero, well you really don't want to screw it up. I wrote myself some briefing notes for the call, as though preparing for a meeting with Bill Gates.

Her voice at the end of line was shy and quiet. I thanked her for the work she had done raising money and told her that so many hundreds of students could now have a better life through the education they'd receive at the new school. She was still quiet, so I went to the second of my "talking points," telling her that everyone at the San Francisco office knew about her and was impressed by her ability to raise so much money. Her voice then broke through at a slightly louder volume: "I want to do more."

I reminded her that she had already done a lot, certainly more than most adults. But she repeated that she wanted to do more.

At this point, her father, listening in on the second line, explained that Kripali already had plans to raise money for a second school. The family would be attending the annual conference for Nepali-Americans living in the southeastern United States, and that Kripali was planning to sell raffle tickets. She had already convinced local merchants to donate a microwave oven and a DVD player, and her goal was to have at least ten prizes. She'd sell raffle tickets at $10 each and hoped to get each of the 800 people attending the conference to buy at least one.

"You're going to go up onstage, aren't you, Kripali?" her father asked.

She assented in a quiet voice.

"She is nervous about being up in front of so many people, but we have convinced her that the easiest way to sell tickets will be to get onstage right before the keynote speech. I've assured her that I will be up there with her. We'll be back in touch afterwards to let you know how it went."

I decided that heroism could be a reciprocal thing. I was in awe of Kripali and her parents and promised to buy some raffle tickets. I hung up the phone and shared the latest installment of this inspiring story with my team. Erin jokingly suggested that we "call Harvard and tell them to save a spot in the class of 2018 for Kripali."

CHAPTER 22

DEMOCRACY IN ACTION IN INDIA

Bᴙ 2004 OUR INDIA PROGRAM HAD GROWN FASTER THAN WE HAD EX-pected. Quick results and rapid growth were needed, given the scale of illiteracy in India. Picture the combined populations of the United States, Canada, and Mexico, all without the ability to read or write, and you have an idea of the size of the work we had cut out for us.

We hired our country director, Sunisha, away from CARE, where she had been working for several years in their education sector. Just as in Cambodia and Nepal, Erin and I had found in India great people who were passionate about education and working in larger aid organizations. We were able to convince them to jump ship because some of these groups were slower-moving than was ideal. Boramy, our country director in Cambodia, told us when he joined that the general belief among foreign NGOs in the capital city of Phnom Penh was that "Cambodians are not yet ready to run their own organizations." In his case, and in Sunisha's, we offered them an opportunity not only to drive the car, but to propel it quickly to high speeds.

During her first year running Room to Read India, Sunisha hired a great staff and forged partnerships with several NGOs. She looked for organizations running schools that lacked a proper library and quickly forged agreements to set up over 300 bilingual Hindi/English libraries. Within two years of our start in India, nearly 100,000 children had access to a vast collection of books. Children could read about Gandhi and their country's struggle for independence, learn how magnets work, or simply enjoy a classic India folktale about a young boy and his desire to one day own the world's fastest horse.

One of the first places we began working in India was in the desert state of Rajasthan. This section of northwest India is one of the poorest areas in a desperately poor country. As in much of the developing world, the parents and the government have all placed a great deal of faith in education as the ticket out of poverty. Yet, as is too often the case, they lacked even small amounts of money to buy or produce books, shelving, chairs, and desks. As a result, Sunisha and her team had many more requests for new libraries than they could possibly handle.

They said yes to as many schools as possible. In Rajasthan's capital of Jaipur, Room to Read formed a partnership with a local NGO named Digantar to set up reading rooms in five government primary schools. The children were enthusiastic, and the new facilities proved popular. Plans were made to increase the size of the collections, as children eagerly read every title they could get their hands on and desired more and more new titles.

At the end of the first year, as summer holiday approached, several of the parents asked whether the library could stay open. During a community meeting, several of them stated that during the six-week summer holiday their children spent most of their time playing around the village. Wouldn't it be better if they could also spend some of that free time enhancing their minds?

As happens too often in this world, a bureaucrat found a reason to say no. The school management was reluctant to give the keys to the school to the staff of Digantar, our NGO partner. Granted, they had trusted Digantar and Room to Read to fund and set up the local library, but were now reluctant to allow any outsiders to run the school library. We did not understand the perceived risks. Even if the library had been poorly run during the summer, it was certainly better than having the library shut down. In my mind I ran through visions of that locked cabinet in Nepal back in 1998, and the teachers' fear of books being destroyed causing them to lock them up in a cabinet.

Fortunately, the brilliant staff at Digantar came up with a solution and found alternative sites. In the village of Kundanpura, for example, they convinced the powers that be at the village temple to be the temporary summer hosts of the library. The entire collection of books was moved from the school to the temple, and children were allowed to read books in the courtyard. This temple, in a central part of the village, was easily accessible to all of the school's children. Best of all, there was open space outside the temple where children could also play. Thus, for the six weeks of summer holiday the students would be able to exercise both their minds and their bodies.

Within a week, 40 to 50 eager young readers from the primary school were visiting the temporary library each day. The village also had a private school, where those parents wealthy enough to avoid the government school would send their children. Once these students heard about the library from their friends, the morning queue for books got even longer. Soon there were 70 to 80 students coming in each day. The local library, just like the ones set up by Carnegie in the United States, was proving to be a spot where people from different socioeconomic classes would intermingle. There were no barriers to accessing knowledge; in the library, caste, gender, and financial resources were irrelevant.

When the vacation period came to an end, a group of ten students from the private school asked Gajanand, the librarian, if the library would continue during the school year. He shook his head and shared the news that the library would now shift back into the government school, and that the private school students would not have access to it. Complaints filled the air as the students, upset about having this newfound enjoyment of books yanked away from them, lobbied to change Gajanand's mind. He explained that it was not his decision, but instead lay with the school's administration, which had proven to be less than willing to think outside the box.

The next day the private school students showed up again and proposed an alternative solution. Perhaps a similar library could be set up in their school. Gajanand, weary of being the bearer of bad news, told them that Room to Read did not typically support the establishment of libraries in private schools.

The students were still not out of options. Perhaps the public school's library could be opened up after regular school hours. The private school kids could then show up in the early evening, before dinnertime. Gajanand, who by now probably appeared in the students' eyes like a Rajasthani version of Dr. No, told them that he had a second job, running a neighboring village's library, during the evening hours.

The students were not finished. The next day they showed up again, this time with a petition. Their letter, which was friendly and fair, requested that Gajanand consider supporting a library at their school or starting a library in the evening hours in their village.

Kundanpura Village
Date: 22 June 2005
Namaste,

Gajanand-ji, we get to read lot of good books in your library. Gajanand-ji, you tell us lots of wonderful stories and also play with us. You teach us drawing as well. Thirty children [from our school] come to your library. Our schools will open from 1st July after the summer vacations, we request you to change the timings of the library to 4pm to 6pm in the evening so that we can also come to the library in the evening after school hours. If you do not change the timing of the library then we won't be able to read wonderful and good books.

We are hoping that you will change the timings of the library as 4–6 in the evening or open library in our school.

Thank you.

Your obedient students,
Nikhil Karadiya
Suraj Chauhan
Class VII

Gajanand explained that he would have to gain approval from both Digantar and Room to Read for this, and that he was not optimistic about either organization's willingness to break the rules. Since he was impressed by the students zeal for libraries, he arranged a meeting with the principal of the private school. He too was eager to have a library and offered to make a teacher available to be trained in library management and to assume the same role that Gajanand had in assuring that the library was well run.

Upon hearing about the students and their passion for books, Sunisha and the Room to Read team in New Delhi decided to make an exception to their usual practice of working only in public schools. A large donation of Hindi and English books was made, with the promise of more books in subsequent years if the library was well run. The team at Digantar offered to train the teacher who would be running the library, and to monitor it to assure high quality and ease of access for the students.

In a distant and remote village in the deserts of Rajasthan, a small group of students experienced the benefits of a peaceful and respectful petition, and of perseverance. Our team learned that it's all right to occasionally bend the rules. And 300 additional students started the school year with access to a brand-new library.

CHAPTER 23

THE TSUNAMI

I HAD PLANNED FOR CHRISTMAS, 2004, TO BE A QUIET PERIOD OF REST after a hectic year. My travels during the year had taken me as far afield as Cambodia, Hong Kong, Singapore, London, and Ethiopia, and I had logged over 100,000 flight miles. It was time for a break, and my goal was to travel for pleasure rather than for work.

To celebrate the five-year anniversary of the official start of Room to Read, I did something quite unusual for me—scheduling an entire week of holiday. The last half decade was a blur of nonstop meetings, back-to-back phone calls, and mountains of e-mails to respond to at the end of each day. Erin and I had mapped out an aggressive growth plan for 2005, so my hope was to take some time off to catch my breath and return to the office ready to dive into the new year.

I first spent three days with friends at their beach house in San Diego, running at water's edge at low tide, cycling up the coast trailing far behind my friend Julie (a professional bike guide), and enjoying some of the best fajitas the city had to offer. Hearing Christmas carols while sitting in bright sunlight at an outdoor beach café was an odd, but welcome, juxtaposition. After San Diego, I headed to my sister's house, just outside of Boulder, Colorado. My parents were also planning to be there, so I had downloaded several gigabytes worth of photos of our new projects to share with them.

My first few days with the family were peaceful, and I counseled myself to stay off e-mail and enjoy a real vacation. I fed my passion for the outdoors with more hikes, long bike rides, and lazy afternoons with my niece and nephew getting wiped out in games of Uno. Unwound, relaxed, and ready to peel back another layer of stress, I received an alarming call from a friend. A tsunami had hit Asia, leaving a massive cut of destruction in its path.

After being totally switched off, I switched back on.

On CNN, BBC, and MSNBC were images of destruction that appeared apocalyptic. I knew that 24-hour news channels could sometimes overdo the "gloom and doom" thing, but there was no denying the images that were being broadcast hour after hour from Indonesia, Thailand, Sri Lanka, and other countries unfortunate enough to be situated along the Indian Ocean.

Thousands had been killed and the number was expected to go much higher. Entire villages had been washed into the ocean. Nothing had been spared—not private homes, nor hospitals, nor schools. Upon hearing that last reference, my mind began racing. Hundreds of schools wiped out. Thousands of orphans survived, but had few adults to help them rebuild their lives. Who would construct new schools and help the children get back to a normal life? As if to answer that question, I speed-dialed United Airlines from my cell phone to book an early flight home to San Francisco. The vacation was over.

THE NEXT DAY, DECEMBER 29, I LOGGED ON TO THE WIRELESS INTERNET at Denver's airport from my departure gate. I fired off an e-mail to my friend Bob Uppington, who ran a Sri Lanka–based educational charity called Shiva. I hoped he was safe and knew that if he was, then he'd be a good source of information from ground zero of the tsunami. The devastation relayed by the television networks seemed incomprehensible to me, and I hoped to get an unfiltered report from someone I trusted inside the country.

Several hours later I returned to a quiet office. We had a skeletal staff on board to handle the usual rush of end-of-year donations, and they seemed surprised to see me. I explained my intention to round up a few friends who would write checks to help out in the rebuilding of schools in tsunami-affected areas. Before I could send a single mail, I noticed that Bob had already replied to my message from the Denver airport. As I gazed out at the Golden Gate Bridge framed against a perfect and calm cobalt sky, I took a deep breath and opened his mail.

The news was even worse than I had feared. Preliminary estimates were that at least 200 villages had lost their schools in Sri Lanka alone. With the devastation in Indonesia of at least equal scale, one could picture a world that suddenly had a deficit of at least 500 schools. We also knew that the count would go higher once communities whose roads had been washed away could finally be reached.

Bob was planning to load a rented van full of food, water, and medical supplies and depart the next morning for Ampara District—an area on the east coast that had suffered particularly heavily. I wished him luck on his journey and encouraged him to "not be shy" in committing to school reconstruction projects. I knew that Shiva's budget was much smaller than ours and did not want him to feel constrained. If he visited ten villages that had lost schools, I did not want him to have to choose only one or two of them for support. So I typed frantically, hoping the message would reach him before he left for Ampara: "If you visit a village that has lost its school, tell them that we will find the money to rebuild it. Repeat as necessary. You have my commitment that I will help out as much as I can with funding."

It felt like the early days of Room to Read, when I had no idea where the money would come from, but knew in my gut that we would not rest until we were able to help these communities. And just like in the early days, I brewed a pot of coffee to prepare for a late night of e-mailing and calling potential donors to ask for their support.

MY CELL PHONE RANG EARLY THE NEXT MORNING. MICHELE, OUR NEWLY hired PR consultant, was calling with good news. She had managed to book me on CNN to talk about our plans to help rebuild schools in Sri Lanka.

I was a bit taken aback. I asked Michele how CNN had even heard we were doing work in Sri Lanka.

"I called them yesterday after getting your e-mail asking for leads on wealthy people who might be able to donate. I know a producer there, so I called and pitched you. They need Asia experts to discuss the impact of the tsunami, and the future of these communities. Once I pitched you, they said it sounded like a great fit, so you'll be on tomorrow or the day after for a live interview."

I protested that I was in way over my head on this one. I did not want to go on television in front of millions of people to talk about the tsunami when our plans were really vague. I had never even been to Sri Lanka and could not yet name a single village that we planned to help. My "war chest" for Sri Lanka was at a paltry $12,000. Indeed, were they to spring a surprise spelling bee on me, I might not even be able to spell *tsunami* correctly.

Michele quickly set the record straight for me. In her laconic yet firm Texas accent, she filled me in on the way things were:

"You covered the Asia region for Microsoft for five years, and you've run an Asia-focused charity for five years that has built more libraries than any charity on the continent. Like it or not, you're now an Asia expert, and this is a really good opportunity for you to tell millions of people about the great work your team is doing."

THE EVENING OF JANUARY 1 MIGHT BE THE IDEAL TIME TO APPEAR ON CNN. After a big night of partying the evening before, many millions are curled up on their sofas, remote control in one hand and cordless phone doing the dial-a-pizza thing in the other. Viewership tends to be much higher as a result, and the tsunami was still generating large spikes in CNN's ratings.

Knowing this made me even more nervous. I called my friend and neighbor Kim to ask if she'd pour me a Scotch to help calm my nerves. In just over an hour, over a million people would be listening to me describe a strategy that was, to put it mildly, embryonic and unformed. Room to Read had no people on the ground, no project sites identified, and at the time only a small amount of capital pledged.

Kim calmed me down. We talked through some potential questions as I sipped the Macallan on the rocks. She gave me a big hug of support as I walked out to the waiting CNN-sponsored Town Car.

Ten minutes later, we arrived at a San Francisco television studio darkened by holiday inactivity. The sole employee, a cameraman whose vacation had been interrupted by the randomness of news events, explained how things worked. Much to my surprise, I would not actually be able to see the CNN anchor during our interview. I would, instead, be staring at a wall. Although split-screen television interviews make it look as if the two talking heads were having a chat with the usual visual cues, the reality is quite different. My only connection to the anchor in Atlanta was an earpiece through which the questions would be delivered.

One other secret was soon revealed. The cameraman asked for my help in changing the large photograph that would appear as the backdrop behind me. A six-by-four-foot daytime cityscape of San Francisco was taken down, and in its place we hung one of the city postsunset, the lights of the Transamerica Pyramid twinkling in the dusk. You'd never know from watching the tape of my CNN appearance that I was not somewhere outside, a roof deck perhaps, with the city's buildings right behind me. In reality, five different backdrops were available, including one of the Golden Gate Bridge.

"Three minutes to air." My musings were interrupted and I scrambled to take my seat and get the earpiece ready. Carol Lin, the anchor, came on to introduce herself and said that we'd be on in sixty seconds. The next four minutes flew by too quickly for me to be nervous. Carol started by asking me about why I started Room to Read, and I breathed a sigh of relief that we were starting with an easy question to answer. We next discussed our plans for Sri Lanka, and when I thought we might be able to get started. The producers were then kind enough to point viewers to our Web site to make donations.

It was all over even before it began.

Within three seconds, my cell phone rang, with friends from Seattle saying how shocked they were to see my face on CNN. They also said that I needed a better choice of tie, but I had to hang up as Erin was calling on the other line. She and her husband were also surprised, and she said I had done really well. My phone continued to ring throughout the night; this was only a harbinger of things to come.

For the next several weeks every cell phone, landline, and fax machine in the office was in hyperdrive. An overwhelming number of CNN viewers wanted to know how they could help. Old friends called to say they were running fund drives within their companies. The angelic daughters of my good friends John and Lauren took advantage of a cold Seattle Saturday by opening a "Hot Chocolate for Tsunami Relief" stand. A high school student in Bethesda, Maryland, was planning a "Battle of the Bands" fund-raising event. Another friend e-mailed to say that she was putting Room to Read on the home page of her company, shopping.com, one of the most heavily trafficked electronic-commerce sites, and that they would be matching the first $25,000 of donations to Room to Read.

My favorite creative idea came from Parkgate, a Montessori primary school in London. Catherine, the energetic founder and headmistress of the school, called to say that her students had invented a new fund-raising technique. They offered their parents the opportunity to pay for what they called the Sponsored Silence. For £10 per hour, the parents could basically hit the Mute button on their children for the evening. Sales of this new luxury item were quite robust. I laughed as I thought about these kids having a much higher value per sale than my sailboat paintings.

We were blown away by the enthusiasm to help us get started in Sri Lanka, and also by the creativity shown by students. Children can be natural fund-raisers, and very entrepreneurial, if given the freedom to think creatively. I think they were also motivated because they would be helping other children to return to school.

The students would continue to inspire us in the days ahead. They were just getting started.

. . .

MEANWHILE, THE TEAM AT CNN HAD BEEN HAPPY WITH THE INTERVIEW and offered me a second appearance—this time on *CNN Headline News.* This promised even more exposure than the original interview, since the one-hour *Headline News* program was placed "into rotation" for six consecutive hours. Knowing that Kara, our office manager, was being overwhelmed with calls, I asked for her permission before saying yes. Fortunately, she had the interest of Sri Lankan kids at heart and said she'd work as many hours as necessary to handle the call volume.

I was more at ease for the second appearance, and as predicted, the multiple showings of the interview led to an even higher volume of calls. I walked into our office and noticed four employees talking on the phone, all frequently invoking words like *schools, tsunami,* and *Sri Lanka.* Our office felt like the Jerry Lewis telethon. I took as many of the calls as I could to help out and was moved by the spirit of generosity and the desire for immediate action. My friend Catherine called from London to say that instead of gifts for her upcoming birthday, she was requesting checks for Room to Read's Sri Lanka program. Julie Trell, a long-lost friend who now worked for the salesforce.com foundation, told me over the phone that her company would be matching any donations made through their site to Room to Read, even if the money came from someone who was not an employee and not a customer. I e-mailed this news to Steve, a longtime supporter from New York, and he immediately made a $25,000 donation.

In between juggling calls with teachers, parents, and donors, I welcomed Bella, our newest employee, to the team. She had been working for us part-time and starting today was transitioning to a full-time role in fund-raising. Having just returned from a quiet ski holiday in Whistler, she was a bit taken aback by the noise of the ringing phones and asked what was happening.

"Uh . . . well, while you were gone, we launched Room to Read Sri Lanka."

"No way."

"Yes, believe it or not, we did. And here's a stack of phone messages to prove it. Kara has been on the phone constantly, and every time she hangs up there are two messages that were left during the last call. We'll need to get you started immediately in giving direction to all the people who want to donate or raise funds."

"I can't believe it. I go away for seven days, and while I am gone, you guys launch a country! I guess I didn't have to worry about my transition."

"What do you mean?"

"I was afraid that transitioning from the equity markets to Room to Read would mean that I'd have to deal with a slower pace. You've nixed *that* worry."

THE NEXT CALL WAS FROM MY FRIEND AND NEIGHBOR KIM, ASKING WHAT she could do to help with the deluge. I proposed that she and her son's nanny, a hardworking 20-year-old named Melanie, spend the weekend in the office with me. We had over 100 schools requesting that we send them brochures and documentary DVDs, and an equal number of parents and teachers who had ideas for fund-raising campaigns, but who wanted feedback and needed to have their questions answered. So over the weekend, Kim, Melanie, Kim's 18-month-old son, Baker, and her black Labrador, Pakse, joined me in the office.

One of Kim's first calls was to the Rasch family in Maryland. Their ten-year-old, Jacob, together with his twelve-year-old Boston-based cousins, had designed a "tsunami wristband." Hoping to capitalize on Lance Armstrong's Livestrong bracelets, Jacob, David, and Danielle had designed a three-color band (blue for sky and water, yellow for sun, green for earth) with the words "Rebuild. Restore. Renewal—Tsunami Relief 2005." Their goal was to get the bands produced for less than $1, sell them for $3, and donate the profit to Room to Read. The three cousins had been on a joint family holiday in Miami on December 26 and had leapt into action at a speed that would have made any venture capitalist proud.

The cousins were initially driven to help but were not sure what to do. Jacob later told us, "We were watching CNN and seeing all the terrible things. We couldn't bear to watch it. We decided that we were going to make an effort [to help]. We didn't know what, we didn't know how, but we knew we were going to do something."

Within a day, they had their moneymaking idea and by the next evening their design concepts were being faxed from Miami to a wristband producer in Guangzhou, China.

They planned to place an initial order for 5,000 bands, which would produce $10,000 of profits. I asked Kim to call both sets of parents to ask if they'd be willing to do PR. To me, this initiative seemed to have all the perfect elements for a good press story—the tsunami, a positive response to it, youthful zeal, entrepreneurship, and a new and timely twist on the wristband craze. The parents immediately gave us their approval. When Kim said they must be proud of their children, they immediately shared credit with the teachers, the principal, and other parents.

I got Michele, our PR person, on the phone as soon as we had the green light. Because the cousins were in Boston and in Maryland, we decided to aim for the *Boston Globe* and the *Washington Post.* "Do you think you can get one of them?" I asked. Michele, in her understated but confident manner, informed me that she was confident that she could deliver both.

Within three days, the story of the entrepreneurial cousins ran in both newspapers. Now it was *their* turn to experience life as a call center. Schools up and down the East Coast were ringing to ask if they could place an order for tsunami bands. The request to the manufacturer was upped from 5,000 to 10,000, then 20,000, then 25,000 then 40,000, and still the phone kept ringing. An e-mail address—tsunamibands@aol.com—was set up. This in-box was soon clogged with over 200 messages from as far away as Hawaii and England. Soon the orders ran above 70,000 units. The hottest fashion trend among teenagers had been designed in less than 24 hours by three cousins not yet in their teens.

MEANWHILE, I WAS RUNNING AT A PACE EMULATING THAT OF THE cousins. On January 10 I hopped on Singapore Airlines flight #1, the midnight departure from San Francisco to Hong Kong. I had planned a round-the-world trip to gain media attention, and donor commitments, with stops planned in Hong Kong, Singapore, Zurich, and London. My board of directors, worried that I was burning out after working through the holidays nonstop, generously upgraded me to business class, on the theory that at least this way I'd get some sleep. Within minutes of takeoff my heavy head fell backward, and slumber overtook me for 12 hours of the 14-hour flight.

The board's decision proved to be prescient, as the blur of activity awaiting me in Hong Kong required me to have restored energy. Edelman, one of the world's leading PR agencies, had taken us on as a pro bono client and had overachieved by booking us three newspaper, one magazine, and two television interviews. In between, I took a phone call from a family foundation that wanted to donate $50,000 toward the rebuilding, and over a breakfast meeting a Hong Kong company chipped in $100,000.

But the most important meeting of the trip lay ahead, in Singapore, even though I did not yet realize it. Edelman's Singapore office had set up additional media interviews, and one of them proved important for our nascent efforts in Sri Lanka. The journalist writing the story, Suba Sivakumaran, told me that she admired our efforts to rebuild schools in the aftermath of the tsunami as she herself was originally from Sri Lanka. She then let slip an important piece of information—she was planning to take time off from work to return there as a volunteer and wanted to find a group with which she could make a difference.

I pounced. I encouraged her not to make any commitments until she'd talked to us about helping to get Room to Read off the ground. The tables quickly turned, as I went from interviewee to interviewer. She answered my questions about her background. Her family had left Sri Lanka shortly after she was born, due to political violence. They had emigrated to Australia, and after finishing high school she left for the UK to study at the London School of Economics. She then took an analyst position with Morgan Stanley and was now "killing time" before starting graduate school in the fall. She was obviously smart, as Columbia, Georgetown, and Berkeley were all competing for her with scholarship offers.

And what could I offer her? An unpaid position with an organization she had known for all of 45 minutes, that had yet to hire its first employee in Sri Lanka? And that was leaving out that we did not yet have a business license to work there, had zero contacts in the Ministry of Education, and had a headquarters that would truly be halfway around the globe.

What the heck, I thought, launching my pitch: "Look, I think you should talk to Erin, our chief operating officer, about getting involved with Room to Read in Sri Lanka. We need somebody to go there as soon as possible to represent us. We're currently working through Shiva, an NGO partner, but we need to have oversight on the ground and find other groups with whom we can forge relationships. I'll admit up front that we don't yet know what we are doing, but hopefully that will make it all the more alluring to you. We are not going to tell you what to do; we are instead going to ask you to figure it out. If you want a chance to help Sri Lanka, this could be it. We have an extraordinary amount of resources flowing in, so you will not be constrained in thinking big. And we have amazing teams in India and Nepal who will be close by, so they can mentor you along with Erin and the team in San Francisco. Think about it, okay, and I'll e-mail you later today and introduce you to Erin."

With that, Jason from Edelman was dragging me away from the coffee shop, on toward an interview at CNBC.

Erin made the call. She was impressed. Within a week, Suba was winging her way northwest to take up the unpaid position of interim country director for Room to Read Sri Lanka. Within a month, she had opened an office, fitted out a book warehouse, and hired our first staff.

MUCH OF OUR ORGANIZATION'S ETHOS AND VALUES CAN BE SEEN IN OUR initial response to the tsunami. True entrepreneurs are not afraid to declare to the world that they are going to fill a market gap or offer a new product or service, even if they are not yet entirely sure *how* they are going to do so. They simply take the leap.

In our case, the Room to Read team decided that if schools had been destroyed, then of course we most certainly had to determine a way to rebuild them. Did we know our exact strategy the day I went on CNN? No. But sometimes if you wait until you have your entire plan figured out and buttoned-up, the world will have moved on and passed you by.

The other important lesson is that once we declared a bold goal, thousands of people rallied around it. Sri Lankans like Suba and my old friend Meera now living in the United States and in Singapore volunteered to go back to their country, at their own expense, to help Room to Read get started. A donor offered frequent-flier miles to get Erin over to view the potential projects. Room to Read chapters threw fund-raising events. Several hundred schools—ranging from Malaysia to Tokyo to Vancouver to London—initiated fund-raising campaigns. Companies like Accenture, ING, Prudential, Credit Suisse, and XL Capital offered large grants. Scholastic, the biggest publisher of children's books in the world, called to offer us half a million books and even volunteered to pay for the shipping.

In retrospect, I believe that the majority of these people were motivated by the fact that we did not yet have a complete strategy or solution for Sri Lanka. In the absence of such, each individual was able to exercise his or her creative muscle and invent his or her own role. Had we been 100 percent buttoned-up, the prospect of volunteering for Room to Read would have been inherently less interesting as it would not have made a demand on people's creativity.

IN APRIL, ERIN LEFT FOR HER INITIAL TRIP TO SRI LANKA. SHE WAS EX-cited to meet Suba, with whom she had only spoken via Skype and e-mail. Suba and the team had already adopted over a dozen projects, and Erin was anxious to visit them and to see the progress and the barriers. She braved the long set of flights: from San Francisco to Seoul, then on to Delhi, then to Sri Lanka's capital city of Colombo.

Meanwhile, I flew east to attend the Skoll Foundation conference on social entrepreneurship at Oxford University. Four days later, I awoke at 6 a.m., my body confused as usual by the sudden change of time zones. I followed my nose to a coffee shop with Wi-Fi and logged on to e-mail. The first message I noticed was from Erin, titled "A Message of Hope from Sri Lanka":

Dear Room to Read Family and Friends—

I have just returned from an emotional trip to the eastern coast of Sri Lanka. The Ampara District is a remote area on the southern half of the east coast. It took us over nine hours by car on a badly paved two-lane road through the central mountain region to get there—a road shared by trucks, buses, cars, motorcycles, bicycles, tractors, and cows! In other words, a typical developing-country road!

We met up with Shiva Charity, who is our partner for rebuilding preschools damaged or destroyed by the tsunami. They have two construction teams working full-time to build the 20+ schools funded by Room to Read. But before visiting the school projects, which are built away from the sea given the new buffer-zone regulations, we toured the tsunami-impacted areas. It is hard to describe how devastated these areas are. As we walked through the piles of rubble just feet from the sea, I tried to imagine what it must have been like on the quiet Sunday morning when the big waves came. It is estimated 12,000 people died in Ampara District, making it one of the hardest hit in Sri Lanka. In some areas there is nothing left standing at all. In others, one brick wall is left to denote where a home used to be. Story after story you hear from the locals about how this house was home to two parents and five kids and now there is only one child left . . . or how a father lost all six of his children and wife. Everybody lost someone near and dear to them that quiet Sunday morning.

There are refugee camps everywhere and temporary tents line the streets. People have tents, clean water, and food in ample supply thankfully. But people complain that nothing else has happened. They have heard much was given but they have received little to rebuild their lives. The government and international relief agencies are plentiful in the south where there are good roads (tourist beach area) and it is a government-controlled area. Ampara is at the border of the Tamil Tiger zone, however, which means the government and the rebel Tamil Tigers have been fighting it out for years. Thus, these areas have not developed as much, and now the government assistance even in the face of this immense tragedy is less forthcoming. The people are attempting to clear the rubble by hand—one piece at a time of their former homes, their former lives. Mostly the women seem to be doing the work. The men point out to sea and say there should be hundreds of boats given how much money has been donated, but they have only received a few dozen.

On the brighter side though, we at Room to Read have just gotten to work despite the challenges and through our partnership with Shiva have managed to have built 3 preschools already with 17+ more in the pipeline. We are one of the first organizations starting reconstruction projects. The schools serve about 50 children each and are a meeting point for the women of the community. Preschools are outside of the government school system, so in partnership with Shiva (who will pay their operation costs going forward) and The Social Welfare Organization of Ampara District (who will manage the teachers and oversee the curriculum), we are quickly building a network of new preschools. The kids are already swinging on the swing sets in three of them with smiles on their faces. The mothers tell us we are helping to bring hope back to their communities after so much sadness. It is indescribable the feeling of positive energy and change we are all helping to bring forth.

A bit of humor on the trip: In a Muslim community in this district (Muslims are some of the most underserved in Sri Lanka) we are rebuilding two schools. We visited one of the construction sites and I was telling the community members our name—Room to Read. The main English speaker of the community said—"Ah, Room to Breed, yes, with the preschools we have more room to breed." After much laughter, I tried to explain we were trying to promote reading, not breeding, and let's hope my message got through!

I could go on about so many other things—the 100+ military checkpoints I have been through already in just a week of being on this very divided island, the tsunami scare the other night that reawakened many emotions in people, the horribly inefficient and corrupt system permeating the tsunami relief work, the helicopter tour I took of the tsunami areas with the secretary of defense and Mary Eisenhower (granddaughter of President Eisenhower), the great Sri Lankan volunteers Room to Read has found to help launch our effort here, or the wonderful evening we had the other night in a girls' orphanage in a small town on the east coast (no hotels to stay in) where the girls taught us some Hindi-style Bollywood dancing and we taught them the hokey-pokey and the Macarena :)

Anyway, this e-mail is too long already so I will just say this country has found a special place in my heart quickly and I feel so blessed to be part of the solution.

All the best to you all,

Erin

There was a separate mail, addressed only to me, in which Erin said that she thought our initial estimate, that we should rebuild 20 schools, was too conservative. She had seen so many villages whose buildings had been flattened and whose people had been demoralized. She and Suba asked if we could double our plan. And as had happened so many times in Room to Read's brief history, I answered yes despite not knowing where the money would come from.

Judging by the 100-plus messages in my in-box—most of which carried titles like "How can I help?"—funding was not going to be a problem. As if to prove that my optimism would be rewarded, a group of Oxford students tracked me down later that day to present a check for £9,000 (about US $16,000) that they had raised to help tsunami-stricken countries. Right there, we had one of the 20 additional schools funded. I just needed 19 more days in a row like this one.

HALFWAY AROUND THE WORLD, THE TSUNAMI FUNDS RAISED BY MANY thousands of students were being put to good use in the rural village of Munamalpe. This small village in southern Sri Lanka was mired in absolute poverty, and life was difficult for its residents. When the tsunami hit and wiped out what few resources the people had, life went from difficult to nearly impossible.

Thankfully, one of the community's leaders, and her family, survived and played a vital role in the rebuilding of the community. Chintha, a qualified Montessori teacher, quickly mobilized three generations of her family to bring hope back to this ravaged village on the coastline. She approached Room to Read to help rebuild the village preschool, which served 35 children. In addition to this school, she proposed the creation of a library in the building, to be used by all local students during the hours after 3 p.m. when the preschool was no longer in session.

Suba and the team in Sri Lanka were impressed with the spirit and resilience of Chintha and her husband, Shantha. At a time when many village residents were understandably traumatized by the destruction, Chintha and Shantha decided that it was their duty to leap into action. Shantha was so excited by the idea of building a combination preschool and village library that he offered to volunteer for Room to Read full-time. He told our team that he did not need money, and that for him it was enough to gain access to resources to help the village's children to begin their journey back to a normal life.

Each morning the couple and their four children came to the building site to organize the day's labor. They were grateful that Room to Read had bought the building materials and wanted to help hold costs down by having as much volunteer labor as possible.

The youngest volunteer was their youngest son, Kavith. At the tender age of four, he carried bricks, one at a time, from the brick pile over to the busy masons putting up the walls. Suba sent us an e-mail in which she reported that "just like his father, there are no complaints, [he is] just doing what he thinks he should be doing."

Kavith also boasted to his friends that the new preschool belonged to him. When told by our local team that the school would actually belong to the entire community, and would he like something else instead, he asked if he could have a new Room to Read school bag like the one all the students would get the day of the school opening ceremony.

Chintha's parents are retired and live near the school site. To do their part, they volunteered to cook a large lunch for the team of laborers. Each day steaming pots would be delivered to the building site, and 10 to 15 people would dig into heaping plates of rice and curry.

Three generations of a single dynamic family had come together, each doing what it could do to help rebuild in a devastated community. In October, only ten months after the preschool had been destroyed, the new school was officially reopened. If ever there was an opening ceremony I regretted missing, this one was it. I vowed to visit Munamalpe one day to meet this extraordinary family. I'm also excited to try the curry.

INSPIRED BY STORIES LIKE THESE, MY TEAM AND I CONTINUED TO WORK insane hours, flying around the world to pitch companies, foundations, and wealthy individuals on the need to help Sri Lanka rebuild. Thankfully, the funding continued to flow, and by the one-year anniversary of the tsunami, Room to Read had reopened 22 schools and had 16 more nearing completion. Not content to stop there, Suba and her team began planning the construction of 60 more schools over the next two years. Each school represented some degree of hope and a return to optimism for each village.

I also think they were emblematic of humankind's unique ability to create order out of chaos. Much of human advancement depends on overcoming setbacks and making progress despite obstacles and tragedy. My personal heroes are the doctors and journalists who throw themselves into war zones, famine-stricken nations, and areas hit by natural disasters such as earthquakes. They are aware that they cannot control or change the past, but believe strongly that they can have an influence over the future. Rather than being paralyzed by tragedy, they are catalyzed into action.

A victim of genocidal violence in Rwanda, or an Iranian woman pulled from a building leveled by an earthquake, may have no idea why a French doctor suddenly appears to tend her wounds, but she is most certainly thankful for this unexplained act of mercy and compassion. Each of these acts is symbolic of the best that exists inside all of us.

In my own life, I had never before responded to a disaster, nor had I expected to. We had to invent a lot of it as we went along. Our first year of work in Sri Lanka proved that people are capable of amazing work when given the latitude. Our team in Sri Lanka spearheaded an impressive number of projects. Thousands of students at 250 schools around the world participated in our Students Helping Students campaign. They raised over half a million dollars even though we were too busy to give them much direction. Our development team in San Francisco, working closely with our volunteer chapters, locked down $2.5 million in capital commitments in just nine months—enough funding to cover our first three years of work in Sri Lanka.

As for me, I will always remember one seminal moment during our initial response to the disaster. On January 4, 2005, we had a team meeting to discuss our plans to rebuild schools in Sri Lanka. Knowing that some of the team were fearful and were walking around the office with a "deer in the headlights" look, I wanted to assure them that we were smart enough to figure this out. I thought of the Ed Harris character from the film *Apollo 13,* who watches his colleagues panic while he methodically determines a way to get the astronauts back to earth safely. His team is pessimistic, focusing on obstacles and doomsday scenarios, while he is reaching deep down to find the Right Stuff that made the original NASA astronauts the American heroes of the 1960s. With this example in mind, I had printed for each team member a handout with a photo of the Ed Harris character, speaking the immortal words:

"With all due respect, gentlemen, I believe this will be NASA's finest hour."

If you ask people to reach deep, to think creatively, and to produce extraordinary results, they usually will. Too often in our modern world, they are simply not asked.

As predicted, Sri Lanka became one of Room to Read's finest hours.

POSTSCRIPT: JACOB RASCH WAS HONORED FOR HIS WRISTBAND CAMPAIGN by the Congressional Committee on Human Rights. He proudly told an assembled group of congressmen how he and his cousins had raised enough funds to build five schools in Sri Lanka (see photo insert).

YOU SAY YOU WANT A REVOLUTION? ADVICE ON CHANGING THE WORLD

Stop Talking, Start Acting

If you are thinking about making some adjustments in your life to allow you to help change the world, my heartfelt recommendation is not to spend too much time thinking about it. Just dive in.

I know that all kinds of practical considerations make this advice difficult to embrace. There might be student loans to be repaid, the need for advice from friends and family, and the desire to write a serious business plan. I am not saying that you should not do any of these things—just that you should not spend too much time on them or you will lose momentum.

The biggest risk is that a lot of people will try to talk you out of pursuing your dream. The world has too many people who are happy to discuss why something might not work, and too few who will cheer you on and say, "I'm there for you." The more time you spend navel-gazing, the longer you give those negative gravitational forces to keep you in their tether.

As an example, I would cite our work in Sri Lanka. After the devastating tsunami, I had to prove to myself that I had the guts to follow my own advice. News reports indicated that hundreds of schools had been destroyed in Indonesia and Sri Lanka. Room to Read did not work in either of those countries, so it was difficult to decide how we could help. But I knew deep in my heart that "We don't work there, it's not our problem" was not an answer worthy of a bold, young charity that had never been willing to accept limits.

So I proposed to our team, and to our board, that we immediately launch operations in Sri Lanka, raise a million dollars to get started, and begin to identify communities whose schools had been destroyed. There was, needless to say, a Greek chorus telling me why we couldn't do this—"We don't have staff there." "Room to Read is not licensed to work in Sri Lanka." "We're already busy enough with our existing five countries."

On January 3, I convened an emergency call of the board of directors, and we included Erin, our chief operating officer, to gain her invaluable perspective. All of us were united in our desire to help tsunami victims, yet also scared of diving into something so new.

continued

I made my case:

"We've been working in South Asia [Nepal and India] for over five years now. We've partnered with over fifteen hundred communities throughout Asia to get new schools and libraries built. We know how to do this. Yes, Sri Lanka will be new for us, but it's not as though we have not launched new countries before. And I think it's important to remember that Room to Read is an organization that has been built on an ethos of bold thinking and direct action. Do we want to say to these devastated communities, "Sorry, but this is not part of our business plan, so we can't help you?"

There was dead air on the phone. I was sweating. This was potentially a moment that would cause me to lose faith in our team's ability to think big about creating change. The silence was broken by a member of our Board, whose opinion I greatly respected. "We know very little about Sri Lanka. If we want to make this decision, we should do a three-month study of the situation, then decide."

More dead air. Now I was really sweating.

Another Board member responded immediately. "With all due respect, if back in 1998 John had decided to do a three-month study of the situation in Nepal, he would have probably never even launched Room to Read. The study would have revealed so many daunting obstacles that he would have become a pessimist, and none of the great accomplishments of the last six years would have been reality. I think that we should go in."

A third member of the Board opined, "You're both right in your own way. We should move quickly because the children of Sri Lanka should not have to wait. But we have to realize that with a fast launch without a detailed study, we will hit obstacles. We should think about them in advance and plan our responses. We also need to trust our team to adjust and to figure things out, just as they always have.

Internally, I cheered, then suggested a vote. The board was unanimous in approving the immediate launch of Room to Read Sri Lanka. In our rookie year there, we began construction on 40 schools and also opened 25 libraries.

Sometimes, it's really important to move with all deliberate speed. If there is something out there that you want to do to make the world a better place, don't focus on the obstacles. Don't ask for permission. Just dive in. Don't let the naysayers get you down.

CHAPTER 24

THE MILLIONTH BOOK

FLYING NORTH FROM BANGKOK TOWARD KATHMANDU, I STARE OUT of the tiny window of the Thai Airlines 777 at a cloudless day. From this height, the coastline of Bangladesh is a place of calm. Yet below struggles a nation short on resources and steeped in challenges. For years, we've had requests to work there. I wonder if we will be able to find the funding commitments and the dedicated local employees we need in order to say yes.

Peering out the window helps me put aside the doom and gloom painted in the international newspaper. The stories are a familiar and depressing roll call of the failures of our modern world, circa November 2005. Suicide bombers in Iraq killed 67 people praying at a mosque yesterday. Tensions between the Israelis and the Palestinians seem to be as high as always. Renewed violence between the Tamil Tigers and the government of Sri Lanka is predicted.

Enough! I throw the newspaper onto the empty seat next to me and return to more hopeful thoughts about the problems of the world that I can actually help to solve.

At the airport, Dinesh is planning to greet me. It has been six and a half years since we first met. On that day my father and I scanned the crowd, wondering what a "Dinesh" looked like and hoping we'd be able to pick our e-mail pen pal out of the crowd of *topi*-topped Nepalis.

It is still difficult to fully grasp how much has changed since that initial meeting. The organization Dinesh and I started is now working in six countries. We've grown from two part-timers to a paid staff of 50 and over 1,000 volunteer fund-raisers. Our initial library in Bahundanda has now been joined by more than 2,300 others. This week we will celebrate a major milestone for Room to Read — the donation of our millionth book.

In August of 2005, when I realized that we were getting close to surpassing this watershed number, I e-mailed Dinesh to suggest that we do something special to publicly commemorate and celebrate the achievement of a dream. We had been working nonstop for years, and I felt the need to slow down for a few days and go back to the country where it had all begun so that we could savor the progress we had made. Dinesh started planning the usual frenzied trip full of site visits, meetings with headmasters, and conversations with village governments that wanted our support. We were planning to visit 21 widely scattered rural villages in three frenetic days to see a full slate of Room to Read projects. On my last day in the country, we'd celebrate the millionth book.

Ahead of our plane, amidst broken clouds, the Himalayan range dominates the land, the sky, and the focus of everyone sitting on the right-hand side of the plane. Indeed, half of the left side seems to have migrated over, and three to four people are queued up at each window. It's rare to hear oohs and aahs on a modern flight, but it happens every day on Thai flight #319 to Kathmandu.

To the east, straddling the border with India, sits Kachenjunga, the world's third-highest mountain at 26,600 feet. I work my way to the left and can make out Mount Everest, with plumes of snow blowing off the top few thousand feet. The view from the plane is unobstructed for nearly 200 miles of glaciated peaks.

These mountains were what originally brought me to Nepal. Now, it is the children.

. . .

A CROWD IS WAITING OUTSIDE OF BAGGAGE CLAIM—AND WHAT A CROWD it is! In America, our busy lives mean that we've largely abandoned the custom of picking up friends at the airport. "Catch a cab, grab the Super Shuttle," we frantically e-mail. "Come straight to the restaurant and we'll meet there. I may be a few minutes late, so sit tight if you don't see me right away."

Here in Nepal, the airport pickup is still taken seriously and is something to witness. Several hundred people await the passengers on the two arriving flights of the afternoon from Bangkok and New Delhi. Spotting Dinesh among the crowd, I startle him with a cry of *"Bai!"*—Nepali for younger brother. He happily shakes my hand, welcomes me back to Nepal, and in his usual "all-business" mode quickly hustles me through the crowd of porters offering their services.

Once the car is rolling through the chaotic streets of Kathmandu, Dinesh and I begin exchanging news both big and small—my recent speech in Bangkok on corporate social responsibility, the current cease-fire between the Maoist rebels and Nepal's government, the rumors of a potential coup d'état that are being taken so seriously that Nepal's king is rumored to be returning early from a foreign holiday, Dinesh's family, and our dinner plans at my favorite *momo* (steamed dumpling) restaurant. Then he springs a surprise on me.

"This Friday will be a big day."

I remind him that I'm well aware of this fact, and that's why I am here.

He laughs and asks if I'm excited to attend the opening ceremony for the library at which we'll also mark the millionth-book milestone. I confirm my excitement and he chuckles, a bit sheepishly this time.

"Dinesh, what's going on? Do you want to let me in on the joke?"

"Actually, we will not open just one library on Friday. We wanted to make the day special. So on Friday between ten a.m. and noon, thirty new libraries across Nepal will have their official opening ceremony."

I am stunned.

"Thirty?"

"Yes, thirty."

"As in three. Zero."

"Yes. Three zero. *Tis.* Thirty."

Many times I have found it hard to fully comprehend our growth. Today I am blown away. I am also proud of Dinesh and his team for thinking big. The depressing news from the day's paper fades from memory as I think about thirty villages across Nepal helping us to celebrate this milestone. As of Friday, they will each have a library full of books and shelves and desks and puzzles and games that will bring a world of opportunities to their children, who would otherwise have so few. I feel blessed to be at the helm of an organization that has so many amazing people, and fortunate to be here to participate in this milestone.

OUR NEPAL TEAM HAS MADE BIG PLANS FOR THE TWO DAYS LEADING UP to the millionth-book celebration on Friday. They are justifiably proud of their work and are anxious to show me as many of the new schools and computer labs as possible. Soon after flying over the mountains that flank Kathmandu Valley to the west, I am traversing them again as we start a kamikaze road trip that will take us to visit 14 schools in just one day.

Our first stop is the Shree Bhagawati Primary School, which is perched on a commanding hilltop overlooking the small plots of farmland that produce the majority of this village's income. The school has just recently opened and already has 151 students in grades one to five, with girls comprising just over half the school's enrollment. But I will have to earn the opportunity to see the school; a steep ascent along dirt paths is required.

Fragrant pine trees line the trail and provide much needed shade. The climb sucks the oxygen out of me and makes my calves burn. Yadav, our School Room construction engineer, ten years my junior, tells me the story of the village as I pant like a dog.

The village residents responded to our challenge grant in two ways. First, they successfully petitioned the owners of the riverside "stone-crushing business" to donate the cement. That was only half the battle, as the plant was by the river and the school was over 1,000 vertical feet above it in the hills. So the parents also volunteered their labor to carry the building materials for the hour of steep ascent. I made a mental note to tell the Room to Read donor who had helped sponsor the project that the village she'd adopted was full of parents who were obviously good negotiators with strong backs and legs.

After a brief visit with the headmaster, and a group photo shoot of the students, we begin the descent to the roadside. A chirping noise in Dinesh's pocket reminds us that we are back in cell phone range. On the other line is Rajeev, the program officer in charge of our library program. Twenty-five more schools have signed on to inaugurate their libraries on Friday and are scrambling to meet this deadline. We are up to 55! Dinesh confidently predicts the number will go higher. I love this team, and their ambition.

As Dinesh simultaneously drives, beeps at Indian lorries, weaves through traffic, and chats on the phone, I grip the door handle with white knuckles. Looking straight down at a steep plunge into the river, I decide that I'd rather look uphill. I notice a large school and ask Dinesh why it looks familiar. Not willing to add one more item to his multitasking list, he tells Rajeev he has to hang up.

Dinesh reminds me that this is the Simle School. We had attended the opening ceremony in the fall of 2003. I propose that we make a surprise inspection. Dinesh comments that the headmaster is not expecting us, and I laugh and say all the better. I often wonder what happens at our schools on the days when I, or the local Room to Read team, are not around, and there is not a ceremony in honor of the foreign visitors. Here lies an opportunity to find out what happens at one of the Room to Read schools on an average day. Do teachers show up? Are the rooms filled with students?

A nightmare scenario plays out in my mind. What if the school is poorly attended? What if the rooms were being used to house chickens in the grade one classroom and goats in grade two? I know that the developing world is littered with projects that had every good intention, but were badly planned and therefore unsustainable.

As we walk into the school's courtyard, I feel that I'm about to experience a referendum on my life's work. But it's immediately apparent that we have nothing to fear. Each classroom appears, even from a distance, to be full of students. An unbroken sea of brown uniforms is in every room. Within minutes, as the lunch period starts, waves of students come streaming out of each room. Soon, we are surrounded by dozens and then hundreds of students who aren't accustomed to having guests. All of them look happy and healthy and seem to have every bit of self-confidence as they yell, "Hello, sir," and ham it up for Yadav's camera.

The headmaster recognizes Dinesh and Yadav and joins our impromptu inspection tour. He tells us proudly that enrollment at the school has increased from 550 students in 2002, to 700 in 2003 (when Room to Read completed the first addition), to over 1,150 today (after Room to Read built a second addition, this time with five new classrooms and a library). Education continued to become more popular as families realized that this was the best hope for their children.

As growth in enrollment increased, so did the need for additional space, and the school had recently completed yet another addition. This time they did not seek Room to Read's support, but instead lobbied their District Development Committee (the local level of government) into funding the project. They were also upgrading the toilets to ensure an adequate supply of clean running water, and constructing a shrine to the goddess of education.

We were happy to hear that the Simle School had done the last addition without asking for our help. Our goal has always been for our schools to be supported by the community, and therefore be self-sufficient in the long run. This was the dream state, because the school would remain for years to come and would be well taken care of. Meanwhile, we could begin working in other villages that also needed our help.

I congratulated the headmaster on the growth in enrollment and told him how proud I was that Room to Read had played a part. Apologizing for stopping by without notice, I said that we knew he was busy and that I hoped to see him again on my next trip to Nepal. As we walked back to the car, I made a note to call the donors who had funded the Simle School projects and let them know that the school was well run, overflowing with students, and being well looked after by the community.

DINESH'S PHONE RANG AGAIN ON THE WAY TO THE DAY'S FINAL VISIT. I could pick up enough of his Nepali to realize that we were adding libraries as fast as the Simle School was adding students. An NGO partner in the Terai region, along the India border, had moved forward the opening date of 15 new libraries. We had reached 70—and counting!

I was excited for the last stop of the day at the Shree Bageshwori school. It was built by the local community and Room to Read in 2003, with funding provided by 85 Broads, the group of female employees and alums of Goldman Sachs who had helped make Alison Levine's Everest climb a fund-raiser for Room to Read. In just over two years, enrollment at Bageshwori had increased to over 1,000 students. The Nepal Room to Read team was impressed by the dedication of the teachers and the continued upward trend in enrollment. This year, the school's request for a computer room was granted in recognition of their progress. I was awarded the fun job—showing up for the opening ceremony as the "chief guest."

The students proved to us that they were ready to make great use of their new computer lab. They had practiced their PowerPoint skills by making welcome signs. As we entered the courtyard, over 1,000 students greeted us. Most were holding flowers, and at least fifty had laser-printed signs mounted on sticks. The messages read, "Thank you for supporting our school," and, "Thank you Room to Read for granting support to establish computer lab."

One adorable sixth-grade girl had a sign reading, "Thank you Room to Read for giving us so much . . . How to express what I have felt? I simply love you very very much!" The daughter of the school's English teacher made me a special "Welcome Jhon Wood" sign.

The ceremony had not yet begun and I was already overwhelmed with the emotion and the sheer joy of knowing that one spot on earth is better off today than it was yesterday. Because of the work of so many people in our global network, these students would have the opportunity to learn how computers worked and to connect with the outside world. To these children, we were heroes. I was reminded of why I work the insane hours, jump on flights when I'd prefer to stay home, and abandon the easy temptation to live a "normal" life. The answer lay with these sign-wielding students. I worked for them and needed to stay maniacally focused since there were tens of thousands of other schools just like Bageshwori that needed our assistance.

FRIDAY MORNING, THE DAY OF THE MILLIONTH-BOOK MILESTONE, IS chilly enough to demand a thick fleece. I wake at 7:30 and walk the streets of Kathmandu for an hour. I love the city at this time of day. The air is clean and retains a chill from the night, the sun is benign, the streets are clean, and there is little traffic. Shopkeepers clean their windows and brush their front stoops with tiny doll-like brooms. It must be a never-ending battle to have a clean store in this perpetually dusty city. I exchange "Namaste" with several. In an alley, a stray dog pounces on a bone, chews, drops it, and stares quizzically, as if wondering about the lack of meat. I wish I had brought Milk-Bones with me.

Back at the Kathmandu Guest House, as I await the arrival of Dinesh and Rajeev, I leaf through the local newspapers. A quote from a story about education in Nepal leaps off the page:

> In my village as well as in the cities, there were local bars in every nook and corner. Roaming around those places, I formed the habit of drinking and I became a drunkard. If only those places [had been] libraries and bookshops, then today I might have been a different man altogether.
>
> —Manu Brajaki quoted in the
> *Kathmandu Post,* November 15, 2005

I hope Manu finds out about what we are up to today; I think he would approve.

Dinesh and Rajeev arrive, and we order a large pot of milk tea. All smiles, they seem to be just as excited for the day as I am. Dinesh announces that he has been up late answering e-mails from our partner NGOs. I can tell by his bemused countenance that he's excited to give me an update. I ask. Seven more NGOs had decided to join us in cutting the red ribbon on their new Room to Read–financed libraries today. In fact, some of them had gotten an early start and were opening the libraries even as we sat over breakfast.

Next I ask for the latest count.

One hundred and eleven.

Rajeev interrupts his mobile phone call to correct Dinesh. Another NGO partner had sent a fax to the office this morning announcing the opening of 12 libraries in the Terai region of southern Nepal, along the border with India.

Today, 123 ribbons will be cut! I am in awe. The entire country of Nepal seems to have caught the millionth-book fever. In 19 different districts, ranging from the flat "breadbasket" of the south, to the shadow of the Annapurna range in Pokhara, speeches are being made and libraries are being opened at a frantic clip. I can only imagine the months of work done in advance of this day. School sites had to be identified, challenge grants negotiated, librarians trained, shelves built, and books transported. Today, in honor of the millionth book, everything would come together. The local Room to Read team reminded me of orchestra players who had painstakingly practiced and were now ready to perform a perfect rendition of a symphony.

We are due to attend three opening ceremonies in the Kathmandu Valley, so I quickly pay our bill. As our team walks to the car, I try to visualize the many libraries and communities being impacted by Room to Read on this one day. Assuming that on average 300 children have access to each library, this means that over 36,000 children will now have an opportunity that had not previously existed in their village. I pat Rajeev on the back and tell him that back in the early days, Dinesh and I would have never pictured Room to Read opening this many libraries in our lifetime, let alone in one day.

. . .

AN HOUR'S DRIVE FROM OUR GUESTHOUSE, ON THE FAR NORTHEASTERN outskirts of Kathmandu, the 135 students of the Shree Ram Janaki Lower Secondary School are preparing for our arrival. Marigolds are being strung into welcome garlands, and the smallest children are in the forest bordering the school picking small flowers to offer their honored guests.

The rutted road almost swallows Dinesh's tiny Hyundai (no Land Rovers at our low-overhead organization), so we park alongside a field of grazing goats. As we walk the last hundred yards to the school, we see children scrambling to their assigned places. We are immediately surrounded by teachers offering the warmest welcomes and greetings. As is the custom in Nepal, the students have formed a human corridor. As we walk through, we are given enough flowers to last for several decades' worth of Valentine's Days. I try to stop long enough to look each student in the eye and say thank you. Some are outgoing and answer with a perfectly enunciated "You're welcome, sir," while others blush and look down at the ground. The youngest students need help from a teacher, who lifts them high enough to place their flower garland around my neck.

We are shown to seats thoughtfully placed in the shade of the school's roof, beneath a large red banner announcing the opening of the school's new bilingual library. A small microphone awaits the speakers, incense burns, and in the school's courtyard students are assembling on rows of long benches.

The headmaster joyfully announces that this is one of the biggest days in the history of the school. In the library lay opportunities for the students to learn about how the world works. They can view maps and photos of far-off lands and oceans, read about their country's rich history, and begin thinking about whether they'd like to be a doctor or a businessperson or an airline pilot when they finish school. In my mind, I picture my childhood visits to our hometown library, and the kinetic energy those hundreds of books unleashed in my young brain. I hope that this school's library is one small part of the repayment for the privileges I have enjoyed.

Next, a group of girl students performs a dance expressing their gratitude to the Room to Read team for our support of their school.

Now we have a Room to Read.
We will study every day.
We will learn Nepali and English.
We will speak them perfectly.

Several teachers and a member of the village government then speak. As they talk to the crowd of students and parents about the importance of reading, and their goals for the future growth of the school, my thoughts drift to different parts of Nepal. I imagine floating 100,000 feet above the country and looking down on 123 villages where crowds are assembling to celebrate the opening of their new village library. In the shadows of the Himalayas, in villages perched on the sides of steep, verdant hills, in narrow river valleys, and in dusty districts of Kathmandu, communities are gathering to mark a milestone in their development. The parents know that a vital part of education that they had missed—access to a wide variety of books in several languages—will be available to their children as of today.

I picture over 30,000 children reading books in these new libraries and think back to how modest my original goal in 1998 had been—just one library, in Bahundanda. From that first small step, progress has snowballed, accelerated, and sometimes left me gasping for breath. Given a choice, I would have it no other way.

In my imaginary spaceship, I go even higher above the earth and look down on India, Laos, Sri Lanka, Cambodia, and Vietnam and think about all the other projects the local Room to Read teams have implemented in these countries: 2,300 libraries across six resource-starved nations; over 200 schools; 50 computer and language labs; 1,700 girls on long-term scholarships; a million books.

I am immensely satisfied with how life has worked out. It seems hard to believe that I had ever worried about whether I would find "life after Microsoft." The company had been a springboard to a new plateau, one on which I was happier than ever with my chosen role in the universe. Through my years at Microsoft, I had been given financial freedom, and a tool kit of management skills that had proved immensely useful while building Room to Read. Rather than seeing a chasm between my old life and my new one, it now seems more of a continuum.

My musings are interrupted by the headmaster. He hands over a pair of scissors to cut the red ribbon stretched across the library's door. I walk slowly, wishing I could slow down time. I desire to preserve this moment forever.

As I cut the ribbon and the two halves flutter downward, the assembled crowd cheers. I put my arm around Dinesh and we walk into a room full of desks, chairs, posters, and shelves of books in Nepali and English. The walls are painted in bright colors. The beautiful room is a harbinger of a brighter tomorrow for the students at the school, this year and every year into the future.

It is also a small piece in the overall mosaic called Room to Read. Today we paused to celebrate. Tomorrow we will get back to work. Tens of thousands of ribbon cuttings lie ahead. With continued focus, tenacity, passion, and sheer force of will, we'll keep marching onward and upward. New tiles—a school here, a library there—will be added to the mosaic until we have created a world in which no child lacks access to education.

Millions of kids are waiting for the opportunity that education brings. I hope and pray that we will not keep them waiting much longer.

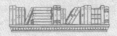

EPILOGUE

THE NEXT CHAPTER OF MY ADULT LIFE

WHEN I STARTED ADOPTING EDUCATION PROJECTS IN ASIA, I DID not stop to think through the long-term implications. I was driven by an immediate desire to do something to help children who did not have access to education. In its purest incarnation, I was simply responding to a need, and a request for help. I had no intention of quitting my job at Microsoft, running a start-up organization, circling the globe on a frequent basis, or working long hours for no pay.

Everything that has come since then has grown out of that first day in the Annapurna range when Pasupathi invited me to visit a school and I said "yes" to the headmaster's request for books.

Over time, I took steps that cemented into reality a simple fact: my destiny was increasingly tied to the quest for global education. There were large steps, such as quitting Microsoft, hiring my first employees, and moving the organization from my back bedroom into a real office. There were also small ones, such as answering the inevitable cocktail-party question of "What do you do?" by talking about schools and libraries in the Third World, rather than my career as a technology executive.

In January 2004, I turned 40. For many people, this milestone is a time for deep introspection and soul-searching. I was surprised to find myself waking up and going to the office as though it were any other day. I felt no need to take the day off to book a vacation, or to reward myself with something "special." All I really wanted was to go to the office, pour a cup of black coffee, and converse with my team.

That night a group of friends celebrated my birthday at a hip Vietnamese restaurant, Ana Mandara, on San Francisco's waterfront. An old friend from my Microsoft days had flown in from Australia. Mark asked if I was freaking out about turning 40.

"No, not really. I thought I would, but it seems normal. I took an hour off this afternoon to write in my journal about it. You know, I think the main reason I am so chilled about forty is that I am really happy with my life and where it is today. It's impossible for me to be anything other than joyful about how things have worked out. I think that someone's fear of a 'milestone birthday' directly relates to how happy they are with their life. If you love what you do and are surrounded by good friends and family, then forty or fifty or sixty is just a round number, not a cause for panic."

Granted, there were trade-offs of which I was painfully aware. I could still not afford a home in San Francisco and had resigned myself to a lifetime of renting. After a series of failed relationships, I was celebrating my milestone 40th birthday alone, without a life mate at my side. I had to beg frequent-flier miles from friends or risk sitting in the back of the plane for 22-hour journeys to remote parts of Asia. Every month I did the math and sweated out whether we'd make the payroll. I spent evenings with wealthy donors who had just made tens of millions by listing or selling their companies, then returned home to open bank statements showing that my balance was continuing its near-perpetual decline.

Yes, there were trade-offs, but there always will be in life. Few people in the world had as much fun at their job as I did. Not many people jumped out of bed on Monday morning excited to be at the office.

My close friend Sarah must have known what I was thinking. Inside my birthday card she had inscribed a quote from St. Francis de Sales:

Do not wish to be anything but what you are,
and try to be that perfectly.

"What I am" has changed markedly since my days at Microsoft. Thankfully, it's a great fit. Turning 40 only emphasized to me how happy I am with the journey and the adventure that life has, thankfully, thrust upon me.

While writing in my journal that day I tried to think about what the next ten years would be like. Assuming that one continues to be blessed with good health, there is possibly no period of life as productive as the forties. By that point, many of us have financial stability, solid networks of supportive friends, and much more certainty about our place in the world. Best of all, we still have a lot of energy, and the world is willing to take us more seriously (indeed, I welcomed the bit of gray that had recently appeared at my temples as it will cause more people to believe I have the maturity to run a worldwide organization).

I gave myself a 40th birthday present—I decided to devote what will probably be the most productive decade of my adult life to the quest for universal education. I have abandoned all thoughts of returning to the field of technology. Having discovered my true life path, I am more ready than ever to embrace it. I feel lucky to know who I am, what I want to focus on, and the yardsticks by which I will measure myself.

I think of Vu, the first student I ever helped. Starting with a $20 scholarship in 1997, we have continued a symbiotic relationship that has allowed him to become fluent in three languages while studying in university, and then to pursue a graduate degree in software engineering. His wife is a well-trained nurse helping the rural poor, and their daughter, Thao, will benefit from having educated parents who believe that girls, as well as boys, should be in school.

I try to imagine all the other students who are still in the early years of being helped by Room to Read. If Vu could make this much progress in eight years, what might become of the nearly 1 million other students now attending our schools and eagerly devouring books in our libraries?

Johann Wolfgang von Goethe once wrote about Beethoven's Fifth Symphony, "If all the musicians in the world played this piece simultaneously, the planet would go off its axis."

That's how I feel about education for the children of the developing world.

UPDATE: 2007

DURING THE EIGHTEEN MONTHS AFTER THIS ORIGINAL MANUSCRIPT was finished in early 2006, Room to Read enjoyed a period of rapid growth. The pace was so torrid that it made everything that occurred from 2000 to 2006 seem glacially slow in comparison. The organization entered a virtuous cycle, attracting a whole new wave of capital contributions. That capital allowed us to grow our programs to a previously undreamed-of scale. It was as if nitrous oxide had been added to the fuel tank.

Keeping this rapidly-accelerating rocket ship on course required a larger team. An entrepreneur I greatly respect gave me succinct advice: "You, John Wood, can't scale. Only organizations can scale." So Room to Read was in a constant hunt for great people. Our website had only occasionally advertised open positions at Room to Read. By early 2006, the "We're Hiring" section became a permanent fixture at www.roomtoread.org.

As the size of our global team doubled, it was inspiring to watch the next generation of leaders dive into their roles with incredible passion. At Microsoft I had learned that the only way to grow quickly, but sustainably, was to hire smart people with strong work ethics, give them bold and specific goals, and stay out of their way. Fortunately, there was a constant queue of amazing people ready to join us. Education experts were welcome additions to our team since both Erin and I are generalists. Others were "corporate refugees," ready, willing, and able to take skills learned in the business world and apply them to the social sector. Our fund-raising team grew to 12 people, with offices opening in London and Hong Kong to cover Europe and Asia. All of the new team members shared a common bond—the belief that in Room to Read they had found a lever with which to move the Earth.

The biggest decision we made during 2006, and the one with the most significant long-term implications for the organization, was to move beyond Asia. Having made several trips to Africa, and having seen so many children lacking access to education, it had long been my dream to bring our programs to the children of this resource-starved continent. Members of our team who had worked in Central and South America made a persuasive case that our education programs were needed in that part of the world. In true Room to Read style, we did not view this as an *either-or* decision. Instead, we said *yes* to both!

Africa was first. We hired a brilliant new employee, Stacey Warner, to undertake a comprehensive study of the African continent. Her goal was to determine the first three countries where Room to Read would be launched. Stacey had spent two years teaching at a rural school in Namibia, so she had experienced at least some of the challenges of education in Africa. Following her recommendations, we started Room to Read South Africa in 2006, then launched operations in Zambia in 2007. With some of my book royalties, I personally funded one of our first reading rooms in South Africa. I chose to endow the library in honor of Nelson Mandela, to recognize and honor the lessons he has taught the world about love, reconciliation, and humility.

Following our model for Africa, we launched our Latin American expansion study in 2007. As these words are written, Room to Read is on the cusp of hiring our Regional Director for Latin America, who will open operations in three countries during 2008–10.

As with our education programs, our fund-raising operations scaled to a global level. Although we are an American-based NGO, it was our strong desire to gain capital commitments from around the world. I joked with my team "Show me a spot on the globe where rich people and companies congregate, and I will get my butt on a flight there." They took me up on this offer, constantly. My body clock struggled to adjust as I flew across oceans and time zones, showing up bleary-eyed for "pitch meetings" in Amsterdam, London, New York, Singapore, Toronto, Tokyo, Vancouver, and Zurich.

My mother, playing the role of concerned parent, asked me how I managed to survive this grueling schedule without collapsing from exhaustion. My secret weapon was simple— donated frequent flier miles! As usual with Room to Read, there was the story of a creative solution. One of our board members pulled me aside at a meeting to say "You looked really worn down. I don't want you flying in the back of the plane any more. When you land in Hong Kong or London and go straight into a day of meetings and a night of fund-raising speeches, I want you to be fresh, relaxed, and ready for action. There is too much at stake in your meetings, and in your speeches to several hundred people."

"But," I protested, "I don't want to spend donors' money on a business class seat. We owe it to them, and to the kids we serve, to get as much money as possible into our education programs, not into the coffers of the world's major airlines."

He chuckled. "Yes, I know well your obsession with low overhead. So I have a solution. I am turning over my frequent flier miles to you—all three million of them. You have *carte blanche*. In return, I expect you to tell other donors that I have done this, and ask them to follow my example. And this does not come free to you, as I am going to expect you to be sending me 'Victory Mails' from around the world."

These mails arrived in his Inbox frequently. Two major trends drove the growth of our capital base—the rise of social entrepreneurship, and an increased focus on corporate social responsibility.

Social entrepreneurship is, to me, a relatively simple concept: the melding of the best practices of the business world with the social focus of the charitable sector. Social entrepreneurs embrace ideas like reporting on their results, measuring the return on their investments, keeping their overhead expenses low, and constantly improving their programs. A new generation of leaders has emerged, eager to break with the historic legacy of large, bureaucratic, top-down solutions. As I've spoken at leading business schools like

Harvard, Stanford, Berkeley, and—my alma mater—Kellogg, I've been blown away by the high quality and passion of students entering the social and corporate social responsibility sectors. Emerging in today's world are thousands of stories like mine, of relatively young people with a passion to change the world, the courage to take the risk, and the business acumen and leadership skills to pull it off.[1]

The social entrepreneurship explosion is being nurtured by funders who applaud the results-driven focus and who are willing to put significant capital behind it. This smart money is being used to build capacity, to replicate programs across more geographies, and to make strategic investments that help to assure the sustainability of the organization. One of the thought leaders in this area is the Skoll Foundation, founded by Jeff Skoll, the first president of eBay. Jeff and his executive director, Sally Osberg, have assembled a brilliant team that focuses on helping social entrepreneurs build their organizations. The foundation offers both long-term capital commitments and strategic advice. During one of our meetings I was told, "We don't want to fund your programs. Anyone can do that. Instead, we want to focus on capacity building. Tell us what you need to make Room to Read not only bigger, but also more sustainable. Give us the non-sexy stuff that no one else wants to fund—the database, phone systems, training, etc."

The foundation was true to its word, and in 2006 we were honored to receive a "Skoll Award for Social Entrepreneurship." This $1.2 million commitment allowed our management team to dream even bigger dreams of expansion. I hope that "the next Warren Buffett" gives his or her money to the Skoll team.

Room to Read's volunteer fund-raising chapters showed their own entrepreneurial spirit by continuing a pace of rapid growth. By the start of 2007, the number of chapters had grown to 25, with start-ups sprouting in Austin, Boulder, Denver, Orange County (California), Paris, Salt Lake City, Sydney, Tokyo, Toronto, and

---

1 Three groups in start-up mode that have particularly impressed me are In The Arena, Kiva, and the One Acre Fund.

Vail. Over 1,000 people, mostly business professionals, carve time out of their busy lives to raise funds and do PR for Room to Read. The power of this network is substantial—by year end 2007, it will have generated over $10 million of capital commitments. Not bad for an idea that had started as a 'back of the napkin' exercise, with just Michael Lindenmayer, myself, and several strong coffees, six years earlier.

Our growth was also fueled by the business community's increased focus on corporate social responsibility. The years 2006 and 2007 saw me in constant motion, meeting up with supporters like Accenture, Cathay Pacific, Credit Suisse, the Financial Times, ING, Microsoft, Scholastic, and UBS. Credit Suisse even went "beyond the check" by providing us with donated office space for our fund-raising teams in London and Hong Kong, two cities where real estate is very expensive. We are proud to have established such a distinguished group of funders. The list got even more blue chip in late 2006 when we announced our first-ever million dollar corporate commitment. The Goldman Sachs Foundation pledged to endow 450 new Reading Rooms in India, a country in which the company is rapidly expanding. As more companies have embraced CSR in a truly meaningful way, I hope to keep hopping around the world on donated frequent flier miles.

All of these factors—a larger group of employees, more countries in which to work, and a rapidly-expanding capital base—allowed Room to Read to do what we do best: deliver the lifelong gift of education to children across the developing world. During 2007, we broke ground on over 150 new schools. Our teams worked with local authors and artists to publish nearly 100 new local-language children's books. Over 1,500 girls were added to our long-term girl's scholarship program, raising the total number of Room to Grow scholars to 3,800. Best of all, the Reading Room program went into a hyper-drive stage of growth, with over 1,400 new libraries opening during 2007. That was nearly four new Reading Rooms per day opening somewhere in the developing world. Each day, over 1,200 eager young readers were gaining their first access to a library. Nothing could make me feel better about this journey that I have been on since leaving Microsoft.

But, as with the technology industry, the best days may be ahead of us. The organization has big plans to continue to scale, and to reach as many children as possible. My faith in our work, and my desire to drive the organization to new heights, is renewed every time I visit the communities where Room to Read works. In Sri Lanka, I hosted a group of 15 chapter leaders and investors to attend the official opening ceremonies of three schools built in tsunami-impacted communities. At one, we were greeted by a corridor of over 300 parents, many holding their children in their arms. Each parent wore a name tag, but instead of identifying themselves, the tags read "Mother of Dinesh" or "Father of Shilpi," etc. Their young offspring, proudly wearing their new school uniforms, greeted us with shy smiles and handshakes. In a rural village in Cambodia, I hosted a roundtable discussion on education with 40 of our Room to Grow scholars. Out of a desire to thank us for the long-term scholarships, 11 of the mothers had joined us, some journeying from as far as 20 kilometers away. When I asked how much education they had received, 9 of the 11 told me, through the interpreter, that they did not have a single day of schooling. The other two had gone through second grade. I asked, "If the Room to Read scholarship program had been in place, how many of you would have wanted to go through secondary school?" They did not even wait for the interpreter. Every hand shot in the air, the women smiled, and began chattering amongst themselves in rapid-fire Khmer. It was obvious that they were talking about what might have been. But rather than being sad about their own missed opportunities, they gazed with love and adoration at their daughters, all of whom were now in eighth through tenth grade. This generation would forever break the cycle of poverty for these families. With tears in my eyes and a warm feeling in my heart, I vowed to myself to aim higher, work harder, and never take no for an answer. This quest for universal, global education is just getting started, and with the momentum currently behind it, the future will be bright for many millions of children. I'm the lucky guy at the front of the parade.

At age 35, John Wood quit his position as Microsoft's Director of Business Development for the Greater China Region in order to found Room to Read. He has never looked back.

John's career at Microsoft spanned 1991 to 1999, where he ran significant parts of Microsoft's international business, as the Director of Marketing for the Asia-Pacific Division, Director of the Internet Customer Unit for Microsoft Australia, and Director of Marketing for Microsoft Australia.

In 1998, John took a vacation that changed his life. Trekking through a remote Himalayan village, he struck up conversation with a schoolteacher, who invited John to visit his school. There, John discovered that the few books available were so precious that they were kept under lock and key—to protect them from the children! Fewer than 20 books, all backpacker cast-aways, were available for more than 450 students.

From a small start—just a simple email requesting used book donations—Room to Read has grown into an award winning non-profit that over the past seven years has established over 4,000 libraries, donated or published over 4 million books, built more than 400 schools, and funded nearly 4,000 long-term girls' scholarships—impacting the lives of over one million children worldwide. John describes these results as "total tip of the iceberg," as the organization plans to expand to at least 20,000 libraries and schools by the year 2020.

John strives to bring the lessons of the corporate world to the non-profit sector. Room to Read combines his passion with the discipline of a well-run global company. He has been described by Fast Company Magazine as "all heart, all business," and by the San Francisco Chronicle as "the Andrew Carnegie of the developing world." He has been selected as a "Young Global Leader" by the World Economic Forum, is a recipient of the Draper Richards fellowship for social entrepreneurs and two Skoll Foundation awards for social entrepreneurship, and was selected by Time Magazine as one of it's "Asian Heroes." He is also a Henry Crown fellow of the Aspen Institute.

John holds a Bachelor of Science, *magna cum laude*, from the University of Colorado, and a Master of Business Administration from the Kellogg Graduate School of Management at Northwestern University. He lives in San Francisco, CA, but travels constantly for Room to Read. His hobbies include running, tennis, skiing, reading, and great red wine. One day, he hopes to author a children's book titled *Zak the Yak with Books on His Back*.

Room to Read's mission is to provide under-privileged children with an opportunity to gain the lifelong gift of education. It was founded on the belief that education is crucial to breaking the cycle of poverty and taking control of one's life. Room to Read operates in countries with a desperate lack of resources to educate their children throughout Asia and Africa and has plans for expansion into Latin America.

Room to Read has a successful strategy for addressing the lack of educational opportunities for children in the developing world that includes:

- *Partnering with villages to build schools*

- *Establishing libraries and filling them with donated English books and local-language books published by Room to Read*

- *Providing computer and language labs to improve employment skills, and*

- *Providing scholarships for under-privileged young girls who cannot afford fees that are required of all students, even those attending public schools*

To increase the likelihood for success and long-term sustainability, Room to Read enlists community involvement and co-investment. Our challenge grants require villages to raise a significant portion of the overall expenditure for building a new school, thereby allowing our cash donations to go further.

Room to Read's long-term goal is to build 20,000 schools and libraries, thereby educating 10 million children in the developing world by the year 2020. Since its inception, Room to Read has impacted the lives of over one million children by:

- *Building over 300 schools*

- *Establishing over 4,000 libraries*

- *Publishing more than 200 local-language children's titles representing over 2 million books*

- *Donating over 2 million English language children's books*

- *Establishing more than 125 computer and language labs*

- *Funding nearly 4,000 long-term girls' scholarships*

Room to Read operates efficiently and has received Charity Navigator's top four-star rating and the Fast Company/Monitor Social Capital Award for four consecutive years. To learn more, please visit: www.roomtoread.org

There are many ways you can help Room to Read reach even more children throughout the developing world, including the vast and growing network of 25 fund-raising chapters around the world. Visit www.roomtoread.org/involvement to find out how you can join one of the world's fastest growing, award-winning organizations. Together, we can change the world for millions of children across the developing world with the lifelong gift of education.

ACKNOWLEDGMENTS

I'VE ALWAYS BELIEVED THAT AN ENTREPRENEUR WILL ONLY SUCCEED IF he surrounds himself with talented and passionate people. I was fortunate enough to meet Dinesh Shrestha and Erin Keown Ganju during the critical early years of Room to Read, and they both deserve full credit for their roles in building out the organization.

Thanks to Dinesh, and also to his wonderful wife, Shobha, for being so supportive of his passion for education for Nepal's children. Thanks also to Pankaj Pradhan for being Dinesh's partner-in-crime during the early years.

To those who work in our San Francisco office, thank you for your fierce dedication to our cause, and for keeping the place running while I'm out on my usual peripatetic travel schedule. I love returning to our office full of smart and funny people, with laughter and good ideas bouncing off the walls. Emily, Kara, Bella, Lisa, Shauna, Jayson, Matt, Jay, Meera, Kelly, Stacey, Dustin, and Pam—each of you has been an incredible addition to the team, and it's now up to you to perpetuate the GSD attitude, the passion, and the focus on results.

Our in-country teams are the true unsung heroes of Room to Read. They ride local buses for a dozen hours to visit villages, they work with communities to determine the best method of co-investment via our Challenge Grant program, and they pilot motorbikes along rutted dirt roads to visit girls whose parents can't afford school fees. To the Room to Read teams in Cambodia, India,

Laos, Nepal, Sri Lanka, Vietnam, and South Africa, I say thank you.

Room to Read's Board members—Marc Andreessen, Christopher Beer, Alastair Mactaggart, Muneer Satter, and Hilary Valentine—have been generous with their strategic direction and financial support. Jenny Stein was a partner in every key decision I made during our formative years. Christine Boskoff, Wynne Leon, Alison Levine, and my father served admirably and with dedication during the organization's early years.

A special thanks to Don and Rachel Valentine and their family for being our first multiyear grant, which underwrote the launch of the Room to Grow scholarship program. I want to recognize the Skoll Foundation for being visionary funders who have encouraged the Room to Read management team to focus on scaling, and for backing up this advice with large-capacity building grants. Thanks to the team at Accenture for being our first significant corporate grant, and for the world-class advice you give to us. Thanks to the team at the Draper Richards Foundation for my fellowship, the seed funding, and all the great advice over the years. Finally, thanks to Marc Andreessen for being willing to invest in a venture run by a Microsoft alumnus!

Our most significant early funding came from Jim Kastenholz and Jennifer Steans, Hilary Valentine, Stuart Kerr, Dena Blank, Sarah Leary and Patte McDowell, and the team at the Cloud Nine Foundation. Our first significant partnership was with the Asia Foundation's Books for Asia program. TAF is an older foundation, and we did not expect them to bet on a new NGO like ours. We're glad they did, and we hope to be partnering together for decades to come! Thanks also to the Brother's Brother Foundation, Charlesbridge Publishing, Chronicle Books, HarperCollins, McGraw-Hill, Pearson, Reader's Digest, Scholastic, and Zaner-Bloser for your generous donations of English language books to our libraries and to Riverdeep and Microsoft for software donations. And kudos to the team at Better World Books for inventing a business model under which university students can sell their used books online and donate the proceeds to Room to Read.

To all of our chapter leaders, past and present, thank you for constantly inspiring me with your passion for and dedication to our cause. You prove that one does not need to quit a job in order to change the world, but instead have to simply be good at multitasking and not be afraid of hard work. I hope you realize that the spirit of volunteerism you exhibit permeates this book.

I also want to recognize all the volunteers. The work is not always glamorous, which means you should be even more proud of having done it. When I attend Room to Read events in various cities, I am always blown away by the quality and the passion of our volunteer fund-raising teams.

I owe thanks to the friends who encouraged me to write this book. The biggest cheerleader for this book was my mother, who did not listen when I said, "Well of course *you* think I am a good writer, you're my mother!" She eventually convinced me that the market for this book was bigger than just the two copies I'd sell to my parents. To her I now say those seven words that few people ever hear me utter: "You were right, and I was wrong."

A number of close friends also believed in this book before I did: Andrew Perrin of *Time* magazine, Kim Anstatt Morton, Martina Lauchengco, and Chris Jones. Michael Lindenmayer read every chapter I wrote at least three times and stayed up until the late hours to quickly turn around editorial passes. Friends like Amy Eldon, Nancy Horowitz, and Bill Lederer were constant cheerleaders for this book while it was still on the drawing board. Other friends who provided critical editorial assistance and a fresh perspective on my work include Cheryl Dahle, Julie Gildred, Tina Sciabica, and Stacy Strazis. Theresa Park gave me advice that stayed top of mind and influenced many of the key decisions I faced as a writer. Lesly Higgins helped me to find a literary agent.

From the moment I first talked to my agent, Jim Levine, I knew his ability to coach me as a writer was surpassed only by his business acumen. Herb Schaffner and the team at HarperCollins were enthusiastic supporters of this project from the moment they met this nervous *wannabe* author. Joe Tessitore opened our meeting with a booming voice by instructing us, "Quit talking to other publishers. We want this book!"

Thanks to Kathleen and Michael Hebert for allowing me to

be the first "writer in residence" of your Seattle boathouse, to Gary and Meryanne for the respite at Jnane Tasmna (stunning—see www.jnanetasmna.com) in Marrakech, to Mike and Chris McHugo for inspiring views of the Atlas Mountains and surprisingly delicious Moroccan wine at Kasbah de Toubkhal (www.kasbahdetoubkhal .com), to Gillian Munson for the cabin in the Adirondacks, to Julie Gildred for the beach house in San Diego, to Clarissa Rowe for the Paris apartment, and to Robin and Chris Donohoe for the stunning digs in Sonoma. If this book had a passport, all of you would have a stamp!

A number of friends have kept me sane during this journey. Mike McSherry was a critical sounding board while trekking in the Everest region. The Friday night dinner group—Angela Hanke, Brett Galimidi, Caitlin Stevens, Elizabeth Cooper, and Jen Dailey—provide a life-affirming amount of laughter on a regular basis. Tim Wood (no relation) has always been full of good advice as the organization grew. And no salute to my friends would be complete without thanking Eric Olsen and Kent Brown.

To close, I want to thank my family for being there for me, even at times when I did not reciprocate. I was fortunate to have a grandmother, a sister, and a mother who all read to me, and for that I am forever grateful.

The final expression of gratitude is to my parents—for all those times that you clipped coupons and stretched budgets to take our family on holidays, to buy us books, and to teach us the joy of skiing, camping, and hiking. I love you, and equally important, I so deeply respect you.

My hope is that many readers will get involved with our continued growth by checking out www.roomtoread.org, or e-mailing me at wood@roomtoread.org. Millions of children in the developing world are waiting for us to bring them the lifelong gift of education.

INDEX